T.C.J.C.-S.C.

The Immigrant Heritage of America Series

Francesco Cordasco, *Editor*

Courtesy of Daughters of the Republic
of Texas Library at the Alamo

Topographisch geognostische
Karte von Texas
by Dr. Ferdinand Roemer

GERMAN CULTURE IN TEXAS

A Free Earth; Essays from the 1978 Southwest Symposium

Edited by
GLEN E. LICH
DONA B. REEVES

Southwest Texas State University
University of New Orleans

TWAYNE PUBLISHERS
A DIVISION OF G. K. HALL & CO., BOSTON

Copyright © 1980 by G. K. Hall & Co.

Published in 1980 by Twayne Publishers,
A Division of G. K. Hall & Co.
All Rights Reserved

Printed on permanent/durable acid-free paper and bound
in the United States of America

First Printing

Library of Congress Cataloging in Publication Data

Southwest Symposium, Southwest Texas State University, 1978.
German Culture in Texas.

(Immigrant heritage of America series)
Sponsored by the School of Liberal Arts, Southwest Texas State University.
Bibliography: p. 281–329
Includes index.
1. German Americans—Texas—Congresses.
I. Lich, Glen E., 1948–
II. Reeves, Dona B., 1932–
III. Southwest Texas State University. School of Liberal Arts.
IV. Title.
F395.G3S68   1978   976.4'004'31   79-26602
ISBN O-8057-8415-2

"Multicultures of the Southwest: A Symposium on the Texas Germans" took place in the Lyndon Baines Johnson Memorial Student Center at Southwest Texas State University. The 1978 Southwest Symposium was sponsored by the School of Liberal Arts, Southwest Texas State University, and supported by a grant from The National Endowment for the Humanities.

Contents

List of Illustrations

Preface

Acknowledgments

Chronology, *Lera Patrick Tyler*

Introduction, *Glen E. Lich*

Part I. *Search for the Garden*
1. Goethe on the Guadalupe, *Glen E. Lich* — 29
2. The Old Homeland and the New, *Mack Walker* — 72
3. Man and His Environment: Ernst Kapp's Pioneering Experience and His Philosophy of Technology and Environment, *Hans-Martin Sass* — 82

Part II. *Civilization in the Wilderness*
4. German Folk Houses in the Texas Hill Country, *Terry G. Jordan* — 103
5. Views of Texas: German Artists on the Frontier in the Mid-Nineteenth Century, *James Patrick McGuire* — 121
6. The German Woman in Frontier Texas, *Crystal Sasse Ragsdale* — 144
7. The Function of the German Literary Heritage, *Hubert P. Heinen* — 157
8. German Cultural Heritage in the Hill Country of Texas, *Gilbert J. Jordan* — 176

Part III. *The Crisis of Ethnicity*

    9. Ethnicity and Politics in Texas, *Joe B. Frantz*   191

   10. *Deutschtum* in Texas: A Look at Texas-German Folklore, *Francis E. Abernethy*   203

Part IV. *Current Dimensions*

   11. The German Language in Texas: Some Needed Research, *Glenn G. Gilbert*   229

   12. The Myth of Texas in Contemporary German Writing, *A. Leslie Willson*   241

   13. Appraisal and Outlook, *Dona B. Reeves*   256

      Notes and References   263

      Selected Bibliography, *Dennis Gibbons and Glen E. Lich*   281

      About the Contributors   330

      Index   335

List of Illustrations

Frontispiece: Antique German map of Texas
Bettina Brentano, wife of Achim von Arnim
Baron Ottfried Hans von Meusebach, 1832
Ink drawing by Elisabethe von Hardenberg
Ferdinand Lindheimer (self-portrait)
Lindheimer's cabin in New Braunfels
Dr. Ferdinand von Roemer
Fossils from Roemer's *Kreidebildungen von Texas*
Congressman Gustav Schleicher
Dr. Ferdinand von Herff
Ottomar von Behr's home in Sisterdale
Pencil sketch of Ottomar von Behr by Richard Petri
Title page of Behr's handbook on immigration to Texas (1847)
Dr. Adolf Douai
August Siemering
Dr. Ernst Kapp
Mr. and Mrs. Leopold von Iwonski
Professor Ernst Kapp's Water Cure Sanatorium at Sisterdale (mid-1850s)
Map of the German Hill Country of Texas
A German "dogtrot" log dwelling at Comfort
A single-pen limestone home in Gillespie County
A "Cumberland" floorplan in Comfort

A limestone "I" house in Blanco County

Story-and-a-half sandstone house in Mason County

Exterior stairs on a story-and-a-half single-pen house in Comfort

Half-timbered house in New Braunfels

Half-timbering with adobe brick nogging

Half-timbered house in Fredericksburg

The Log Cabin, by Carl G. von Iwonski

New Braunfels (1857)

Kabale und Liebe, theatrical sketch (1856) by Carl G. von Iwonski

Elise Haseloff (1869), by Carl G. von Iwonski

Carl G. von Iwonski (ca. 1865–70)

Indian Maid, by Richard Petri

San Antonio de Bexar (1857), by Hermann Lungkwitz

Paggi's Mill on Barton Creek (1876), by Hermann Lungkwitz

The Pioneer Cowpen, by Richard Petri

Kindermaskenball in New Braunfels

Music Festival Poster, by Richard Petri

"Answer of the Germans to the Above" (1868), cartoon by Carl G. von Iwonski

Location of present-day speakers of German in Central Texas

He came with me./ St. Ger. *Er kam mit mir.*

He's helping me now./ St. Ger. *Er hilft mir jetzt.*

Dative and accusative usage by age

Preface

German colonization in Texas reflects the motivation of several varieties of ethical and political idealists to remake their world, in other words, to re-create an environment in their own image in opposition to what they foresaw as emerging reality. For them, Texas became a "last frontier," more a state of mind at first than a place, a notion colored with romance, adventure, and exploration. In current parlance, this was a "space odyssey" or "star trek" into a New World. These radical liberals and revolutionaries were products of a youth rebellion unparalleled in Western history except by the youth movement of this country in the 1960s. They were alienated from their own society even before they left; the uprooting had occurred in Europe. They came to the frontier of Texas filled with hopes that could not be realized within a single lifetime, and they reacted badly to their inevitable disappointment. For many disappointment turned to despair; a number of them once again "copped-out" and most of the others felt alienated from American life. Socially, many Germans considered themselves superior to the Anglo-American frontiersmen, distanced by several generations from Virginia, the Carolinas, and Europe. Politically, they felt themselves ostracized by the Civil War. That conflict, in a sense, was the symbolic death blow of the German dream of creating a "transatlantic Germany," or a model state from the Texas wilderness.

For various reasons, these intellectuals transplanted poorly in the soil of Texas. The common people were the ones who succeeded as merchants, artisans, workers, and farmers. It was this class which produced the new leaders after the Civil War— the safe, conservative, yet progressive successors of the earlier nobles, scientists, and thinkers whose written records reveal their utopian dreams and their quest for community. It was the new class of leaders which reformulated those ideas and realized those dreams.

Still, all together, they were a thoughtful people who encountered many of the problems current today—issues like environment, survival, progress, and future shock. Their example sensitizes a thoughtful person confronting seriously the human dilemma of today with one example in history of how a group took a very radical posture toward the whole way of living which is hardly viable for a modern person but yet does have some striking parallels with some of the more alienated groups of our society.

This utopian venture, which combined ethical idealism, directed economy, and mercantilism in order to effect controlled social evolution, was not unusual in the context of the troubled 1840s—the inchoate years of communitarianism, Darwinism, and Marxism. For many colonists—intellectuals and peasants alike—the migration satisfied an often unconscious need to reconcile social myth and reality. Under normal circumstances, people change their world-view to accommodate a changing reality. Migration, like science fiction, affords an opportunity to alternate on reality while preserving a deteriorating status quo—a solution at once radical and reactionary.

The present volume is a localized study of how this relatively small group of migrants, holding in common perhaps little more than the most rudimentary forms of a world view, attempted to assert their own claims, variously manifested in actual experience, over the claims of a changing world as they perceived and conceived it. This collection of symposium essays is taken from an interdisciplinary conference on art, architecture, music, language, literature, folklore, geography, education, politics, sociology, and values of the Southwest as these subjects relate to the broader context of life and culture in America. The essayists attempt to go beyond what *happened* with the Germans in Texas to what these events *meant* in the lives of people. The aim is the preservation of the image or ideas which an ethnic subculture has of itself. That picture derives from the context of how a particular group sees itself chronologically and how it compares or contrasts itself horizontally with other subcultures and the mainstream culture. The assumption is that the forces and movements of the large world are discernable on a regional level in the way people resolve the crises of

Preface

their own lives and adjust to the demands of the larger culture. How people conceptualize these crises of identity and destiny, and then set out to convert others, affords an insight into the social construction of reality. It is the lives that are lived that are a place and its history.

Acknowledgments

Perhaps the most satisfying part of finishing such a study is the opportunity to thank the many people who helped make it possible. Foremost among those who supported the project in its incipient stages was Clarence C. Schultz, Acting Dean of Liberal Arts, Southwest Texas State University. William H. Goetzmann, Robert M. Crunden, and Hubert P. Heinen offered many valuable comments which helped to define the problems addressed by the 1978 Southwest Symposium. The presiders at the five sessions were Professors Emmie Craddock, Vernon E. Lynch, Ingeborg McCoy, Manfred Kremkus, and M. L. Brunson. Lera Patrick Tyler handled most of the correspondence and many of the local arrangements for the meeting. Special thanks also go to the staff of the Lyndon Baines Johnson Memorial Student Center, and to our many students who assisted with manuscripts, mailings, information, museum displays, and numerous other tasks—Terry Dalrymple, Jim Fagan, Shirla Hutchins, Deborah Hinkle, Teresa Elzey, Robert Frazier, and Linda Kern, as well as other members of the SWT chapter of Delta Phi Alpha, National German Honor Fraternity. Without their help, the conference would never have run so smoothly.

The meeting itself was enhanced by a combined display of Texas-German paintings, sculpture, documents, books, and artifacts from regional immigrant ethnic museums. Our hearty appreciation is extended to the following individuals who contributed their time and resources: Helen Martin and Paula Ingenhuett from the Comfort Museum; Al Lowman, John Davis, and James Patrick McGuire from the University of Texas Institute of Texan Cultures at San Antonio; Mary S. Carnahan from the Texas Memorial Museum; Margaret Bracher from the Pioneer Museum of Fredericksburg; Linda Dietert from the Sophienburg Museum in New Braunfels; Gloria Jaster from the Winedale Museum of the University of Texas at Austin; Hugh Black from the SWT Special Collections; and Susan Woolfley

Lich, Emmie Flach, Loel Green, and Selina Saur from the Comfort Art Guild.

Many of the initial arrangements for facilities, information, registration, and printing were made by Pat Murdock, Patteann Daniel, Jim Hamm, Robert Jones, Lilly Dees, Michelle Scallorn, and Eva Goodnight—all of Southwest Texas State University.

Substantial support for the 1978 Southwest Symposium came from the German Consulate General in Houston; the departments of English and Modern Languages and the Advisory Committee for University Activities of Southwest Texas State University; and ultimately from The National Endowment for the Humanities, Washington, D.C.

Chronology

Lera Patrick Tyler

1831 Friedrich Ernst receives land at Mill Creek in Austin County and begins writing letters to friends in Oldenburg and Westphalia.

1832 The German settlement of Biegel develops along Cummins Creek in Fayette County.

1834 Renewal of Anglo-American colonization in Texas.
Several German families, including the Klebergs and the von Roeders, are encouraged by the Ernst letters to come to Texas. They settle at Cat Spring in Austin County.

1836 Texas Independence.

1838 Friedrich Ernst founds the town of Industry in Austin County.
William Frels establishes the German settlement of Frelsburg in the northern corner of Colorado County.

1839 L. C. Ervendberg holds the first recorded religious services among the Germans in Texas at Houston.

1841 Texas government grants land contracts to immigrant agents.
Charles Sealsfield (Karl Anton Postl) publishes *The Cabin Book*, a popular novel about Texas which influences the immigration of German-speaking Europeans more than any other single work or effort.

1842 The Adelsverein (The Society for the Protection of German Immigrants in Texas) organizes at Biebrich on the Rhine, near Mainz.
Henri Castro contracts with the Texas government to establish a colony of 600 families.

1842 Shelby (Roedersmuehle) becomes a small German farm community in Austin County. A number of families sponsored by the Adelsverein populate the village in 1845 and 1846.

1843 Count Boos-Waldeck buys a plantation in Fayette County

	for the Adelsverein. On this purchase, Nassau Farm, a "manor house" retreat for the society's officials, is built.
1844	Voyage from the Continent to Galveston or Indianola takes about twelve weeks.
	High Hill, first known as Oldenburg, Wursten, and Blum Hill, develops as a German community in southern Fayette County. In 1860, however, Czech families arrive there to start a Catholic settlement, the mother colony of Schulenburg.
	Henri Castro lays out the town of Castroville west of San Antonio on the Medina River. By 1847 over 2,000 French, Alsatian, and German colonists live on Castro's grant.
1845	Carl, Prince of Solms-Braunfels and first commissioner-general of the Adelsverein, founds the town of New Braunfels with about 200 German immigrants on Good Friday.
	Ross Prairie, another small German settlement, develops in eastern Fayette County.
	In Austin County, the German community of Millheim, an offshoot of Cat Spring, grows as some Adelsverein settlers venture into the more populous eastern regions of Texas.
	Johan Reinert Reiersen's colony of Normandy in Henderson County attracts Norwegian immigrants.
1845	New Ulm is settled by former inhabitants of Nassau, Industry, and Shelby.
1846	Annexation of Texas.
	United States and Mexico at war.
	Baron Ottfried Hans von Meusebach, second commissioner-general for the Adelsverein, leads German families farther into the Hill Country of western Texas to establish Fredericksburg.
	The *Galveston Zeitung*, the first German newspaper in Texas, begins publication.
1846–1847	Geologist Ferdinand von Roemer visits the German-populated areas of Texas, recording his scientific and personal observations.
1847	Meusebach ventures into Indian territory to conclude a

Chronology

      treaty with the Comanches allowing Germans to settle on Indian lands. The tradition of the Easter Fires begins as an explanation to the Fredericksburg children of the Indian negotiations.
      "The Forty," a fraternity of young students under the leadership of Dr. Ferdinand von Herff and Gustav Schleicher, establish communistic Bettina on the north bank of the Llano River.
      Four other settlements—Castell, Meerholz, Leiningen, and Schoenburg—are attempted by the Adelsverein on the lands of the Fisher and Miller grant.

1848 The United States and Mexico conclude the Treaty of Guadalupe Hidalgo, ending Mexican claims to Texas and a large portion of western North America.
      The Forty-Eighters, refugees from the revolution of 1848, arrive in Texas. A number of prominent and well-educated Germans from this group of refugees settle at Sisterdale on the Guadalupe.
      The town of Yorktown in DeWitt County is planned and settled by Germans.
      Swen Swenson returns to Texas with about twenty-five Swedes. Between this date and 1861 over 200 Swedes come to the state under the leadership of Swenson and his uncle Swante Palm.

1849 Viktor Witte and other German intellectuals establish Latium in Washington County.
      Five members of "the Forty" organize a German communistic farm named Tusculum which develops into the town of Boerne in the Hill Country.

1850 Germans comprise approximately 20 percent of the white population of Texas. The boundaries of Texas are fixed by U.S. Congress in the Compromise of 1850.

1852 Sixteen Czech families journey inland to start the New Bremen community in Austin County. Fayetteville, originally a German town, becomes a center of Czech settlement.
      Four Oldenburger schoolmasters establish the town of Welcome in northern Austin County.
      German farmers disperse from the towns first established

by the Adelsverein. Small farm communities like the Cypress Creek settlement begin as these immigrants are drawn by cluster migration and by availability of land into the fertile river valleys.

The *Neu-Braunfelser Zeitung* starts publication with Ferdinand Lindheimer as editor.

Steamships begin to replace clippers in trans-Atlantic passenger traffic.

1853 The first Texas-German *Saengerfest* is held at New Braunfels.

Der freie Verein organizes at Sisterdale. With Dr. Ernst Kapp as president, the society takes a strongly worded stand against slavery.

Dr. Adolf Douai edits the *San Antonio Zeitung*. A year before, he was driven from New Braunfels for his radical views, and in San Antonio he rouses the violent opposition of Southerners with his abolitionist platform.

1854 Texas legislature sets aside $2 million for a state school system, but not until the 1880s does the system become a reality. (Throughout the decade, Germans call for compulsory public education.)

Ernst Hermann Altgelt organizes the Cypress Creek settlement as the town of Comfort, a community of Freethinkers and political extremists.

Influenced by the socialistic philosophy of Fourier, 350 Frenchmen led by Victor Considerant and Francis Cantagel found the North Texas community of La Reunion.

Norwegian immigrants acquire land in southwestern Bosque County and begin settling in that area, with the establishment of Norse.

Hermann Seele and others organize the New Braunfels Dramatic Society.

Pastor John Kilian brings a group of over 500 Wends seeking religious freedom from the area of Dahlen (Saxony) to Texas. These colonists establish Serbin in Lee County.

Father Leopold Moczygemba, a Silesian priest in New Braunfels and Castroville, along with Johann Twohig, a

Chronology

       San Antonio merchant, bring Polish settlers to the confluence of the Cibolo and San Antonio rivers.
       Panna Maria, the first homogeneous Polish community in the Western Hemisphere, is founded by 100 families from Upper Silesia.
       The *Deutsch Texanischer Saengerbund* organizes.

1855 Swiss immigrants, led by Carl Burkli, settle with the French at La Reunion. Shortly afterward, these twenty-five Swiss settlers disband to form their own neighborhood in Dallas, which continues to draw Swiss to Texas.
       Under the leadership of Father Felix Zwiardowski, the parish of St. Stanislaus is established by Poles in Bandera.
       A German settlement develops at Round Top in Fayette County.
       The Polish parish of St. Hedwig is founded by John Demmer.

1856 Near Schulenburg, Czech immigrants settle Navidad and rename it Dubina.
       Agricultural Society of Austin County is chartered at Cat Spring.

1857 Trans-Atlantic voyage to New York takes less than two weeks.
       The poet Johannes Romberg organizes the *Prairie-Blume*, a literary society for young German Texans near Black Jack Springs, Fayette County.
       The Casino Association of San Antonio forms to promote social entertainments.

1858 Praha (Prague) in southern Fayette County develops as Czech immigration to the area continues to increase.

1859 The first Jewish congregation, with a membership derived from France, Alsace, Bavaria, and other German-speaking lands, is chartered in Houston.

1861 Secession and Civil War.

1862 Homestead Act.
       In Comfort, several hundred male unionists reorganize the "Union Loyal League" into a German battalion with companies from Kendall, Gillespie, and Kerr counties.

GERMAN CULTURE IN TEXAS

When these counties are declared in open rebellion, the German cadre assembles for movement into Mexico and is ambushed by a massive Confederate force. This Battle of Nueces eliminates what remains of the radical German element in Texas.

1866 Reconstruction.

After twenty-five years of caring for Jewish and non-Jewish families in Galveston, the Hebrew Benevolent Society formally incorporates.

1867 Mayor William C. A. Thielepape founds San Antonio's *Beethoven Maennerchor*.

Ernst Hermann Altgelt constructs a home on King William Street, starting a fashionable residential district for San Antonio's German elite.

1872 First extensive railroad connections between Texas and other states.

1873 Cestohowa, a filial of Panna Maria, is established by forty Polish families.

1874 Cattle drives become more profitable, and by 1885 millions of head of cattle are sent north.

End of Reconstruction.

1875 Indian raids into Texas cease.

1878 The sale of railroad lands stimulates settlement of western Texas. Approximately 32 million acres (an area the size of Alabama) are disposed of in this way.

Swedes start coming to Texas again. By 1895 over 5,000 settlers join their predecessors in Houston, Austin, Manor, and Palm Valley.

1880 Ten Swiss families settle on the Guadalupe River near Seguin. Like the other Swiss colonies in Texas, it quickly disperses to already established towns and cities.

1880s Windmills appear in western Texas.

German farmers begin to settle the divides and plains of West Texas where water is now available, turning their farm operations into ranches.

Germans from Colorado County found Westphalia in Falls County.

1881 The *Texanischer Gebirgs-Saengerbund* organizes.

1889 Muenster and nearby Lindsay in Cooke County, founded

Chronology

by Emil and Carl Flusche, become the fourth and fifth German-Catholic colonies started in the New World by six brothers from Westphalia.

1890   The Grand Order of the Sons of Hermann, a benevolent fraternal society, organizes in San Antonio.

1890s   German farmers from the older colonies of eastern Texas move into the area around Rosenberg in Fort Bend County.

A small group of Russian Germans leaves Rorbach, near the Black Sea in Russia, and settles at Hurnville, Clay County, Texas.

1891   Father Joseph Reisdorff brings German Catholics from the Midwest to Windthorst in Archer County. By 1911, five other colonies are established by Father Reisdorff.

1892   Kosciusko in Wilson County is founded by sixty-five Polish families.

1903   German Lutherans settle southwestern Haskell and eastern Stonewall counties, where the towns of Brandenburg (renamed "Old Glory" during World War I) and Sagerton develop.

1905   German-speaking Mennonite congregation (sixteenth-century Swiss Anabaptist origin) is established at Tuleta, Bee County, Texas.

1910   Germans primarily from out of state are attracted to the southern regions of Texas. Forty German-Catholic families from the North settle Vatmannville in Kleberg County.

1911   Deutschburg near Matagorda Bay is founded by Pastor Gerhard, a Lutheran minister from Wisconsin, and settled by Germans from the Midwest. Pastor Gerhard is only partially successful in his plan to create a health resort and gardening center there.

1911–1914   A larger body of Mennonites settles temporarily in Dimmit County.

1914   World War I begins in Europe.

1915–1918   One hundred sixty Mennonites establish a colony near Littlefield.

Introduction

The facts of history are a fleeting succession of images flashed onto the mind. That successive generations interpret and arrange and weigh these images differently, in light of their different experiences, loads the past with a fruitful variety of dynamic meanings.

The past is never finished, never final. It lives on, changing from generation to generation. Each new generation must rewrite its own history to explain an ever-changing present. Each generation looks to discover in its past the combinations to unlock the possibilities of its future.

In a larger sense, then, history is a progression of metaphors, never static, but constantly changing as the light strikes them differently. These metaphors illuminate the present and reflect the future. They grow from our need to believe, to create myths and heroes, to chalk our way into a better tomorrow.

This was the ethical dream of many nineteenth-century German colonists in Texas: to rearrange the pieces of their past so that they would have a new future—in short, to make a new world. In a very active way, they took history into their own hands.

Part I

Search for the Garden

CHAPTER 1

Goethe on the Guadalupe

GLEN E. LICH

> We must not go from here without realizing a national idea or at least making the beginnings toward its realization; the foundation of a new and free Germany in the great North American Republic shall be laid by us; we must therefore gather people about us when we emigrate, and we must, at the same time, make the necessary arrangements providing for a large body of immigrants to follow us annually, and thus we may be able, at least in one of the American territories, to establish an essentially German state ... a territory which we shall be able to make a model state in the new Republic.
>
> Giessener Gesellschaft, 1830

HOPELESSLY repressive conditions on the Continent between the Revolutions of 1830 and 1848 diverted the minds of many German intellectuals to the sweet dream of building a model homeland in the New World. This ideal of making a corporate fresh start led to the organization of the Giessener Gesellschaft in 1830 by Paul Follenius and Friedrich Münch. These reformers eventually settled thousands of Germans in the Mississippi Valley, and the success of their colonization convinced a number of more highly placed men of the practicability of their New World vision. "Germany" in

The author wishes to acknowledge the gracious support of the University of Texas Institute of Texan Cultures at San Antonio.

the silence between the revolutions was hardly more than a geographical expression. Industrialization had set in, but a multiplicity of little states labored under an almost medieval economy. The population had always been dense; now it rose sharply while an antiquated agriculture struggled to keep pace. The golden age of German culture was drawing to an end as the German states (and indeed all Europe) tried desperately to dress up a new society in old clothes. The union in the eighteenth century of intellectual and political leaders had been complete in such men as Goethe, Frederick the Great, Duke Karl August of Weimar, and the Humboldts. Now society was fractured and political reversion radicalized liberal intellectuals. Casting themselves in roles as poet-priests, reformers at first hoped to minister to the needs of state and populace from within, but the extremes widened and police repression led to open revolts against autocratic authority and to the revival of external utopian socialism.

I The Ideal of America:
A Transition from Literature to Politics

Most of the New World plans were ephemeral, and initially the largest emigration was undertaken by individuals. Gradually, however, some of the dreams became more practicable. All of them, in a sense, derived from a model in German literature. Goethe's *Wilhelm Meister* (1795-96, 1821, 1826)—called by Friedrich Schlegel one of three "greatest tendencies of the age" along with the French Revolution and Fichte's *Wissenschaftslehre* (1794) because it embraced the manifold phenomena of the epoch, like an "encyclopedia of an age, a mirror of the entire surrounding world"[1]—engaged in a utopian fantasy directed by a benevolent prince and a mystical society. Futuristically expressive, *Wilhelm Meister* presents an ideal of the perfectibility of society through a teleological process of the awakened spirit striving after Truth.

In his essay "Goethes Amerikabild. Wirklichkeit und Vision" (1975),[2] humanistic scholar Victor Lange implies that Goethe's New World idealism was imported from America and based on his observation of American examples. In 1810 Goethe met with Aaron Burr in Weimar. Furthermore, according to Lange, Goethe's *Dichtung und Wahrheit* (1811–33) reveals an interest in the political and scientific work of Benjamin Franklin, whom he admired somewhat for his practical achievements during the American Revolution but primarily for his enlightened understanding of natural laws. Goethe sustained a friendship with the American mineralogist Joseph Cogswell of Harvard, as well, because it afforded him an opportunity to keep abreast of American research. Goethe's firsthand knowledge of America grew during the North American travels of his royal student Duke Bernhard, who called upon Thomas Jefferson in 1825 and saw Robert Owen's New Harmony settlement in Indiana. Goethe's diary notes the young duke's impressions from these visits, and later Goethe read but never commented on Jefferson's *Memoir* (London, 1829). Apart from his readings of Cooper during this time, Goethe's interest in America centered, by and large, on scientific investigation.[3] Otherwise "America" was for him an allegory, an Eldorado for those in distress, and as such he invokes its name in *Wilhelm Meister*.

The novel stops short of counseling overt emigration. What Lafayette did for America, his German emulator might better do for his German homeland. *"Here or nowhere is America!"* Goethe's Prince Lothario exclaims as he surveys his lands,[4] and with that emigration is internalized and utopianism directed inward upon the corporate state. Goethe's criticism of the machine age, "his aversion to social change," and "his opposition to the 'economic man,'" led him to this myth of renewal, and exodus to a Utopia of constructive humanness.[5] His ideal community, which recent scholarship links with George Rapp's Harmony Society,[6] refocused attention on the purpose of society to serve human ends, to enable man to reach that calmness of soul which Goethe deemed the highest accessible good. The disciples of Goethe's community are emigrants to this new society.[7] Goethe's insistence upon an unfragmented, dynamic social organism transformed *Wilhelm Meister* into a moral aesthetic. The novel reflects its age, as Schlegel correctly perceived, but shining out through it is the prophet's idealistic resolution of the age.

The futility of this lofty solution slowly became apparent,

even to Goethe himself, after the Congress of Vienna. Radicalized by reaction, German intellectuals spouted their ideas of national unity and political freedom. Their responses to suppression varied. A few desisted momentarily from political activity. Some of these, like Wilhelm Schlegel, toyed with the thought of going to America with Madame de Staël but realized that the "utilitarian thinking of Americans" and their own severance from literature in the German language would spell the end of their careers.[8] A larger number of the writers—men like Brentano, Eichendorff, and the Grimms—embraced Romanticism and thus moved into a new arena of active politics since their interest in folklore and folklife dovetailed with the tendencies of emerging nationalism. Their transition from German Classicism to Romantic individualism was somewhat an outgrowth of Fichte's new philosophic system of practical and productive idealism. He preached "that every man must, in the most literal sense, carve out his own destiny. This invigorating individualism was a chalybeate spring, in which the German spirit bathed itself, to emerge again with new strength to face the struggle for national existence that lay before it."[9] From Fichte, the first rector of the new Berlin University, these Romantic nationalists derived the best of their ethical ideals.

The response to suppression took other forms as well. Several of the greatest minds sublimated their idealism in travel and science, so that they withdrew into their own minds and into the physical world around them. Here the foremost examples are the Humboldts. The German literary critic J. G. Robertson calls Wilhelm von Humboldt (1767–1835) "one of the makers of modern Germany," a man to whom "more than to any other, Germany owed a practical realisation of the ideals of her classical poets and thinkers."[10] A minister in the Prussian movement, he was the founder of the new University of Berlin. He conducted a voluminous correspondence with Schiller and Goethe, wrote a metaphysics of language as structure rather than sound, and formulated a philosophy of speech with emphasis on speech differences and human development. His younger brother Alexander (1769–1859) was a geographer and ethnographer whose fame rested on comparative studies of earth sciences and the development of ecology. Alexander worked closely with the

German chemist Justus von Liebig (whose discovery in Giessen of chemical fertilizers revolutionized European agriculture) and the Swiss zoologist Louis Agassiz. Like that of his older brother, Alexander von Humboldt's ideal of scientific exploration was to discern natural laws and discover in them the future course of human destiny. To this end he traveled extensively through Central and South America (1799–1804) and actively sponsored the travels of a succession of young explorers and scientists in the New World.[11]

While not as prodigious as the Humboldts, two lesser explorers exerted a more direct influence on the development of popular New World idealism in Germany. In 1832–34 Prince Maximilian von Wied-Neuwied traversed the expanses of the Southwest, the Rocky Mountains, the Great Plains, and the Mississippi with Carl Bodmer, an alpine artist whose mythic Western landscapes engraved on German minds an exotic image of the new land. Duke Paul of Württemberg was accompanied on a later trip through the Rockies by Heinrich Balduin Möllhausen, who came to him with an introduction from Paul's mentor Alexander von Humboldt. Called the "German Fenimore Cooper," Möllhausen was a prolific and tremendously popular writer (and watercolorist) who, it was said, "never allowed facts, or the demands of literalism, to interfere with his romantic imagination."[12] Like the Humboldts and many other explorers, Prince Wied and Duke Paul were liberals who shirked political responsibilities and avoided reactionism by traveling abroad (though others say the reasons were much simpler: Duke Paul was avoiding his wife, Sophie). The travel accounts of these men fired the German imagination and made it all the more difficult for the "new radicals" to await gradual social evolution at home.

This younger generation was no longer content with "utopianism directed inward." Most of them, except those protected by high birth, lived in exile and so were, in effect, already emigrants. Their view of Germany was bitter. Writers like Büchner, Heine, and Börne announced that the readiest cure for the country's ills would be found outside Germany, and they had large followings among Young German liberals, as they were called. Inside Germany, in the midst of the Berlin

Bettina

Courtesy of University of Texas

literary and political circle, the same sentiment was expressed by Bettina Brentano. The widow of von Arnim and a youthful correspondent with Goethe, Bettina carried her message to the king of Prussia for redress of social grievances. Leading a charmed life, Bettina could attempt what few others dared, but her plea in *Dies Buch gehört dem König* (1843) did not relieve the suffering of Germany's masses, and even in high government, though few there spoke of it, the alternative of leaving was obvious.

To attribute this circumstance to one cause would be simplistic and inaccurate. The immigration of ideas in the North Atlantic community was leading to parallel developments throughout Europe and in the United States. America and England had little real political oppression, but utopian socialism thrived there. German utopianism, originally also social in origin, had run a curious circle, and though Goethe was by no means alone in shaping its development and delaying its political application, his concept of a mystical society directed by a benevolent prince furnished the intellectual construct for the new union in the 1840s of German princes and radical liberals. Disillusioned with the hope of overcoming reactionism, these men dreamed of a "transatlantic Europe," as one put it,[13] where they would be free to realize their ethical and moral ideals, however vaguely they may have conceived them.

II *Philosophy, Science, and the Practical Vision*

A peasant working on the hillside above the Rhine outside Biebrich on the morning of 20 April 1842 might have been astonished to see a procession of fine carriages moving along the road from Mainz into Biebrich. On that day, five sovereign princes and sixteen nobles dissatisfied with internal reform assembled there for the purpose of organizing a society to direct a massive transplantation of German farmers and artisans to the New World.[14]

Chief among the philanthropic concerns of this Adelsverein was the problem of overpopulation, which alone, in the years before Liebig's agricultural breakthroughs, would have precluded the sweeping social reforms Bettina advocated before the Prussian king. In the preface of his book published in 1829, Gottfried Duden, a German traveler through the Midwest, wrote that "most of the evils from which the inhabitants of Europe, and particularly of Germany, suffer arise from overpopulation and are of such a nature that all remedies remain without effect unless a thinning out of the population precedes them."[15]

The political motives of these nobles, however, are clouded in accounts left of the Adelsverein. Whether they hoped to found a "New Germany" in America can only be conjectured. Similar attempts in Illinois and Missouri had failed because Americans were already numerically superior in these regions. At any rate, that same day they dispatched two members to represent the society before President Sam Houston in Texas and to secure a grant of land from the young republic.

Texas was by no means unknown in Germany at that time. In political circles, the future of its independence had caused discussion, especially in the French and British governments, and several princes of the Adelsverein were closely allied with the British crown. Texas had been popularized as a mythic, fabulous, and wild land in the novels of Charles Sealsfield (Karl Postl), another romantic rebel from reactionary Europe. The Texas coastland prairie was a "boundless sea of green," an unspoiled garden in "God's world immaculate."[16] It was an immeasurably beautiful and rich land where "nails grew overnight into horseshoes" (p. 117), and where "hopes for the future grew taller by the mile" (p. 28). Sealsfield admitted there was "indeed a lot of rabble in Texas" (p. 26), but he assured readers that the bones of the Texas rabble would "pave the road into a better tomorrow just as, once upon a time, the skulls of the rowdy Normans paved roads in the wilds of Britain" (p. 77). "Why do we love America?" Sealsfield asked. "Because she makes us love Freedom for the whole human race, and stands for the progress of all civilization" (p. 20). Furthermore, a small number of German families, diverted from other goals, had filtered into Texas during the previous decade. Robert Justus Kleberg recounts the curiosity touched off in Germany by the widely circulated letter of one of these early settlers.

We had accidentally got hold of a letter written by a gentleman, who had emigrated some time before us from the Duchy of Oldenburg and who lived where now is Industry, Texas, Fritz Ernst, by name. In this letter . . . he had described Texas, then a province of Mexico, in very glowing colors, mentioning also the advantages offered to immigrants by the Mexican government, namely, a league and labor for every man with a family and ½ league for every single man. This letter caused us to change our first intention to go to one of the northern states and to choose Texas for our future home. At the time we left, hardly anything was known of Texas, except that my ideas and those of my party were formed by the above mentioned letter, in which Texas was described as a beautiful country, with enchanting scenery and delightful climate, similar to that of Italy, the most fruitful soil and republican government, with unbounded personal and political liberty, free from so many disadvantages and evils of old countries.[17]

No sooner had a somewhat favorable report come back from Texas in 1843 than the Adelsverein determined upon a colonization scheme. The next year the members incorporated as a stock company, their number having grown now to twenty-four, and "a resolution was adopted that speculation and political projects were not contemplated and that the society, out of purely philanthropical reasons, would devote itself to the support and direction of German emigration to Texas.[18] Four objectives were formulated:

To improve the lot of the working class who are without employment, thus controlling their increasing impoverishment;
To unite the emigrants by giving them protection through this Association in order to ease their burden by mutual assistance;
To maintain contacts between Germany and the emigrants, and to develop maritime trade by establishing business connections;
To find a market for German craft in these settlements, and to provide a market in Germany for the products of these colonies.[19]

Shortly after he was named commissioner-general of the society in Texas, Prince Carl of Solms-Braunfels proclaimed, "The eyes of all Germany, no, the eyes of all Europe are fixed on us and our undertaking: German princes, counts, and noblemen stand at the head, and no doubt can remember the historical glory of their ancestors and bring new crowns to old glory while they at the same time are ensuring immeasurable riches for their children and grandchildren."[20] With that the major part of the undertaking was completed. All that remained was getting the emigrants together in Antwerp or Bremen, provisioning, transporting, lodging, and finding a suitable place for settlement (since it was decided that 4,000 acres purchased for this purpose in Fayette County were too close to existing American towns for the Germans to preserve their identity). Upon his arrival in Texas, Solms negotiated the purchase of a tract of land on the Guadalupe River, where, on Good Friday, 1845, New Braunfels was established.[21]

In Germany the response was stronger than anticipated, perhaps for the reasons explained in the memoir of a clergyman's daughter:

It does not require any vast psychological knowledge to understand that Pastor Fuchs wished to provide greater opportunities for his children, rather than allowing them to be stifled, body and soul, through the miserable conditions prevailing in Germany. To understand this, one needs only to visualize the rigid bureaucracy of the thirties and forties, when Metternich was in power, to sense the impending storm in the political atmosphere precipitating in the year of 1848; to recall the tyrannical suppression of the writings of the Young German writers, as well as the then prevailing oppressive rule of the Church. Was he to watch his girls at most attain positions as governesses, the boys starving themselves to struggle through a university in order, perhaps too by God's will alone, to earn a scanty living, thus perpetuating the old miseries and wants from generation to generation? Or was it not better to go to found a new home? The choice must have been a difficult one, resolutely faced.[22]

Nearly 10,000 colonists came to Texas under the auspices of the society in the first two years. For its leaders, though, the venture was not financially rewarding. The members of the Adelsverein seem to have lost interest in the colonization of Texas after its annexation, and in 1847 its directors declared bankruptcy. The emigration wave continued, however, and by 1850 Germans in Texas numbered over 30,000 (20 percent of the total white population).[23] This compares with about a quarter million German immigrants between 1845–50 to the rest of the United States.[24]

Even after the demise of the Adelsverein, developments progressed in Texas on two levels at once along patterns equally characteristic of nineteenth-century social and intellectual history. At first glance, German settlement of the interior of Texas distinguishes itself in no way from what was the most massive migration of Germans from their homeland since the fall of Rome in the West. In the nature of its origin, however, this colonization effort in Texas had more in common with the sectarian and Owenite phases of communitarian socialism than with other numerically significant German settlements in North and South America. In short, what one observes in Texas is the only organized transplantation for philosophical and ethical purposes undertaken by Germans in Europe. In that sense it differs from the overall pattern of German migration to the New World. It differs furthermore from other utopian settlements in America on the basis of its practical success.

It succeeded because its goals could be realized for the majority. Prince Solms was the notable exception, but apart from him the men who saw to the society's affairs in Texas acquitted themselves well. Utopian idealists for the most part, they were motivated by the ethical ideal of starting a model society, not only for themselves but also for their fellow men.[25] Early leaders like Meusebach, Lindheimer, Roemer, and Ervendberg had come to Texas at different times and to escape a variety of problems at home. They were young, recent university graduates, with little experience in the affairs of the world, much less in the political and socioeconomic requirements of establishing frontier settlements. Although they made mistakes in these areas, what they did best, unlike the sectarian socialists in America, was correctly gauge the needs of the majority. Although they were intellectuals, they did not place intellectual demands on their followers until much later, when a reaction set in. They led, but did not outdistance, the mainstream of farmers and artisans, and they measured their idealism by practical success. It was a cooperative and mutually supportive venture. While the colonists progressed socioeconomically, these leaders moved ahead gradually in implementing their New World vision.

In *Backwoods Utopias*, Arthur E. Bestor cites an interesting observation. "The American Republic, remarked the aging James Madison to an English visitor, is 'useful in proving things before held impossible.' ... Here the social dreams of the Old World,"

Bestor continues, "were dreams no longer, but things of flesh and blood."²⁶ In this sense, the utopian venture in Texas succeeded also because its leaders, with all their European antecedents, were moving with the main current of American history. The myth of the West as a virgin land exerted a powerful influence on the course of American domestic politics during the decade before the Civil War. As a part of this

Baron Ottfried Hans von Meusebach, 1832
Von Meusebach, von Witzleben, and von Polenz Familien-Album
Courtesy of Irene Marschall King

expansion, the Germans were helping to bring about "the agrarian utopia of hardy and virtuous yeomen which," according to Henry Nash Smith, "had haunted the imaginations of writers about the West since the time of Crèvecoeur."[27]

The outstanding example of the German leadership in Texas was the second commissioner-general of the Adelsverein, Baron Ottfried Hans von Meusebach (1812–1897). The scion of ancient service nobility, he was educated for the same brilliant career achieved by his brother, a Prussian officer, consul, and foreign minister. He first studied mining and natural sciences at the academy in Clausthal, and then he graduated from the universities of Bonn and Halle after studies in law, political economy, and finance. He read five languages and spoke English fluently. More than any other, young Meusebach was the embodiment of Goethe's benevolent prince. On his voyage across the Atlantic to take charge of the Adelsverein settlers, he carried with him a passage copied from *Faust*, the other work which, like *Wilhelm Meister*, Goethe struggled with for more than fifty years. This passage, in translation, became a theme of the German exodus: "Aye! Such a throng I fain would see/ Stand on a free earth, among a people free."

Meusebach's father, first president of the court at Koblenz and later chief justice of the Superior Court in Berlin, was a friend of Goethe, Clausewitz, Wilhelm von Humboldt, the Grimms, Bettina von Arnim, Varnhagen von Ense, and Hoffmann von Fallersleben. Their political views were far ahead of the time in Prussia. In this circle, young Meusebach heard the first echoes of utopian socialistic experiments in faraway America, and he shared the concern of this group that Metternich's Europe had effectively closed the door on liberalism and nationalism, the twin daughters of the French Revolution. His political idealism derived during this period from Goethe, the poet-liberator, whose hand "stretched out in benediction to give them grace and strength."[28] In practice, as jurist and mayor of a small town, he applied Humboldt's dictum that "the state should be no more than an agent to secure protection and freedom for its citizens."[29]

His journals record more than passing interest in the colonization efforts of the Giessener Gesellschaft and the Adelsverein.

With his brother Meusebach debated the advantages of emigration, and with his father he discussed Sealsfield's story of the promising life in Texas. To another member of the Adelsverein he admitted in 1844, "For several years I have been considering going to America to obtain a large enough property to be the basis of nature study and furtherance thereof in those rich fields. I have had my eyes especially on Texas."[30]

An ink drawing by Elisabethe von Hardenberg of the Berlin circle depicts a curious fantasy, fed in part by Sealsfield, of life in Texas
Meusebach Family Files

Courtesy of Irene Marschall King

Meusebach was at once a practical and visionary leader in Texas. He recognized that the future welfare of the German settlers depended upon their political and socioeconomic assimilation, rather than upon isolation and self-sufficiency. Because he found the climate and geography of Texas not conducive to traditional European farm-villages, Meusebach encouraged dispersal into the fertile valleys of the hill country. Within a year five new colonies were established in a network stretching 150 miles northwestwardly from New Braunfels into previously unsettled lands of the Comanche Indians. To secure

Goethe on the Guadalupe

additional land for his settlers, he rode into the Indian hunting grounds, accompanied by a small party including a geologist from Berlin, and negotiated a treaty with twenty Comanche chiefs which opened over three million acres beyond the San Saba River for German colonization. He had taken the citizenship of Texas immediately upon his arrival (when he also relinquished his hereditary titles), and he assisted the swarm of newcomers in becoming citizens. Petitions were circulated for the organization of new counties around the German settlements, and in 1850 Meusebach was elected from them to the state senate. Until the Civil War, he held a number of state appointments regulating headrights, surveys, immigration, public education (the Germans favoring compulsory attendance at nonsectarian schools), and state affairs.[31]

Even during the early years when he was impeded on every hand by the tottering Adelsverein and by the Mexican War, which disrupted domestic transportation, Meusebach's correspondence attests to his conviction that "German knowledge at the side of American freedom"[32] was creating a haven in the New World. His curiosity led him to investigate the land. He undertook geographical surveys, classification of fossils and fauna (sending specimens to Halle and Berlin), and horticultural research. His extensive library he placed at the disposal of other naturalists. In particular, he supported the scientific research of Ferdinand Lindheimer and Ferdinand von Roemer, two other scholars thoroughly inculcated with the Humboldt quest to recover the meaning of the whole by discovering the relation of the parts.

Lindheimer (1801–1879) was a younger cousin of Goethe from Frankfurt. A botanist and naturalist trained at Bonn and Jena, he had taken part in the abortive Frankfurt putsch of 1833 and fled to the United States in the company of close associates—the Bunsens, Berchtelmann, Koerner, and the Engelmann brothers.[33] These men, called the "Dreissiger" because they were political refugees of the 1830s, gravitated toward the village of Belleville, Illinois, across the river from St. Louis. Von Hagen writes that these Latin farmers "carried over their political romanticism from Europe. Their ideal," he says, "was Cincinnatus, leaving his plow and hurrying to the Forum to

Ferdinand Lindheimer (self-portrait)
Courtesy of New Braunfels Conservation Society

save the Roman Republic from invaders."[34] From Belleville, the more adventurous Lindheimer flatboated with five friends down the river in 1834 to New Orleans, where they intended to provision themselves for an expedition into Texas. The promise, however, of taking part in a Mexican coup lured three of them to Vera Cruz. For the next sixteen months, Lindheimer was variously employed in Mexico as a distiller on a coffee plantation and as overseer on a banana and pineapple plantation. He still found time, though, to make an extensive collection of insects and plants. In the last months of 1835, Lindheimer was caught up in the agitation before the Texas Revolution. Because of his hatred for political oppression, Lindheimer supposedly declined a commission in the army of Santa Anna and started for Texas: "I recognized that this was the moment to carry out my original plan of going to Texas before the decisive battle."[35] Blown off course and shipwrecked just off the coast of Mobile, Lindheimer joined Houston's army one day after San Jacinto.

He remained in Texas as a botanical collector until the winter of 1839–40, when he returned to St. Louis to work out an arrangement with George Engelmann and Asa Gray of Harvard for extensive botanical investigation in Texas. Back in Texas in 1843, Lindheimer bought a two-wheeled horse-drawn cart, a supply of pressing paper, flour, coffee, and salt, and set out with two dogs. The trips often lasted a month as Lindheimer explored the Brazos, Colorado, and Guadalupe valleys. On one of them, he made the acquaintance of Rev. Louis Cachand Ervendberg, whom Prince Solms invited to become pastor of the Adelsverein colony, and through this association Lindheimer became the prince's guide into the wilderness.[36]

Ferdinand von Roemer, a young geologist dispatched for two years to Texas by the Berlin Academy of Sciences, left a colorful description of Lindheimer's way of life in New Braunfels.

At the end of the town, some distance from the last house, half hidden beneath a group of elm and oak trees, stood a hut or little house close to the banks of the Comal. It furnished an idyllic picture with its enclosed garden and general arrangement and position. When

Lindheimer's cabin in New Braunfels
Courtesy of Sophienburg Museum

Dr. Ferdinand von Roemer
Courtesy of F.W. Simonds

I neared this simple, rustic home, I spied a man in front of the entrance busily engaged in splitting wood. Apparently he was used to this kind of work. As far as the thick black beard, covering his face, permitted me to judge, the man was in his early forties. He wore a blue jacket, open at the front, yellow trousers and the coarse shoes customarily worn by farmers in the vicinity.... The description fitted the man I was looking for.... It was the botanist, Mr. Ferdinand Lindheimer, of Frankfort-on-the-Main. He had acquired for himself an enduring reputation through his many years of assiduous collecting of plants and through his study of the botany of Texas, which up to this time was almost unknown.[37]

After this meeting early in 1846, the paths of Lindheimer and Roemer crossed frequently as the two explored the region bounded by San Antonio, Austin, the San Saba, and the Enchanted Rock. They often conferred with Meusebach at his farm in the hills west of New Braunfels. More even than Meusebach, whom the Indians connected with the sun because of his flowing red beard, the legendary Lindheimer cast a spell over the natives, who considered him a powerful medicine man and associated freely with him in town and on his travels.[38] By the conclusion of these travels in 1851, he had organized the flora of Texas into a system. About twenty species of plants were named after him by Gray at Harvard, and Engelmann honored him by giving his name to a genus of Texas wildflowers.[39]

The geologist Roemer of Hildesheim, whose introduction from Alexander von Humboldt read "Dr. Roemer, like a book, needs but to be opened to yield good answers to all questions,"[40] was sent to Texas at the request of Prince Solms for a complete geological survey. Apart from the geological and paleontological work which made Roemer an eminent geologist of the nineteenth century,[41] the observations in Roemer's *Texas* (Bonn, 1849) are filled with the fresh wonder of a traveler transported into a strange landscape. He explained,

In gathering objects of natural history, I was assisted by practically the entire population of New Braunfels, especially the younger generation, since the peculiar types of animals, unknown in the native land, aroused their interest as much as mine. Nearly every

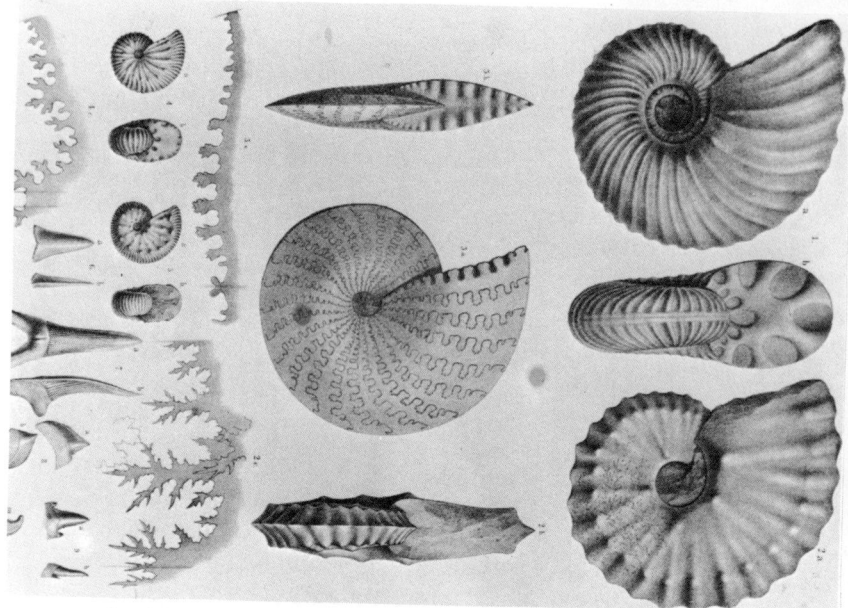

Fossils from Roemer's *Kreidebildungen von Texas*
Courtesy of Institute of Texan Cultures

day, birds, snakes, lizards, turtles, fish, etc., were brought to me, and by rewarding the finders with a small coin, I was able to stimulate them to renew their search.[42]

With an abundance of detail, he tried to pin down the exotic in terms of the familiar, to incorporate the unknown into the known. Responding to an ancient trait of man, he attempted to name the new creatures he saw, to "place" them in known contexts, to sort out the pieces, to categorize them, so they would have value in general terms. The roadrunner, for example, was described as a cross between a magpie and a pheasant. The church and the pastor of the colony were presented with a similar realism:

On the same main street is located the Evangelical Church of the place, a moderately large frame building with openings for the

windows, but without windows proper.... Close by stood a tiny
house, the modest home of the Evangelical minister, Pastor Ervendberg, who does not perform his spiritual duties with the ease of
most of his colleagues in Germany. He receives a very meager
salary, which the Adelsverein pays. He must preach on Sunday,
teach on week-days and furthermore, cultivate his corn field and
his garden in the sweat of his brow. I was filled with sincere respect
for the man when I saw how untiringly he sought to lead his congregation in diligent work and cheerful endurance of the trials and
hardships that are inseparably linked with the first settlement in
the wilderness; especially also, how, in the evil days, when virulent
climatic diseases decimated the population, in true understanding
of his sacred calling, he exercised himself without ceasing to give
support and comfort. (p. 95)

Life for his class in this new world was basically different from
what it was in Germany, and Roemer looked for causes.

I noticed a similar irregularity and romanticism in regard to the
clothing of the young German colonists, recently come to Texas.
It seems as if they wanted to compensate themselves in the land
of the free for the restraint which the manners and customs of the
homeland had imposed upon them. The almost total absence of
cultured women also helped to encourage this recklessness in dress.
(pp. 99–100)

He analyzed adaptation to the new geography by classes of
society:

The colonist who has not farmed in the old country or who had
not brought along a large enough capital to purchase slaves, thus
enabling him to carry on agriculture on a large scale as a planter,
must have an unusual amount of endurance and will-power.... I
have seen quite a few German peasants and laborers, who had come
here without any funds, come into possession of little farms through
their industry. These supplied them with the necessities of life and
even gave promise of future affluence and comfortable living. On
the other hand, I have hardly seen ten people of the higher class,
supplied with moderate funds, who within a year were able to
acquire a house with a fenced-in field and of whom one could hope

that they would be able to sustain themselves through their own efforts.

Many educated young men lived in New Braunfels at the time of my arrival. The majority of them belonged to prominent noble families who had come here for the purpose of making their fortune, without first having gained a clear conception in what manner.... Although the majority of them did not leave home for dishonorable reasons, but for financial ones, hoping to become financially independent here through hard work, still I have seen very few reach this goal, but most have ended tragically or in degeneracy, and this during my short stay in Texas. (p. 100)

In completing his report, he predicted eventual success based on geographical determinants:

Among the advantages and attractions which would argue in favor of settling in Texas, I would like to place above all the mild and excellent climate. The climate of Texas is surely one of the best in the world. During the greater part of the year the sky is clear and blue. A real winter is unknown and only during a few months of the year does the temperature at times go below the freezing point. Whereas it is in itself a great advantage to live under such a clear sky during the winter months, the mildness of the climate offers also other advantages and relief to the European colonist. Shelter and clothing are more easily obtained than in the rough climate with a severe winter. (p. 26)

In February, before he departed Texas in May 1847, Roemer persuaded Meusebach to permit him to accompany his peace mission into the uncivilized region of the San Saba River. He saw in these expanses the vision of a farming empire and he left the state in euphoria. Through his far-seeing eyes, the ethical dream had become a thing "of flesh and blood."

I had grown to love the beautiful land of meadows, to which belongs a great future. It moved me to sorrow that I must say farewell to the land forever. To me there still remain rich and pleasant memories; and from afar I shall always follow with lively interest the further development of the country. May its broad, green prairies become the habitation of a great and happy people![43]

Later that year, in September, Lindheimer also pilgrimaged into this same wilderness on the San Saba. He returned in the following February, though, after having seen Utopia wither.

III A Search for the Ideal in Texas: The Forty at Bettina

The winter of 1846–47 found the directors of the Adelsverein planning the establishment of its seventh and last colony in the New World by a fraternity of communitarian Freethinkers. The visionary undertaking began when Prince Solms addressed members of the fraternity, telling them "that there was no demand in the old country for all the professional men whom the universities were turning out, and that they must find a new and developing country where their services would be in demand."[44] The directors were attempting to recover losses by concentrating German emigration upon Texas through the successful transplantation to that state of a highly visible group of young activists. "They have the trust of their German countrymen, and if their settlement succeeds, there can be no doubt that the stream of emigration will be directed toward Texas," explained one of the directors to Meusebach.[45]

Known as "The Forty" from the size of their membership, the fraternity had chapters at Darmstadt, Giessen, and Heidelberg. While the association itself was patterned on Etienne Cabet's Icarian dream of a communistic utopia (1840), the reform philosophy of the Forty derived from Charles Fourier's idea of "social inventiveness cultivated by communitarians" (as opposed to "Marxist reliance on historically generated forces").[46] The students "had no regular scheme of government," so far as one of the members recalled. "In fact, being communistic, the association would not brook the tyranny of a ruler." Instead, there were guiding spirits by common consent, this member continued. "Being the youngest of the whole company—I was thirteen—I was, of course, rarely consulted."[47] The association first considered Wisconsin and Iowa. No doubt remained, though, after Prince Solms's words, that the place to seek their ideal community was Texas—"a land of milk and honey, of perennial flowers, of crystal streams rich and fruitful beyond measure, where roamed myriads of deer and buffalo, while the primeval forests abounded in wild fowl of every kind."[48] With the intent from the start of living in community, the Forty brought with them diversified skills to clear the land for settlement: two physicians, one engineer, two architects, seven lawyers, five foresters, two mechanics, two carpenters, one butcher, one blacksmith, one lieutenant of artillery, one ship's carpenter, one brewer, one miller, one hosteler, one theologian, one maker of musical instruments, one agriculturist, and one botanist. None spoke English. In Texas they were joined by Lindheimer as guide.[49]

The commune established by the Forty in September 1847 on the Llano was named *Bettina* after Bettina von Arnim of the Berlin circle. Unlike most other communitarian experiments in America, the Bettina settlement was agnostic and not sectarian. Opposed generally to revolution and impatient with gradual internal reform, "what these enterprises had in common," according to Arthur E. Bestor, "was the idea of employing the small experimental community as a lever to exert upon society the force necessary to produce reform and change. The ends might differ, with economic, religious, ethical, and educational purposes mingled ... but the means were uniform."[50] Their approach was through voluntary, experimental collectivism. In Robert Owen's words, "the change from the OLD system to the NEW must become universal," proceeding "solely from proof, in practice, of the very great superiority of the new arrangements over the old."[51] Writing of their mentality, a visitor to the Forty observed,

In Bettina I found an organization of mostly highly educated men who naturally were unaccustomed to manual labor and understood little about farming but loved the hunt, and classic lectures. Had a well constructed roomy house in which all resided and slept jointly, therefore well furnished with campbeds. A small building at the side served as the kitchen.

The cooking chores here ... were the first source of discord. For me it was interesting and instructive to see communism tried practically. At classical school in Hamburg I attended Professor Wurm's lectures on communism and socialism and had there learned the beautiful reform-ideals of Fourier and Louis Blanz. But here, experience taught me, that an organization of communism requires a capable organizer and leader and that the old adage: "many heads, many-sided-ness" still holds true.[52]

Within less than a year, the Bettina experiment "went to pieces like a bubble."[53] Some had given themselves up entirely to intellectual speculation while others had quibbled about work details. "Most of the professional men wanted to do the directing and ordering," recalled the thirteen-year-old botanist, "while the mechanics and laborers were to carry out their plans. Of course, the latter failed to see the justice of this ruling, so no one did anything."[54]

After they abandoned Bettina, most of the Forty retired in 1848 to the *Darmstädter Farm*, a Latin colony offshoot of the fraternity. Five of these split away the next year and settled twelve miles from Sisterdale on a third commune called *Tusculum*, where every man was to live as he pleased. They sold this place two years later for a fourth of the purchase price, bought more land nearby, and then gave up the venture entirely. On this last land, Gustav Theissen, another German intellectual—one of the Forty-Eighters at Sisterdale—laid out the town of Boerne, naming it for the archradical German journalist Ludwig Börne.

As they grew older, most of the Forty eventually settled into occupations for which they had been trained with lives distinguished in no way from their fellow townsmen other than by their former connection with the fraternity. Some achieved positions of prominence in the state. One of these, Jacob Kuechler (1823–1893), from the university of Giessen, first became a West Texas surveyor. Then, after escaping from the German unionist uprising, he waited out the Civil War in Mexico. Upon returning to the state, he became a delegate to the constitutional convention of 1868–69. For about a decade thereafter he was commissioner of the General Land Office in Austin. Another prominent member of the Forty was Gustav Schleicher (1823–1879), from Darmstadt. Educated at Giessen in civil engineering and architecture, he was drafted to build the Frankfurt-Heidelberg railroad shortly before the group's departure. After Bettina failed, Schleicher established a shingle

Congressman Gustav Schleicher

Courtesy of Sophienburg Museum

mill outside New Braunfels. He gave this mill up to become a surveyor in 1850, and two years later he was elected to the state legislature. During the Civil War, he held a commission in the Confederate corps of engineers. Later he practiced law in San Antonio and superintended construction of the San Antonio and Mexican Gulf Railroad. Between 1875–79 he served three terms in the House of Representatives.

The most distinguished of the Forty was Ferdinand von Herff (1820–1912), son of a privy-councilor of Hesse-Darmstadt and a cousin of Meusebach. Trained first at Bonn, he was introduced to a social circle which included Alexander von Humboldt (from whom he carried letters of introduction to Texas), Prince Albert, and Prince Frederick of Prussia. At court in his native city he frequently met Maria Alexandra, a future czarina of Russia. Later, in Berlin, Herff continued his studies in pathology, surgery, and physiology, and in 1843 he graduated from the university of Giessen. Already famous as a surgeon, the twenty-seven-year-old Herff negotiated with the Adelsverein and led

Dr. Ferdinand von Herff

Courtesy of August Herff

an advance party of the Forty to Texas.[55] Having seen the failure of undisciplined personal freedom at Bettina, Herff retained his faith in the future of the New World, but became now a proponent of gradual political reform. When he returned to Germany to marry, he was impressed into the army during the Revolution of 1848 and witnessed the final suppression of German radicalism of the nineteenth century. Late in 1849, Dr. Herff and his young wife departed Germany for Texas. At first, before they settled into the physician's fine home in San Antonio, his wife was not overly taken with the promise of America. Herff's biographer, Henry B. Dielmann, cites a letter written to Germany in 1850 by the wife of Professor Ernst Kapp of Sisterdale:

The Mrs. Doctor von Herff, who arrived a week sooner than we did, is still very unhappy. She thinks her husband, who had been here several years, had not told her about everything. He, however, remarked very dryly: "When one speaks in Germany of great privations and hardships, one takes it to be a generalization and regards it as nothing; when, however, privations and hardships come in specific cases, then they are considered unbearable."[56]

In 1850 Herff published his mature political philosophy in *Die geregelte Auswanderung des deutschen Proletariats mit besonderer Beziehung auf Texas*, a treatise on the incremental transplantation of the German proletariat to Texas by a heavily financed national organization. This grandiose scheme, derived in parts from Fourier, Cabet, and probably Engels and Marx, called for a directed economy, controlled production and distribution, and curtailed personal liberty designed so that the lower classes could rise by their own efforts to become decent and worthy citizens of their new fatherland.[57]

IV *Refugees from Reaction: The Forty-Eighters in Texas*

With the establishment of Sisterdale and the arrival of the Forty-Eighters, the last of three nineteenth-century German reform movements reached antebellum Texas. The first of these grew from Goethe's individualistic morality expressed in *Faust* but was tempered by the corporate ethical idealism of

Wilhelm Meister, the moral aesthetic of internal and gradual progression through successively higher stages of reality. Meusebach, Lindheimer, and Roemer were the major proponents of this idealism in Texas during the Adelsverein colonization. The second of these reform movements, communitarianism, was an offshoot in Germany of Goethe's corporate philosophy, filtered through the philosophical constructs of Fourier, Cabet, and perhaps Marx and Engels. In this category are the Forty, whose youthful idealism saw reform alone—the mystical society without the benevolent prince—as showing a path into the future. The third of these movements, and the other extreme, included the most articulate and radical nineteenth-century German reformers. These were the Forty-Eighters, individualists without a corporate base, revolutionaries who rebelled against utopianism turned inward in the form of human perfectibility, who demanded immediate social changes, and who stayed in Germany until their defeat in 1848 forced them to get out.[58]

The Forty-Eighters left with a sense of impending disaster for Germany. They reached America unencumbered by any notions of a "transatlantic Germany" or a model state in the New World. America was for them the ideal, and with all their energy and experience in revolutionary politics, they set about to become super-patriots of the land which took them in. A letter to Germany from a Forty-Eighter in Texas summarizes the mood:

Much land around here has been bought by people ... who want a place of refuge ... during the bad times which will soon come to Germany. All people in America are agreed that there will be a mighty clash in Germany, yes in all of Europe, in which not even the child in the mother's womb will be safe. America will not remain neutral in the coming revolution, but will help the republicans. Our country gains strength every year and could show the Old World who is boss.[59]

In his study of the Forty-Eighters Carl Wittke writes, "When western Europe exploded into revolution in 1848, all the liberal forces west of Russia hailed the occasion as the beginning of a new springtime ... and the bright new dawn after a long night of reaction. When that springtime ended in a killing frost, political refugees scattered to the far corners of the western world."[60] Another eminent historian, Veit Valentin, explains the failure in *1848*:

The German Revolution of 1848 erected no guillotines and held no extraordinary courts of a purely political nature.... No one in Germany thought that in order to combat the past, its representatives must be made personally defenceless and economically impotent. Outwardly it was nothing more than a purely political reversal, borne aloft by representatives of pure humanitarianism; a humane revolution is necessarily a semi-revolution. This was probably the deepest error of the men of 1848.[61]

As part of the ensuing exodus which found Marx, Kinkel, Freiligrath, and Mazzini in London and Garibaldi and Kossuth temporarily exiled in New York, the Forty-Eighters who sought refuge in Texas included Ottomar von Behr, Julius Dresel, Friedrich Kapp and his uncle Dr. Ernst Kapp, Dr. Julius Froebel, Dr. Adolf Douai, Gustav Theissen, August Siemering, and Baron von Westphal (the brother-in-law of Karl Marx). These men built homes at Sisterdale in the hills west of New Braunfels, where according to Rudolph L. Biesele "the woods resounded with the 'classic' strokes of the Latin scholars."[62] A traveler through the village remembered that farmers gathered from a wide area to attend meetings of a Freethinkers' Society and that often one saw several of them resting from their work under a clump of live-oaks while they engaged their minds in discussions of St. Simon and Fourier.[63] A partisan rivalry eventually developed and sometimes spilled over into politics between these Latin Farmers, called the "Greens" (or greenhorns), and the earlier Adelsverein settlers known as the "Grays" (or oldtimers).[64] But for the most part, the Forty-Eighters were content to leave the views of their neighbors undisturbed and they kept to their own in the idyllic community. There they remained from 1849 until secession drew them again from isolation.

Sisterdale's existence actually dated from 1847 when Nicolas Zink, a German engineer who had taken part in the Greek

Ottomar von Behr's home in Sisterdale

Courtesy of Mrs. J.R. Cade

Pencil sketch of Ottomar von Behr
by Richard Petri

Courtesy of Sophienburg Museum

Revolution, settled up the Guadalupe in the valley of the Sister Creeks. He had been followed by Ottomar von Behr (1810–1856), son of the premier of Anhalt-Koethen and an acquaintance of Alexander von Humboldt and Bettina von Arnim. As a member of the landed gentry, Behr's singular interest apparently was agricultural reform. His book—*Guter Rath für Auswanderer nach den Vereinigten Staaten von Nordamerika, mit besonderer Berücksichtigung von Texas* (Leipzig, 1847)—was a guide for German immigrants to Texas. His research at Sisterdale resulted in the development of a new breed of sheep especially adapted to the climate of the Southwest. His log and half-timber home on the Guadalupe was the stopping place of Duke Paul of Württemberg and Frederick Law Olmsted. It contained a harpsichord, possibly

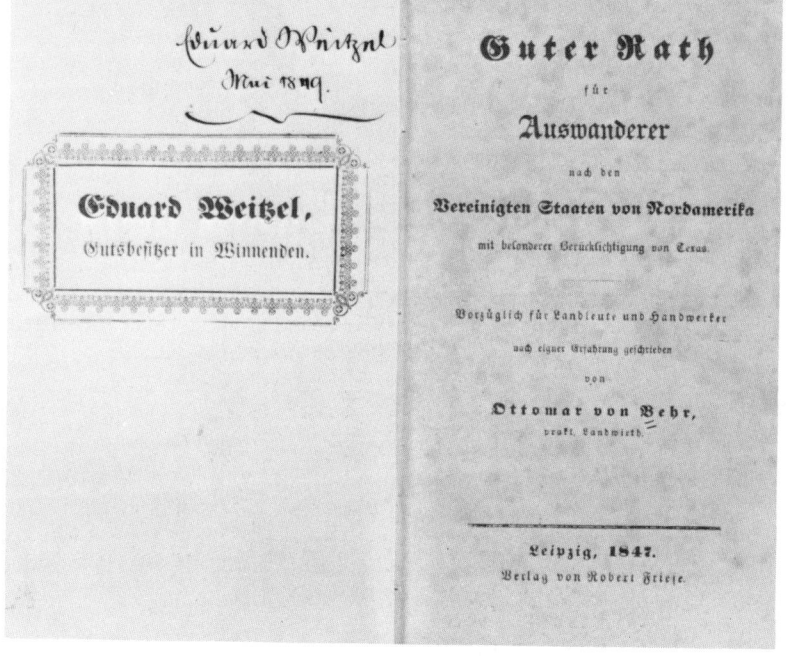

Title page of Behr's handbook on immigration to Texas (1847)

Courtesy of Ottomar von Behr

Dr. Adolf Douai
Courtesy of Sophienburg Museum

August Siemering
Courtesy of Sophienburg Museum

the first lending library in Texas, the post office, and Behr's own office as justice of the peace.[65]

One of the next settlers at Sisterdale was Julius Dresel (1816–1901), a member of a prominent family in the German freedom movement. With friends among the Forty and a brother who was consul of Nassau in Texas and Meusebach's successor as commissioner-general of the Adelsverein,[66] Julius Dresel was one of the most colorful and widely known of the Forty-Eighters in Texas. The family of Dr. Ernst Kapp (1808–1896) fled directly from prison in Germany to Texas. Kapp was a professor of cultural geography in Westphalia when he published a liberal political treatise—*Der konstituierte Despotismus und die konstitutionelle Freiheit*—which led to his arrest after the revolution. His nephew Friedrich Kapp joined him in Texas before he became prominent in the Republican party during Lincoln's campaign and administration.

Later Forty-Eighters in Sisterdale included Edward Degener (1809–1890) from Brunswick. A man of great wealth, Degener worked on the international level for the advancement of liberal, democratic ideals. Professor Julius Froebel (1805–1893) taught mineralogy at Zurich before he became involved in the revolution in Vienna, where he was condemned to death but pardoned on the condition that he leave Europe. Julius Froebel was a nephew of the pedagog Friedrich Froebel. Dr. Adolf Douai (1819–1888) was a private tutor and revolutionary tractarian before he arrived in Texas. Called the earliest popularizer of Marxian ideas in the United States, Douai's outspokenness resulted in his near ruin on several occasions. Driven from New Braunfels as a teacher, he became the editor of the *San Antonio Zeitung*, in which he advocated the abolition of slavery. When he was drummed out of the state in 1856, he went to Boston. His first school there was destroyed after an allegedly atheistic commemoration of Humboldt.[67] He survived, however, to become known as the introducer of Friedrich Froebel's kindergarten system in America. The last of the significant Forty-Eighters in Texas was the journalist August Siemering (1830–1883), from Berlin, who, despite myopia and chronic illness, eventually won all his political battles by outliving his opponents.

Goethe on the Guadalupe

Siemering's vignette of Sisterdale shows a life distinguished by "a certain politeness in manners" and by "the cultivation of science." Here in the village, "Nearly every farm had a good library, the latest publications in literature were always available, and Sunday was often devoted to free lectures." The farms were named from German folk tales—the "Polished Boot," the "Lion's Citadel," even a "Paradise." Still the visit of Paul of Württemberg to the village caused the Latin Farmers considerable consternation. Siemering wrote of a neighbor:

One morning he had found the prince polishing his boots and watched the prince for quite a while trying hard to make his boots shine. "What a pity," he told him, "that Your Royal Highness is a prince. It would be a pleasure for my boys to do this work for you if you were an ordinary farmer, but they would not think of polishing the boots of a prince!"

Siemering admitted that "the old revolutionaries were in a fix as to how to address the prince, since they did not recognize any title or nobility. One suggested 'Mr. Württemberg,' another 'Mr. Paul.' Eventually," Siemering concluded, "they agreed to call him 'Prince' and this they did. Only the ladies continued to call him 'Your Royal Highness,' and they were always rewarded with a 'Madam.' "[68]

Of Professor Kapp, Siemering recalled that "within his book-covered walls he used to serve his guests with self-grown wine . . . and home-grown tobacco," while he philosophized about "the advantages of life in the country." The professor was recognized by European scholars for two works, a comparative cultural geography (1845) and a philosophy of tools and technology (1877). In these works Kapp postulated, a century ahead of his time, that the human organism (humanity) was determined by environment rather than history, and that the future was threatened by pollution and dehumanization resulting from man's reckless search for better machines.[69]

After his release from prison, Ernst Kapp announced, resuming the theme from Goethe, "I leave Germany, exchanging comfort for toil, the familiar pen for the unfamiliar spade, but I will be a free man in a free earth."[70] The "free earth" of

Dr. Ernst Kapp
Courtesy of Institute of Texan Cultures

Texas overwhelmed the professor's wife as the family journeyed inland toward Sisterdale. Writing home, she described a strange, psychic landscape.

Everybody tries to stop you, to hold you, by painting the next succeeding region as horrifying, but up to now as far as we have come, the land has become more and more beautiful.
 I find that ... one is overcome with an amazing change; the farther one comes inland, the more civilization ceases, but one transforms with the changes and begins to think it must be so.[71]

While the professor cleared their farm, wrote, and experimented with natural cures for physical illnesses, his wife told of the change which had come over him.

How contented, healthy, and happy Ernst here is, I cannot describe to you; you would not know him anymore. I am delighted about it everytime I look at him. Daily he extols how fortunate it is for him that he came away from tired old Europe. (13 January 1850)

The whole family, in Ida Kapp's words, seemed transformed by the new surroundings and infected with energy and purpose.

If someone portrayed life the way we here are living it—we sleep with a cover and a pillow on the floor of a semi-furnished room, do our cooking with one pot, one cauldron and one cornbread pan for which we have to build a fire out in the yard, etc. Eating and drinking utensils consist of a few tin plates and tin cups, we have rented... an ordinary kitchen table... for chairs we use baskets and trunks... yes, would someone have portrayed it to me, I would have laughed.... And yet I don't know how it happens, but I never before have been more content and in better health. I now have the courage to tackle any and all things and... I know now that everything will take root. (13 January 1850)

Ida Kapp was not alone in observing a change in human nature brought on by the new land. A father wrote of his young son, who appeared "determined to live his own way," taking orders from no one,

Otto... has shown little desire for physical labor when given a job to do, although for his years he shows a remarkable skill and untiring eagerness in cultivating a small plot in our garden given him to till all by himself. However, he insists upon doing it his own way absolutely, which leads me to believe that republican principles, the love of freedom, have already taken root in him....[72]

In short, the Forty-Eighters believed they had found the qualities they had searched for in Germany. As their existence became more and more comfortable, they lost the sense of disaster which had impelled them to America, and they set their minds to preserving the promise of their new homeland. Not all of them concurred, however. When Friedrich Kapp left Texas he ridiculed his former companions, these law-givers, dictators, provisional governors and regents, ministers, civil commissioners, triumvirs, generals and staff officers—in what forests and blockhouses have they found asylum, where have they settled and where are they living out their monotonous lives? They wished it so, and they are disintegrating of and by themselves.[73]

But at the same time, Friedrich Kapp encouraged their acculturation when he warned that "the well-being of the Germans does not lie in the separation from the American educational interests, nor in fantastic dreams of founding a German State in America."[74]

For all their avowed liberalism, the Forty-Eighters had difficulty understanding democratic processes and republican government. Above all, they could not tolerate compromise. With the exception of Behr, and perhaps of Kapp (whose Texas experiment foundered because of his poor health), the Forty-Eighters were too individualistic, too impatient, to succeed. They outdistanced their potential following, overtaxed democratic processes, at least in the South, and alienated people needlessly. August Siemering touches on this problematic attitude in his sketch of life in Sisterdale. Frequently the conversations there turned from science to politics, he explained, and although the Latin Farmers had settled in a Southern state, they were strong abolitionists. "They did not try to conceal their political catechism and even went so far as to agitate openly against slavery in 1853."

At first the inhabitants of Sisterdale united in a "Free Association" whose President was Professor Kapp, and in the following year this Association invited the Germans of Texas to a convention at San Antonio. The convention actually met in May 1854 and was attended by delegates of nearly all German settlements. Among other things it was decided that "slavery was an evil and had to be abolished."

In a public statement they called for "federal aid," meaning financial compensation to former slaveholders, to abolish it. To a Southerner, however, in 1854, "federal aid" implied something quite different. An insistence upon absolute human liberty was at the root of the antislavery fervor of the Forty-Eighters.

Goethe on the Guadalupe

Friedrich Kapp quickly perceived the universal implications of the issue:

> The problem of slavery is not the problem of the Negro. It is the eternal conflict between a small privileged class and the great mass of the nonprivileged, the eternal struggle between aristocracy and democracy.[75]

Many Forty-Eighters saw it as the destiny of the Germans and Americans "to reunite in the common struggle to extend the frontiers of human liberty."[76] In this perfectionism was the seed of a great danger to their political idealism. "The 'Latin Settlement' did not survive the Civil War," concluded Siemering. Its vitality turned to reactionary despair.

V Cut off in the New World

The Civil War blighted German idealism and culture in Texas, although that was not symbolically clear until the unification of Germany in 1871 when Bismarck concluded the national goal of a century of German intellectuals and radical liberals. While the Germans in Texas rejoiced along with the rest of the German homeland, they somehow sensed that the unification, achieved without them, left them no part in the old country while the war in the United States had cut them off for at least a generation from a part in their new country. The idealism of a young girl quoting Wilhelm von Humboldt in 1846, "We associated home with two worlds,"[77] had turned to the despair in 1871 of being citizens of neither country, of finding neither "rest nor peace" in this world or the old.[78]

At the outbreak of the war, Meusebach retired from state politics to contemplate the natural order on his farm, withdrawing much as Goethe had into an inner existence.

Lindheimer, on the other hand, became not only the cultural but also the political spokesman of the German majority. As editor of the *Neu-Braunfelser Zeitung* (1852), he attacked German unionism, calling it impolitic to antagonize the American settlers and dangerous to meddle in their affairs. Opposed to slavery, he nonetheless protested against the San Antonio platform of men like Douai because of their theoretical and often abrasive language, as in the example of their demand for "federal aid." Lindheimer aggressively countered a slaveowner and nativist backlash to restrict the political rights of German settlers. When the American press accused Germans of organizing singing societies and debate clubs as abolitionist bases, he wrote that the Americans were acting in "an unrepublican, inquisition-like, and illogical manner in casting suspicion on the German settlers" as a whole for the actions of a few. Furthermore, he counseled Germans to fall in step, exhorting them to find that quality of humanity required of frontiersmen on the edge of a savage wilderness.

Despite Lindheimer's efforts to avert armed conflicts between Germans and Americans during Secession, the radical posture of the Forty-Eighters prevailed in the western German counties of the hill country. Unionism was strongest in the freethinker villages of Sisterdale and Comfort (1854). Through firsthand observation, Siemering reported of this area after the war:

Part of the German youth had followed the Confederate flag, though mostly under pressure. It can be said that until 1862 it was a rare exception for a German to join the Confederate movement out of conviction. The Texas Germans believed in the Union and its final victory.... Whoever had a chance to listen to the conversations at the camp fires of the German companies by night could see that they were friends of the Union in spite of their grey jacket.[79]

The impetus for German unionism throughout the state derived from Douai's *San Antonio Zeitung*, which Siemering described as "decidedly Republican and abolitionistic," serving "a movement that was supported by at least part of the Germans," in opposition to Lindheimer's paper which "gradually shifted to extreme southern politics ... and remained strictly Democratic." Biesele writes that anti-German hostility might have ended under Lindheimer's influence had Douai "not kept on agitating for abolition."[80] Siemering even admits that the *San Antonio Zeitung* was the only German paper in Texas which "regularly published articles in English against slavery" so that "the attention of the Americans was soon drawn to it."

The war destroyed the Sisterdale movement. Douai left Texas

for the better climate of the North. Julius Dresel was, in his own words, taken in chains to San Antonio. The distinguished old Degener (later congressman from Texas) was kept in San Antonio under arrest. Part of Professor Kapp's family returned to Germany for a visit but remained there permanently, for their health, they said. Gustav Theissen had become prominent in New York financial circles but later took up residence in Linz. Siemering, though decidedly a unionist, was drafted into the Confederate army as a lieutenant. He was subsequently discharged because his eyes grew so weak by the "constant exposure to the cold air" that he could see no farther than "two to three steps."[81]

In Comfort, several hundred male unionists reorganized the "Union Loyal League" into a German battalion with companies from Kendall, Gillespie, and Kerr counties on 4 July 1862. When letters were intercepted allegedly connecting the German officers with Southern unionists like A. J. Hamilton (later military governor) and E. J. Davis (last Reconstruction governor), these counties were declared in open rebellion.[82] Believing that a safe-conduct had been issued, the German cadre assembled for movement into Mexico and was ambushed by a Confederate force on the early morning of 10 August 1862. This Battle of the Nueces, as it came to be called, effectively eliminated what remained of the radical liberal element in Texas.

"To the German colonies," Siemering wrote, the war "had been like a nightmare. No more immigrants from Europe had come since 1860. On the contrary thousands ... had left the state. A considerable number of them had settled in Mexico," where German life "was strengthened at that time by the Austrian troops."

Most of the German Texans went to the northern states, where they enlisted in the army, or to Germany. Many a house in Texas stood empty and many a field remained uncultivated. The small places were empty, and in others there were only women and children left. When the Union flag was flying again on the capitol in Austin the question was raised whether or not the Germans could find their home again in Texas.[83]

The reaction solidified the culture. At the same time, the German unification in 1871 aroused great celebration in the state. One proud Texas-German father named his firstborn after the victory at Sedan. Bismarck saloons popped up all over German Texas, and the Iron Chancellor's likeness was displayed here and there, probably with no deeper implications than, say, a picture of Queen Victoria hanging in St. George's Church at Wakefield, Kansas, at the turn of the century. Reflecting on the events of 1870–71, a German grandmother, Ottilie Fuchs Goeth, whose parents had come with the Adelsverein, wrote,

"The Watch on the Rhine" had taken to the field and the news of its victory spread around the world. . . . Finally there came the renewal of the German Reich at Versailles. It was difficult to fathom and one feared to be imagining it. . . . Germany was an empire as large and grand as in the days of the Hohenstaufen. Young dreams had been fulfilled. Old people were glad to have survived long enough to experience it, and even those living in Texas, where so many had fled from their fatherland.[84]

Germany was now a new political reality, something different from what they had left and no longer a part of them. The great majority were content to leave it at that and to get on with the tasks nearest at hand. Because they were able to take the Ironclad Oath, Germans played an important role in municipal and state politics during Reconstruction in Texas. Their cultural life bloomed one last time during the 1870s, but then that headed downhill. During the whole time, however, their socioeconomic assimilation moved ahead with great strides. Some, though, like Friedrich Kapp, "could not shake off the 'demon thought'" of being cut off.[85] He returned. German culture in America could no longer draw sustenance from an old homeland. In Texas, being German was something suspicious, as it was again in World War I, and again in World War II. New generations grew up with two cultures existing side by side but rarely mixing. The German culture became a private thing, closed to outside influences. It fed off itself.

In a sense, Friedrich Kapp saw clearly where this dream of

a "model state" in the New World was headed when he wrote of the atrophy of these intellectuals on the frontier. In 1920 when his son Wolfgang Kapp overthrew the Weimar government and established a rightist dictatorship for a week, the grandchildren in Texas of Dr. Ernst Kapp managed their sawmill, store, and farm uninterrupted by the immediacy of this news—if indeed it ever reached Comfort or if they knew who Wolfgang Kapp was. Fifty years later, the wife of one Kapp great-grandchild in Comfort would write,

There are no available statistics, but it is a shrewd guess that even today seventy percent of all German-Americans still marry within the Germanic family and this is the fifth (sometimes the sixth) generation since pioneer days. The community approves of this. It keeps the bloodlines clean.

Now that this culture is nearly at an end, one looks at the older generation, still speaking the beloved language, maintaining their identity, preserving their antiques in museums, reading yellowed letters and diaries, and one speculates about them.[86]

CHAPTER 2

The Old Homeland and the New

MACK WALKER

ABOUT 130 years ago, at a time when the emigration to America was arousing great interest and concern in Germany, there was a saying going around that writers seemed to pick up and repeat in varied forms and contexts: "Newark," if it was Newark, "is a city in the American state of New Jersey inhabited by five thousand Germans and one Irishman. Every two years they have an election and make the Irishman mayor."

I tell the story again not so as to nourish German national self-pity, which at that time at least needed no special encouragement, but because it points to an ethnic model or stereotype taking form and widely believed in Germany then; and this allows a point of departure for some general observations about the social and cultural quality of the German emigration from Central Europe to North America, which took place principally in the nineteenth century, and especially in the years

---

This lecture is based on my work in *Germany and the Emigration, 1816–1885* (Cambridge, 1964), and *German Home Towns: Community, State and General Estate 1648–1871* (Ithaca, 1971). For its preparation I have also read Ethel Hander Geue, *New Homes in a New Land. German Immigration to Texas, 1847–1861* (Waco, 1970); Peter Marschalk, *Deutsche Überseewanderung im 19. Jahrhundert* (Stuttgart, 1973); and La Vern J. Rippley, *The German-Americans* (Boston, 1976).

The Old Homeland and the New

from about 1830 to 1890. The story suggests a link perceived between the origins of the German emigration and some characteristics of German-American culture. Notice that it comes from informal German sources, around the time of the frustrated and generally futile revolutions of 1848. A modern American counterpart might be that when modern American historians or sociologists go to describe the role of ethnicity in American life, they have little to say about German-Americans. Generally speaking, there is little to find out about German-Americans in the places where these scholars tend to look: aggressive political action, social dissatisfaction or unrest, organized ethnic politics.

What the factors for this may be, on the American side, I am not prepared to argue. One is probably the religious diversity among the Germans, so that their religious community or association has not coincided with the ethnic or linguistic one—compare Irish Catholic organization and its relation with Irish urban Democratic politics, for example. Then of course came the two world wars of our century, which made German-Americans pull in their heads and play down their European national identity.

Our subject here, though, is the migration—why Germans migrated to America, and inseparably from that, who they were: what kinds of people, what kinds of aims and hopes propelled them. In any effort to say general things about this, surely particular instances may not fit; but more troublesome still, if we do find some broad economic or demographic cause that seems common to large masses of people in migration, it still might not be the single most important motive for any one of them. We want here a theme for characterizing the German migration of the nineteenth century that connects their situation in the land they left behind with their culture in the land they came to—from a place we might now describe as a "developing country," where growth of industry and population were just taking hold (a "modernizing" country, in some contemporary jargon), to a land of what might be called a modified or gentled frontier, with space for nearly everybody but yet a reasonable level of personal security. The German journalists I quoted picked up that anecdote because it fit something about their own country and society, which their emigrating countrymen were telling them and bearing with them to America.

Let us begin then with some general observations about the historical context of that great nineteenth-century German migration. That was a time of massive transformation in the Atlantic world, changes of a magnitude far greater than any we have experienced in our own time if only because people saw them but did not understand them and were not equipped to deal with them. Here was the onset of population growth, with the graph pointing toward straight up, leaving people without houses or shops or trades or farms to build their families on, for the social economy was static and could not accommodate growing numbers of people. Here were the revolutionary changes in technology, the large factory and the wage-labor force, imposing styles of life morally and culturally painful to accept. Here were accumulating pools of wealth, providing active and aggressive financial and industrial capital for new, imponderable centers of economic and political power. Along with these changes in Europe came new systems for mass communication, for transportation of goods and people, and for exchange of information— the railroad, the cheap newspaper, the steamship, and so on— with their pressure for economic and cultural and social conformity; and coming out of all of these, the political and economic unifications of both Germany and the United States in the 1860s and 1870s. This was a wrenching, a baffling, and often a terrifying experience in western history, but one which in German society struck a special sensitivity and elicited a particular response.

There are many reasons for this and many facets of it. For shorthand we may use a term from cultural or artistic history: the Biedermeier. This name for a cultural style that emerged in the Germany of those years sheds light on the causes and nature of the great emigration which was a main social phenomenon of those years. For the Biedermeier style and the German migration of the mid-nineteenth century seem to me genetically related, pointing back to a common origin in social and cultural conditions. The hallmark of the Biedermeier style is its home-seeking, quiet-seeking quality, its preoccupation with private things, and with stability. It seems fair to interpret this

The Old Homeland and the New

Mr. and Mrs. Leopold von Iwonski
Pencil Drawing by Carl G. von Iwonski

Courtesy of Mrs. H.B. Dickenson

as a recoiling against the violence and change that seemed to be developing in the world (as part of the "modernizing" historical process); it was an expression of retreat, of cultural "inner migration," maybe, to stable values of the family, the small traditional community, to the eternal patterns of nature. In Biedermeier painting we find mature and quiet landscapes, and small-town scenes, home interiors, and especially the family group, harmoniously depicted making house-music, for example, with Papa at the piano, Mama plucking a guitar, the children tootling away on their wooden flutes. Or cutting out silhouettes, around the table in the lamplight, or reading aloud to one another. In Biedermeier home furnishings: the popularity of simple, domesticated designs, useful and quiet, in contrast with ornate public representation and ostentation. In the writing of fiction the Biedermeier style was characteristically the village novel or tale, celebrating the simplicity, virtue, and truth of the small and stable community, put in deliberate contrast with the rushing, clanging, changing great world that came to be called "modern times," times and ways which almost by definition were set upon destroying the homelike values that the Biedermeier style located by the contrast. For the converse of this conscious style of family, home, stability, and simplicity was, in the cultural dialectic, fear and anxiety about where Europe, where Germany, where one's own native home was going and how to get away from where it was going.

The German emigration that came out of that Biedermeier world was especially marked by its home-seeking, peace-seeking, stability-seeking qualities. The word "uprooted" is a cliché of American immigration history, fairly enough; but to get its meaning fully one should remember that the uprooting took place in Europe, something happening to people before they moved, which made them move; and from that it follows, particularly in the German instance, that what impelled or propelled the emigrant was this uprooting process, his intolerance of the uprooted condition, and his hope to find a place to resink his roots, a society where he knew who and where he was, the society and values depicted in the Biedermeier style. In this way the act of emigration, that central formative and identifying event of German-Americans, was a profoundly preservative, conservative action; and if it turned out that the emigrant and his family could not in fact recreate in America the idealized, utopianized old world being destroyed in Europe (that question we cannot try to manage here) it was not for want of wishing and trying.

We can come a little closer to concrete detail, in this cultural and moral picture, by making a social analysis of the German emigrants. The German emigrant was not a rich man, or a very poor man; he was rather the small family farmer, or the independent artisan or small merchant with a steady family trade, or the young man for whom that was the proper expectation or the young woman for whom that was the proper marriage. For the German small farmer, modern growth of rural population, pressure on land, and the development of large-scale commercial agriculture were shrinking the chances of the small subsistence farm: in America, though, he heard, he could find or recreate one. For the small craftsman, or a family businessman, modern industry and transportation and capitalism were exposing him to a scale of competition that threatened to overwhelm his economic independence, tossing aside his shop, the dignity of himself, and his calling in the society, trying to make a wage-laborer out of him: perhaps in the modified frontier, the premodern regions of America, he could find his place and dignity and honor again. The wealthy German businessman did not emigrate because he had no reason to emigrate; the industrial wage-laborer did not emigrate, partly because he had too little money to pay his way, but also because working in an American factory was no better than working in a German one.

Another reason was that the industrial worker and industrial employer both had accepted the modern condition of things and found a place in it. The German emigrant to America characteristically was somebody who did not want to go to the German city and its way of life. Notice that among the immigrant nationalities of the nineteenth century, comparing the German with, say, the Irish, Italians, and East Europeans, or the more recent black or Spanish-American migrants, the Germans seemed least likely to aim for and to congregate in the great metropolitan centers of North America (though that might be where in the course of events he stuck, along his road), nor did he aim for the wilds of the true frontier (though as in the case of the earliest Texas Germans he might find himself there). There is, to be sure, a partial exception here: German Jews commonly did locate in American cities; but the background of German Jewish immigrants was usually urban or urban related, or if rural then from the relatively poor and socially oppressive areas of Eastern Germany and Europe (compare Ireland) which they had no wish to recreate. So the Jewish exception supports the general proposition. On the whole, then, the Germans headed for the slightly populated, open but gentled areas of the Midwest and the old Northwest, countryside and small towns, and other areas like them as such areas were developed in other parts of the continent. Once there they established their homes and they stayed, again unlike some immigrant nationalities who often worked and saved their money in order to return to the old country.

The German-American group activities and associations were

like those of small-town life in Germany: the singing society, Wednesday evening or Sunday afternoon at the tavern, and so on—simple points of association among themselves rather than instruments formed for ethnic politics—again unlike urban Democratic party clubs, for example. Where one sees German ethnic politicians like Schurz or Koerner at work they are working with preexisting German cultural or recreational associations to build bases for their own political ambitions. Where one sees a serious and widespread German interest in American national politics it seems to be on the issue of free soil or of temperance—or, rather, antitemperance. Free soil meant the establishment and protection of communities of independent small farmers or artisans; this seems the background of the hostility toward the slave economy, against blacks and their owners, often associated with German-Americans. German-American hostility to the temperance movement in the United States defended German rights to that homliest of social solvents —beer around the table and around the room. In Germany beer and the tavern have long been focal points of village and small-town life; and if anything focuses German-American identity, perhaps it appears there, in the passions and the ethnic solidarity which the temperance issue aroused. Most national political issues did not do this, even including American entry into the two major wars against Germany in the twentieth century, where German-Americans did not provide the solid barrier against American entry that the governments both of the Emperor William and of Adolf Hitler hoped for, and where their concern was not with international issues or the rights and wrongs of Germany but how to protect the homes and attachments they had achieved in America.

Let us now try to slice up this description in still another way, a historical form setting down the stages through time of the German migration to North America, to see what each of them was like and was about. The early birds, of the seventeenth and eighteenth centuries, are difficult to generalize about; the rhythms are not marked. Commonly we find particular religious associations and connotations—Palatine Calvinists to upstate New York, Quaker and other Pennsylvania Dutch, Pietists, and Moravians—but remember that religion was the main group-forming criterion in the political and social life of Germany in those centuries; religious association defined the boundaries of community toward the outside and enforced social discipline within. German migration then often took the form of group migration organized on religious bases, for mutual protection and discipline. Groups pushed out of Germany because they were deemed alien and hostile to the prevailing governments and societies there. This migration was sporadic and particular; it did not flow from the massive social dynamics one can identify in the nineteenth century.

After the end of the revolutionary era of the late eighteenth century, German emigration resumed in 1816–17 in something like the older pattern—many religious groups, coming especially from southwestern Germany—but in ways forecasting future patterns, too, with famine, the beginnings of industrial competition and mass markets, technological unemployment of artisanry. In the 1830s and 1840s began the "social" migration, whose impetus and context in Biedermeier Germany I tried to establish earlier, and which set its cultural imprint on the German-American migration generally. Its sources were this steady and growing pressure of population on land, and these pressures from industrial development on the artisan economy, both of which pressures in combination now came to be perceived as permanent, irreversible threats imposed by the future on the German home and community in Europe; and the emigrants went seeking family farms and communally circumscribed crafts and businesses in the relatively safe but open lands of Ohio, Illinois, and Missouri.

Now the "hungry forties" and the "Forty-Eighters": here we ought to distinguish—as contemporaries clearly did—between the great bulk of migration in the late 1840s and early 1850s, which was composed and motivated much in the way just described (but intensified by crop failures in potatoes and other things) and the political émigrés from the revolutions of 1848. The latter were a handful of educated and politically active people whose backgrounds and expression of goals were quite unlike those of the bulk of their migrating countrymen, who now were preeminently the Biedermeier emigration. This mid-century wave peaked in the mid-1850s, at the rate of a quarter-million German emigrants a year; then it was interrupted or slowed by such hindrances as American nativism, economic troubles in both countries, making it harder and riskier to move, and the civil wars of the 1860s in both countries.

When emigration revived in the 1870s and 1880s it began to show other symptoms, signs of having another character. The German emigrants were a bit poorer than before, more likely to have been wage workers in Germany, where industry was booming, and more likely in America to enter the urban work force of American cities where industry was also booming. The shape of the societies in both countries and their economic relations were changing, and even though the German emigrant and immigrant were culturally close to their predecessors of only thirty years before, fluctuations in volume of migration began to follow fluctuations in the business cycle more closely and positively. Transatlantic transportation was cheaper and safer than before (the steamship); so was inland rail transportation. Wage-earning people could follow opportunities for industrial work more closely. Consequently emigrants with that background and expectation now began to flow in increasing numbers into the older social categories of displaced farmer and artisan; and there was another crest in the volume of migration in the early 1880s, again at around a quarter-million.

That changing pattern of the 1880s foretells the end of the great nineteenth-century migration. It tells how the migration, by the end of the nineteenth century, was taking place between two industrial nations, two "modern" societies, as we have used that word to distinguish modern from traditional societies. The older German-American is still there, with his traditional awareness of status and dignity, within family and community; and the tone he has set for German-American-ness seems to prevail. But migration from one industrial society to another looks different, and I daresay it feels different. Where earlier we saw the migrants in terms of their relations and concerns with family, home, and community, we now tend to see them in terms of social class, in the German case, especially, that badly defined and often puzzling stratum sometimes called the "lower middle class"—which indeed we may be wrong to think of as a "class"; perhaps even now it is more like the Biedermeier after all.

After the mid-1880s, then, with the victory of modern industrial patterns on both sides of the Atlantic, German emigration dropped off precipitously to a tiny fraction of what it had been; and when it did sometimes revive (notably after the end of World War II) it is hard to see in it that nineteenth-century character of anxiety about change and dislocation, that concern for family, home, and community. The near-disappearance of German emigration to America late in the 1880s marks an end to the very painful throes of transition in both countries from one kind of world to another, or at least an accommodation to it: a shift or adaptation, perhaps (remembering Newark, New Jersey), from what the nineteenth century called the Biedermeier toward what the twentieth came one day to call the silent majority.

CHAPTER 3

Man and His Environment:
Ernst Kapp's Pioneering Experience and His Philosophy of Technology and Environment

HANS-MARTIN SASS

ERNST Kapp, who was a farmer, carpenter, and hydrotherapist at Sisterdale (Kendall County), had another occupation —he was a philosopher. He was an outstanding philosopher, too. As early as 1845 he developed what is still a very important philosophy of environment. In 1877 he presented the world's first concise philosophy of technology. The fact that he could be one of the most excellent philosophers of his century indicates that a person can be a philosopher without being a pro-

---

Ernst Kapp's most important books—*Vergleichende allgemeine Erdkunde* (1868) and *Grundlinien einer Philosophie der Technik* (1877)—are available in 1978 and 1979 reprints, with introductory and bibliographical notes from Stern-Verlag, Düsseldorf. The best *biographical* information is given by Vera Flach (married to a great-grandson of Ernst Kapp), *A Yankee in German America: Texas Hill Country* (San Antonio, 1973); and S. W. Geiser, "Chronology of Dr. E. Kapp," *Southwestern Historical Quarterly* 50 (1946), 297–300. For Kapp's *political* activities see R. L. Biesele, "The Texas State Convention of Germans in 1854," *Southwestern Historical Quarterly* 33 (1930), 247–61, and H. M. Sass, "A Hegelian in Southwest Texas," *Owl of Minerva*, ed. for the Hegel Society of America by L. S. Stepelevich, Vol. 9, No. 2 (1977), 5–7. For

fessor of philosophy. It is a common prejudice in our times that only academic people, preferably doctors or professors of philosophy, can *do philosophy*. The contrary is true: we are all doing philosophy whenever we raise ultimate questions about the meaning of life and what is essential in the world; when we wonder about the reasons for values and aims in our life, we are doing nothing else than philosophy. Doing philosophy is a natural predisposition of all human beings, though only a few of us do so professionally at a certain level of accepted standards and techniques. Yet inasmuch as professional philosophers often live in an ivory-tower intellectual environment, they sometimes represent more the intellectual fashions and fads in the academic world than the needs of the human being in general. Overintellectualized academic communities tend to produce fictitious problems. As a matter of fact, many of the most important philosophers in the history of ideas were not professors of philosophy.

More than formerly, intellectuals in our post-Enlightenment time have a fatal tendency to fabricate and dream up new frameworks and horizons for secure and simple orientation in our very complex world. In creating those new intellectual religions they demonstrate a lack of understanding of the philosophical questions of everyday life and a lack of self-awareness of their own limits. There is a difference between philosophical questions rooted in our human experiences of everyday environments and those questions rooted only in the sometimes artificial and esoteric intellectual environments of academic life. Doing philosophy always answers the challenge of a given environment, first for orientation, analysis, and creating world views, and, second, for predisposing our actions in evaluating

---

Kapp's *philosophy* see E. Lenel, *Friedrich Kapp* (Leipzig, 1935), pp. 16–25; H. M. Sass, "Die philosophische Erdkunde des Hegelianers Ernst Kapp," *Hegel-Studien* 8 (1973), 163–81; H. M. Sass, "Meaning in Geography versus Meaning in History," *Proceedings of the Bicentennial Philosophical Symposium*, ed. P. Caws (New York, 1977). A copy of the letter from Friedrich Kapp to Ludwig Feuerbach, dated New York, December 10, 1852, is in the Universitätsbibliothek Helsinki (Finland), depositum Wilhelm Bolin.

moral norms and standards and setting up goals for emancipation or colonization as a sort of self-fulfilling prophecy.

Ernst Kapp's philosophy of environment and technology answers the challenges of modern times. It presupposes the results of the sciences and raises ethical questions. It represents a humanistic answer to questions raised in interdisciplinary fields of economics, history, social sciences, and politics.

Ernst Kapp, born 1808 in Ludwigsstadt (Oberfranken), was a sophisticated professional philosopher, yet he was open-minded enough to distrust academic fads. He was a brilliant student of geography, history, and philosophy at Bonn University, where he took his doctorate in 1828. After passing his examinations and becoming Gymnasial professor and Oberlehrer at Minden (Westfalen), he wrote several textbooks as well as books on how to teach geography and history. In his most scholarly work, *Philosophische oder vergleichende allgemeine Erdkunde als wissenschaftliche Darstellung der Erdverhältnisse und des Menschenlebens nach ihrem inneren Zusammenhang*, 2 vols. (Brunswick, 1845), he developed a philosophy of *environmental orientation and action*.

Kapp's philosophy of environment employed Hegel's dialectical method. However, Kapp's dialectic was not fully identical with that of Hegel in which Nature was seen as being derived from and dependent only upon the Absolute Idea. With Kapp both realities, *idea and nature*, were interdependent. The process of humanizing and developing nature was dialectical. This method of dialectic as a metascience was intended to "fluidify" the ossified material of positive science "and to rekindle the living idea (*Begriff*) in such a dead substance."[1] So, to Kapp, the dialectic mediated between Spirit and Nature, method and material, humanity and earth. This had to occur in such a way that nature would not be enslaved, material would not be alienated, and the earth would not be exploited. Nature must be *transfigured* according to a program of "emancipatorial spiritualization" and of "internal colonization" (*innere Kolonisation*). Not only external nature, but even human nature with its psychological and physical structure was in need of "internal colonization." This universal dialectic had four tasks: 1) analyzing and describing the factual correlations between spirit

Man and His Environment

and nature; 2) setting up goals for "internal colonization"; 3) overcoming the actual conflicts between man and nature, need and soil, techniques and material; and finally 4) dialectical criticism of scientific methods and philosophical positions. As Kapp himself wrote, nature, or environment, is the precondition of man; man's duty is to generate the consciousness of liberty both within the political state and within individual self-determination; man's duty is also "the liberation from the naturalness of his existence by means of work.... Therefore, environmentology is, according to the elements—nature, man, work—*physical, political and cultural environmentology.*"[2] Kapp combined the traditional philosophies of nature, politics, culture, and technology within a philosophy of environment. The center point of this combination was the demand for an "internal colonization" of both man and nature. Politics and culture were the fields for that colonization.

Not just the individual, but even the state had a "natural side," a geographical and anthropological expression which Kapp developed into a theory of Political Aqua-Geography. Through this construct, he dealt successively with Oriental, Greco-Roman, Oceanic, and modern global political history. In this system he indicated how rivers, inland seas, and oceans influence not only state-formations and constitutions, but military and economic formations as well, along with how cultural achievements and the scope of consciousness correlate to the given water-environment. This remarkable epistemological theory dealt in the final analysis with psychology and human evolution based upon environment, especially that of water. It was ultimately the aquatic environment that challenged and encouraged the individual to develop his intellectual capacities. This Political Aqua-Geography became the principle of Kapp's phenomenology of the mind and for his social and political history of mankind. It was his "internal colonization" (*innere Kolonisation*).

The subject of *Cultural Geography* was the emancipatorial "transfiguration" of nature—both internally and externally—as the embodiment of the mind, which Kapp designated with the Hegelian term "spiritualization" (*Begeisterung*). There was first the *cultivation of space* which consisted of 1) the spiritualization of the soil through agriculture, mining, and architecture;³ 2) the transformation of natural resources and of organic and animal products from raw materials into artificial products,⁴ and 3) the transfiguration of space through roads, waterways, and airways.⁵ This culture of space aimed at overcoming the given fragility of nature through appropriating, transforming, and establishing roadways. Nature, as raw and virgin, was not sacred but fragile, and needed transfiguration by cultivation and culture.⁶ The *cultivation of time* transfigured space-times and time-spaces through 1) communication on land, sea, and in air; 2) communication by mental powers (e.g., language-study, translations, universal languages, and the further invention and exchange of international and global economic and technical achievements);⁷ and finally 3) communication on its highest level by "universal telegraphics" (*universelle Telegraphik*) which would link universal language, semiotics, and inventions to global earthly transfiguration, unifying nations and spiritually transfiguring space as well as time through internal colonization.⁸ This program of universal telegraphics remained rather abstract, but it served as a concrete utopia of a general technology which, however, should not dominate nature but rather emancipate and transfigure raw nature.

Finally, this universal "transfiguring of nature" was concerned with "the vital functions and ways of exchange in human society, which emanated from the vital exchange between the cultural human being and the cultured earth" through "work turned into art."⁹ The nature of man and humanity, with regard to internal colonization, was the subject of the last chapter of Kapp's universal philosophy of environment. The political state of the future, in which, Kapp wrote, "everything is mediated through everything, law, religion, morality, art, and sciences, one through the other ... into a multimembered organism of true humanity," is governed by the "perfect shaping of the nation's moral substance." Historically this state was "the unity of nature and spirit, of earth and man, mediated through man's work," while geographically it was "the historical transfiguration of nature."¹⁰

The philosopher Hegel had argued that laws of history predispose the human being and his society to particular social, moral, or technological activities, but Kapp thought that history could only be understood as man's attempt to meet the challenges of the given environment in order to overcome his dependence on raw nature and to build up those rural, urban, social, cultural, and political environments in which human beings can feel at home. It was not the fulfillment of fictitious aims of so-called world history but the cultivation and spiritualization of the soil by means of human labor that Kapp saw as the challenge for mankind. But he did not mean simply the soil of raw outside nature. There was a "human soil," too, which needed cultivation into educational, social, and political environments adequate for man's development. This is what Kapp called the program of internal colonization, and he saw internal colonization as a parallel to the external colonization of lands that had never been plowed before. The concept of internal colonization expressed Kapp's awareness of the need for cultivation of human soil in every new situation and in every new generation not being backed by "fictitious laws" of history. The internal colonization concept was bound to nature and to the natural side of the human being.

Modern concepts of happiness tend to forget the limitations of human growth and change. A steadily progressive concept of outstanding perfection and emancipation is unnatural; furthermore, it is typically intellectual and unrealistic. People with views of unending unilinear progress also tend to forget that one task in colonization is always the protection of the soil already cultivated against its regression into wilderness or steppe. This is a seriously underestimated fact today, when most of our problems in decayed social, urban, and even bureaucratic environments require recultivation instead of further progression beyond our limits.

The other task of colonization was, naturally, the demand for further cultivation, but this demand was to respect the limits to exploitation of natural, as well as human, resources. Further growth was always to reaffirm the actual standard of culture and to search for those techniques which did not waste already-acquired resources. Instead of developing methods for avoiding side-effects or retarding the consumption of scarce resources, new methods were to stimulate and strengthen the self-developing process of nature—both nature's nature and man's nature.

Ernst Kapp maintained that there is a strict difference between man and machine. In his 1848 critique of Prussian bureaucracy, *Der konstituierte Despotismus und die konstitutionelle Freiheit*, he argued that bureaucracies behave like megamachines dominating people and finally making them parts of a machine, too. He thought that the citizens of a state should govern themselves by means of democratically controlled authorities and by the self-responsibility of citizens. Stated simply: mechanism is despotism, organism is liberty. His plea for liberty and for an end to excessive bureaucratic control in Prussia landed him in jail in 1848–49 and led him to emigrate in 1849 with his wife and four children to southwest Texas, where he settled at the Latin colony of Sisterdale in the Guadalupe valley.

His philosophy of internal colonization was not just a fantastic idea; after having written a book about it, he tested it by building up a cultivated environment at Sisterdale. First, there

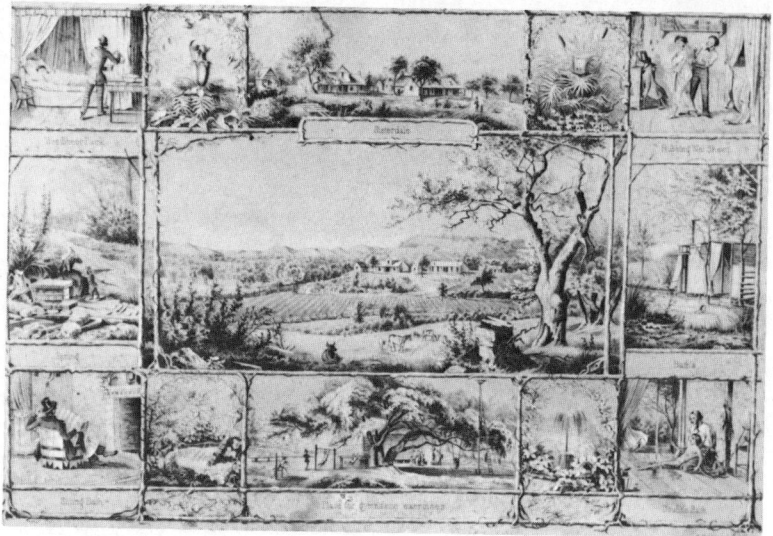

Professor Ernst Kapp's Water Cure Sanatorium at Sisterdale (mid-1850s)
Hermann Lungkwitz

Courtesy of Comfort Museum

was the cultivation of the soil for growing cattle and cotton. Second, there was the cultivation of housing to make it a homelike place for the family, the natural center of social activities and companionship. Even though he was an excellent philosopher, Kapp was said to have become an excellent carpenter as well. Third, there was the need to cultivate a sense of neighborhood and friendship. We have many testimonials to the brilliant intellectual and cultural environment at Sisterdale in the 1850s and 1860s. Fourth, there was the cultivation of the human body by sports and gymnastics. To that end Kapp established a hydrotherapeutical center at Sisterdale which served the human body's self-regenerating and self-developing powers in contrast to the allotherapeutical medicine introducing foreign substances into the body. Fifth, and finally, there was the cultivation of the social and political environment in a greater context; as president of *Der Freie Verein* he served these purposes and was especially involved in the drafting of a call for political, social, and religious reforms in preparation for the great convention of the Texas Germans held in San Antonio in May 1854.

Then, at the appointed time, a large number of Germans gathered in San Antonio and adopted Kapp's platform, qualifying some harsh formulations against Negro slavery in the following statement for political, social, and religious reforms:

POLITICAL REFORMS

1. The constitution of the United States is the best now extant, but like all existing things it is susceptible to and in need of improvement. We therefore demand:

a. Direct election of the President and United States senators.

b. Direct election of judges and of postal, tax, and all other administrative officials, with the exception of cabinet members and foreign ministers.

c. Removal of officials, not for party considerations, but only on the ground of incapacity or violation of duty, according to law and justice.

d. Eligibility without reference to the place of residence of candidates.

e. The right of the voters to recall representatives whose conduct is unsatisfactory.

2. In order to secure for the United States their proper position

toward foreign countries, and to enable them to exert their influence for the growth of liberty, we claim:

a. Acknowledgment and maintenance of republican states by actual assistance.

b. Adequate protection of American citizens who may be abroad.

c. Adherence to the Monroe Doctrine.

d. Abrogation of all treaties for the delivery of fugitives.

3. The naval and land forces are instituted for the protection of the country and its citizens. They should, therefore, be established and maintained as popular bodies within the State. In this regard we claim:

a. Only citizens, and those who have declared for at least one year their intention of becoming citizens, shall become soldiers.

b. Abolition of all corporal punishment.

c. In time of peace the soldier shall be amenable to the law like other citizens.

d. Abolition of all institutions for the education of cadets.

e. Establishment of institutions for the training of officers and examination by the State of officers both in theory and practice.

SOCIAL REFORMS

1. Legislative enactments and the administration of justice have the object of protecting and extending the rights of the citizens, in accordance with the demands and spirit of the age. Punishment should not extend beyond the requirements of such protection. Therefore we demand:

a. A general code of criminal and civil laws, which, by virtue of their simplicity and certainty, should be intelligible to every citizen and dispense with the intervention of attorneys.

b. The meeting in open court of plaintiff and defendant and, therefore, the abolition of the grand jury system.

c. Abolition of imprisonment for debt.

d. Certain property, necessary for making a living, shall be exempt from judicial sale.

e. Equality of labor and capital in all laws relating to them.

f. Abolition of capital punishment.

g. Further laws for the encouragement of and greater protection to immigration.

h. Repeal of all temperance laws.

2. Slavery is an evil, the abolition of which is a requirement of democratic principles; but, as it affects only single states, we desire:

a. That the federal government abstain from all interference in the question of slavery, but that, if a state resolves upon the abolition of the evil, such state may claim the assistance of the federal government for the purpose of carrying out such resolve.

3. The soil should not be an article of speculation, but should be regarded as a means of compensating labor. In this matter we ask:

a. That not only every citizen, but also everyone who has brought himself within the protection of the government, shall on application be entitled to a proper quantity of public land, free of charge, for his own use.

b. Prohibition of the sale of public lands, except to actual settlers.

4. Taxes have no other object than to defray the expenses of government. They should, therefore, be fixed with a view to the amount of these expenses and should be equalized, as much as possible, according to the possessions of the citizens. We demand in this particular:

a. Direct taxation.

b. Taxes on incomes in such manner that the larger income shall be taxed proportionately higher.

c. A progressive inheritance tax.

d. Higher taxation of uncultivated lands in order to check land speculation.

e. The greatest possible freedom of trade.

5. Banks can have only the object of affording protection to the poor against the power of capital and to support commerce. We demand, therefore:

a. Abolition of banks in their present establishments.

b. The establishment of institutions of credit upon a secure foundation.

6. Although internal improvements of general utility should be left to the federal government, yet we ask:

a. Their construction by private industry and public competition in order to avoid speculations heretofore practiced.

b. Public supervision and proper guarantees to contracts with laborers.

7. It is the duty of the State to provide for the education of the youth as republican citizens and to remove, as much as practicable, all influences of a deteriorating character. We therefore advocate:

a. Free schools supported by the means of the State.

b. Total exclusion of religious training, as well as of religious books, from schools.

c. No preacher may be a teacher.

d. No child shall be withdrawn from the free school, unless it is satisfactorily shown that a sufficient education is otherwise furnished.

e. Establishment of universities with free admission to all.

f. Examination of teachers, physicians, and apothecaries by the government.

RELIGIOUS REFORMS

1. Religion is a private matter. The United States are political states and have no right to interfere in matters of religion, either favoring or restricting. We therefore demand:

a. Abolition of the religious oath.

b. Abolition of Sunday laws and thanksgiving days.

c. Meetings of Congress and of legislative bodies shall not be opened with prayer.[11]

A storm of protest centered immediately on the slavery plank. The German minority group came under such great pressure that finally in 1856 their political efforts tired; they concentrated then on building up their farms and cultural activities in the Texas Hill Country neighborhoods. Even today, descendants of the radical 1848 immigrants know of these political, social, and religious reform platforms of the mid 1850s. These radical Hegelian—or, in some aspects of the call for religious reforms, Young Hegelian—theses require analysis as important contributions of Hegelian political and social thinking to nineteenth-century America.

Furthermore, while farming, carpentering, and running his hydrotherapeutical center in Texas, Kapp worked also for the Smithsonian Institution and formulated a general theory of utility and tools. This was, after all, the first time in his life that the professor was confronted with tools and everyday jobs. But he, his wife, and their six children became familiar with tools and did a good job.

Kapp's American stay lasted from 1849 to 1865. Then, after the Civil War, he went to Germany for a visit and remained there, having fallen ill, but the multiple experiences of developing cultivated environments in the early Texas pioneering situation enabled Ernst Kapp to write his final scholarly book, *Grundlinien einer Philosophie der Technik* (1877), and to publish a second revised version of his philosophy of environment based on his Texas experiences.

While Kapp's philosophy of environment developed a totally new framework in 1845 for general philosophical patterns within the traditional semantics of Hegelian transcendentalism, this other chief work, the *Philosophy of Technology* of 1877, used Kapp's pioneer experiences in Sisterdale as its basis. In it, Hegelian language was gone. Even the term "dialectic" was not used. In this book, the mission of philosophy is intended to bring "speculation and reality to mutual completion."[12] Because of his strictly anthropological approach to technology, and as a result of his fifteen years as a pioneer farmer in southwest Texas, he developed a thesis of tools and techniques as projections of human organs. His first thesis was that the human hand—the prime instrument for orientation, touch, seizing, and moving—is the prototype for all artificial instruments and tools which serve the same purposes.[13] His second thesis asserted that all human visceral organs and activities, such as the circulatory and nervous systems, heart and head, had served as examples for all sorts of mechanical and sociopolitical techniques. His third thesis was that this process of tool-making found its examples in the human body or organs partly in a conscious way, partly and more probably, however, in an unconscious way.[14] In this, he extended Darwin's theory of biological evolution to a theory of technical development. This continuation of biogenetics into technogenetics was prefigured, of course, in Kapp's concept of internal colonization. The model-machine for describing the conceptual theory of an organ projection was the locomotive; since Stevenson's invention, he pointed out, steam engines and systems of roads were no longer unconnected. "In this analogy of railway and steamship lines to a closed system, the network of the traffic on which the materials for the sustenance of mankind circulate is based on the model of blood circulation in an organism"; systems of telegraphy were projections, on the other hand, of the nervous system.[15]

Kapp's *Philosophy of Technology* was introduced with the motto, "The history of mankind in general, precisely examined, is identical with the history of inventing better tools." To make the advantages of the *tool-use-history* approach clearer, it is helpful to compare this approach with another general approach to the history of mankind created ten years earlier, namely Karl Marx's *class-war-history*.[16] Both of these general theories are metasciences, combining and evaluating the materials and results of other sciences, e.g., anthropology, ethics, political philosophy, economics, and social sciences. Marx's theory of class-war-history, however, is rooted in a rather vague preconception of alienation and "scientific historical laws." All this has a rather weak relation to reality and normally requires a large expenditure of hermeneutics to adapt it to reality.[17] The less pretentious concept of connecting the process of humanity and culture to the process of creating techniques and of cultivating the environment contrasts with the Marxian view. It is rooted more solidly in the factual challenges of the environment and in human needs.

To compare Kapp's general theory to that of Marx is not absurd. The comparison shows how misleading an orientation can be if it is tested only within the framework of "history." The degree to which we are unaccustomed to the concept of tool-use-history could be a measure of how we ourselves, in the twentieth century, have lost our natural spatial orientation in favor of a relatively dangerous historical orientation. Not the fulfillment of pretended laws in history but a human transfiguration of the environment—that is the real concept of Kapp's theory of looking for man's future in his environment rather than in his history. Environmental programs will still have to be realized in a time parameter, but when such programs are grounded in earth and space they are immunized against contagion from eschatological utopias. The human and his environment should become the framework, measure, and goal of Kapp's new humanism outlined in his theory of organ-projection.

It is an improper approach to Kapp's "organ-projection" thesis to ask whether or not the behavior of human organs has factually been the prototype for the development of techniques or whether organisms and machines both depend on the same natural laws for self-regulating systems. One should ask what the *intention* might have been to bring the creation and development of technology so close to the functions of the human mind and body and to relate the question of human culture to the question of the human body, the cultivated environment, the house and cultivated land, factories, and systems of traffic and information. The central thesis of the organ-projection theory stressed the self-emancipation and self-realization of man and humanity. Within this process, technology has an important but limited contribution. Just as a disfunctioning organ leads to the sickness or death of the organism, so the disfunctioning of dominating machines and techniques leads to the sickness or death of the enslaved, exploited, and misled individual and his community. According to Jacques Ellul in *La technique ou l'enjeu du siècle* (1954), techniques have the fatal tendency of encroaching into *all* sections of life by bringing all things into the order of operational laws.[18] Kapp in 1877 had a clear and instinctive insight into this expansive tendency of technology. On the other hand, the essence of technology is "methodical limitation" (*planvolle Beschränkung*). Methodical limitation is the conceptual framework for discussing the question of the limits to growth. Kapp generalized this thesis: "The essence of the machine in general is the result of a methodical limitation; the perfection of it means the increasing ingenious narrowing of the movement until the definite suspension of every indetermination. Mankind has worked on this increasing of limitation. If we are looking for a model for that we can find it in the great problem of human ethics."[19] In short, culture has an aspect of limitation; it is not limitless. The more special problems of modern operationalistic planning, the avoiding of side-effects, not only in techniques of production but also in techniques of social organization and human technique, are not yet treated with such a precise and universal method as Kapp's concept of technique as projected restriction.

Kapp's anthropological approach to a philosophy of environment and technology contradicts the *Mega-machine theory* developed by L. Mumford.[20] The best illustration is that both general theories and environment technology developed by Kapp end with a last chapter dealing with the theory of the organic and democratic state. In a special essay, "Constituted Despotism and Constitutional Liberty" (*Der konstituierte Despotismus und die konstitutionelle Freiheit*), written in 1848 as a contribution to civic rebellion against repressive administration, Kapp contrasted the state which asserts its natural side with the bureaucratic-mechanical state. In his words, "to the machine-man the state is also a machine, until it has destroyed him.... Bureaucracy represents the misled and unhampered machine-side of the state.... Every attack on bureaucracy from below strengthens and irritates it even more; for it is irritable, violent, irascible, sensitive, comparable to the weakened nervous system.... The more a state is governed, the more despotically it is governed; the more organically a state governs itself, the freer it is. *Facit: Mechanism is Despotism, Organism is Liberty.*"[21] In 1877 Kapp noted that "being a state means behaving like an organism. Therefore it can never be totally mechanical; however, there are within it machines which must be differentiated as distinct mechanisms within the whole organism."[22] The constitution of the state has to reflect the bodily constitution of man if the social and political environment are to be functional. So anthropology serves as a metascience not only for enlarging the fundamental structures of a philosophy of environment and of technology, but also for developing standards for measuring social and political institutions. In this way it becomes obvious that man's destiny and dignity and nature's destiny and dignity are bound together, but when extending the organ-projection theory from isolated organs and tools to man and state in general, Kapp understood the state to be both: an organ-product and a tool of culture, i.e., of man's will. Culture, i.e., cultivating man's nature and nature's nature, was the only way of preserving and establishing the good life and of overcoming the natural fragile cycle of life and death. Kapp's *principium individuationis*, which was his general concept of individuality and democracy, prevents him from following the panlogical temptation which would subordinate the individual to the state.

Mumford is in agreement with Kapp when he describes techniques as a means "to the deliberate cultivation of all those parts of the organic environment and the human personality that have been suppressed in order to magnify the offices of the Mega-machine." But the theory which Mumford vaguely called the redevelopment of techniques as "biotechnics," within which the tool-techniques are a specialized and limited section, had already been formulated by Kapp in a more lucid manner as organ-projection, but in regard to the analysis of the limits and diagnosis for the development of technics and techniques essentially there is no difference between Mumford and Kapp.

The most important aspect of history as a history of humanity's performance in inventing and using tools would be an investigation of the proper and righteous design and use of tools. Emphasis has to be laid on the fact that not only the construction and possession of tools but the right and proper use of them will enable the human being to cultivate his environment in a uniquely human way.

Ernst Kapp was a master not only in developing and using agricultural and woodworking tools, he also was a master in developing and using ideational tools, that is those tools we need to live a good life (for analysis and for setting up goals and values). His skill at this shows up particularly well when he criticizes the modern intellectual's slavery to misleading ideas about history. His concept of internal colonization and his tool-use-history were developed within the philosophical context of the nineteenth century, especially the thought of Georg Wilhelm, Friedrich Hegel, and Carl Ritter. However, his general tool-use-theory, based on his pioneering experiences, overcame both positions. Inasmuch as Hegel's one-sided ideas on history in their many variations—Karl Marx's thought is one of them—are still very influential, Kapp's philosophy of environment and tool use really is still a challenge even for some fads in contemporary intellectual behavior.

In the hills of German Texas, as elsewhere, we find important testimony for the craftsmanship of the early Texas Germans in establishing cultivated environments. One of these is a recent discovery. The well-known German philosopher Ludwig Feuerbach, author of "Das Wesen des Christentums" (1841) and "Grundsätze der Philosophie der Zukunft" (1843), decided to leave the decayed old Continent after 1850 and discussed this question with a young friend who was Ernst Kapp's nephew, namely Friedrich Kapp (a lawyer in New York, later U.S. Commissioner of Immigration, and author of several books). Friedrich Kapp described in detail, in a letter from New York, the problems a forty-six-year-old intellectual like Ludwig Feuerbach would confront in the New World.

But then, in 1852, after Friedrich had visited the Texas Hill Country he wrote again to Ludwig Feuerbach:

Am meisten hat mich mein Aufenthalt in Texas befriedigt; namentlich der Teil, welcher fast ausschliesslich von Deutschen bewohnt ist, der Umgebung von San Antonio, Neu Braunfels und Friedrichsburg. Ich besuchte dort einen Onkel von mir, denselben der die philosophische Erdkunde geschrieben hat und jetzt mit seinen Kindern am Guadaloupe Farmer ist. Wenn ich ueberhaupt Lust haette, mein spaeteres Leben in gottseliger Kartoffel- und Viehzucht zu verbringen, so wuerde ich in diesen Teil von Texas gehen. Namentlich glaube ich, wird ein Familienvater gut daran tun, der seinen Kindern mit wenig Mitteln eine unabhaengige Zukunft sichern will. Es wohnen dort schon verhaeltnismaessig viel Gebildete und wenig deutsches Gesindel. Ich mache Dich auf Texas in Deinem und im Interesse der Kinder Deines Bruders aufmerksam.

(By and large my sojourn in Texas put my mind at rest; especially that region which has been settled almost exclusively by Germans, the area around San Antonio, New Braunfels, and Fredericksburg. I visited an uncle of mine there, the one who wrote the philosophical geography and who now is a farmer with his children on the Guadalupe. If I had any thought of spending my later years as a pious plowman and stock farmer, then I would go to this part of Texas. I particularly believe that a father of limited means would do well there if he wanted to secure an independent future for his children. The region is populated by a relatively large number of educated Germans with very little German riffraff. I call Texas to your attention for your sake and for that of your brother's children.[23])

Feuerbach seriously contemplated emigration. Furthermore, his daughter Eleonore was engaged to Friedrich Kapp's younger brother Otto, who was a New York engineer. But then too Feuerbach was nearly fifty years old and deeply undecided about what to do. So finally he stayed in Europe. The daughter's engagement broke and she died unmarried in Germany. The fact, however, that Friedrich Kapp recommended Sisterdale as the only congenial cultural environment in America in 1852 for an outstanding German philosopher is indeed remarkable.

Since we human beings have only a very limited lifetime

Man and His Environment

for establishing cultivated environments for ourselves and for the following generations, there is always a challenge for pioneering efforts at internal colonization. The Texas Hill Country people of the nineteenth century set challenging examples for our times. Particularly Ernst Kapp's philosophical theory of the proper and righteous use of tools, indeed the *human use of tools*, in constructing human environments may serve as an *ideational tool* in our times, for philosophical as well as for practical purposes. Affirmatively I quote the sentence from Goethe engraved on the Pioneer Monument in Landa Park at New Braunfels:

> Was Du ererbt von Deinen Vätern,
> erwirb es, um es zu besitzen.
>
> (What you have inherited from your fathers,
> Earn that anew, so that you may own it.)

Part II

Civilization in the Wilderness

CHAPTER 4

German Folk Houses in the Texas Hill Country

TERRY G. JORDAN

FOLK architecture is based in traditional rural cultures. Such buildings spring from the common people, who erect them without the assistance of blueprints or professional architects. The modest beauty of these structures represents both a visual expression of traditional culture and a harmony with the physical surroundings. It is not surprising that artists and kindred sensitive souls are often attracted by the surviving specimens of American folk architecture.

But quite aside from their aesthetic qualities, folk buildings reveal much about the people who built and occupied them. A modern observer can learn a great deal about the life-style, heritage, socioeconomic status, and aspirations of vanished generations of pioneers by inspecting the remnants of their domestic architecture. Perhaps most revealing of all is the dwelling, the single most important structure erected by members of any culture. The house, in the words of a German scholar, "is the embodiment of a people's soul."[1] Especially is this true of the houses built by immigrants settling in a new cultural and physical environment. Observe closely the homes of such uprooted people and you will obtain a visual statement of the immigrants' attitudes toward their Old World cultural heritage and the alien host culture surrounding them, of acculturation and the possibility of eventual assimilation. Truly, the folk house permits a posthumous look into the very heart of the immigrant.

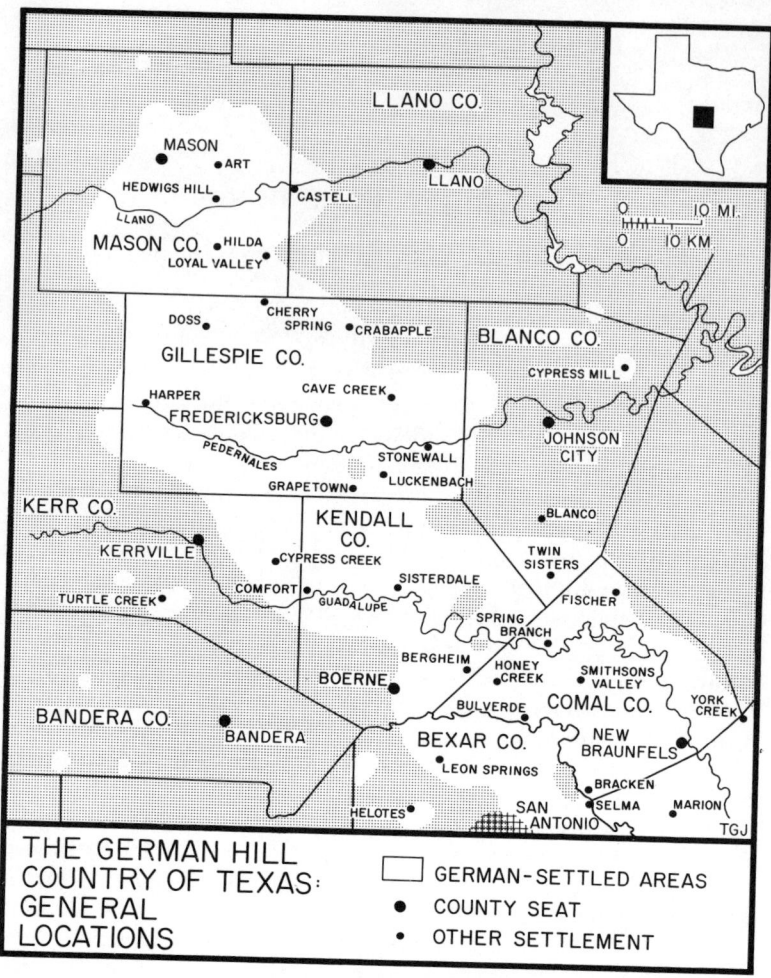

Figure 1

When viewed from this perspective, the nineteenth-century dwellings erected by German colonists in the Texas Hill Country are most instructive.[2] The region in question, a hundred-mile belt stretching northwestward from San Antonio and New Braunfels, is one of the most purely German districts in America (figure 1). The story of its settlement is a well-known facet of Texas ethnic history and requires no elaboration here.[3] Suffice it to say that the German Hill Country was settled in the 1840s and 1850s, mainly by thousands of Hessians and Saxons recruited from farm villages in the Westerwald, the Taunus, southern Hanover, Brunswick, and other districts of central and western Germany.[4] Most had been landed peasants and farmer-craftsmen, but some were university-educated intellectuals and city folk. While the Teutonic settlements in the Texas Hill Country were somewhat isolated, regular contacts with Anglo-Americans and Mexicans occurred from the very first. On both east and west, the German-settled area was flanked by the domain of southern Anglo-American yeoman farmers derived from the mountains and hills of Appalachia and Ozarkia. These neighbors were Tennessean, Kentuckian, and Arkansan backwoodsmen wise in the ways of the frontier. Immediately south of the Germans dwelt the long-established Mexican-American population of the San Antonio River valley. Bearers of a mixed Hispanic and Indian culture, the Mexicans had been resident in the region for well over a century prior to the arrival of the Germans.

What house architecture emerged from this curious confluence of peoples, this juxtaposition and interplay of Teutonic peasant, Anglo frontiersman, and Mexican peon? And what does the resultant domestic architecture tell us about the early German experience in the Texas hills? Those are the central questions of this essay. A brief consideration of the Old World architectural heritage of the German settlers is a necessary point of departure.

Central Europe is a crazy-quilt of folk architecture. Every small district can boast its own distinctive house and farmstead types, producing a highly complex map of building styles, methods, and materials.[5] Still, it is possible to generalize and render some order out of the seeming chaos. Such generalization permits us to reduce to three the number of traditional rural house types common in the German source areas of the Texas settlers. These are 1) the courtyard or *Frankish* farmstead; 2) the single-story unit, or *Saxon* house; and 3) the multi-story unit house. Many who immigrated to the Texas hills, particularly Hessians from better farming districts, had lived in Frankish-type farmsteads in the Old Country. An enclosed, rectangular courtyard was the central focus of the Frankish farmstead. Tightly clustered around two or three sides of the courtyard were the dwelling, stables, and barn, while a formidable wall pierced by a gate occupied the fourth side, facing the village street. The house was typically two full stories in height, usually with an additional half-story in the attic space, and it stood either to the left or right side of the courtyard, at right angles to the street. A massive, steeply pitched gable, often partly hipped, looked down on the street.

Hessians from poorer hill districts had a rather different housing tradition. They lived in multi-story unit farmsteads, in which people and farm animals occupied different stories within the same structure. Immigrants from regions further north in Germany, in particular Lower Saxony, had known another type of single-structure farmstead, the Saxon house. Instead of humans and animals occupying different stories, as in the Hessian hill house, they cohabited a single story. The gabled front end of the Saxon house contained stalls for the cattle, while the rear portion, separated from the stalls by an open hearth, was inhabited by the farm family. Above, under the tall, steep roof, was space for feed and food storage.

In spite of these basic differences, the Hessian and Saxon houses had some elements in common. All were normally built of half-timbering, or *Fachwerk*, in which a framework of braced oaken beams formed the weight-bearing skeleton of the structure. In the Hessian regions, the spaces between the beams were typically filled in with wattle-and-daub nogging, a webwork of dowels, sticks, and twigs onto which a moist mixture of clay and straw was pressed. Plaster and whitewash were then applied to both exterior and interior, with the beams left exposed. Saxons more often used kiln-fired bricks to fill the interstices, in which case plastering was unnecessary.

Figure 2

Figure 3

Figure 4

Figure 5

German Folk Houses in the Texas Hill Country

Figure 6

Figure 7

Hessian and Saxon houses lacked fireplaces with connected chimneys. Instead, a stove, usually tiled, or an open hearth provided heating and cooking facilities. Casement windows were typical of both Hesse and Saxony, as were "Dutch" doors and steep, thatched roofs. The large majority of Texas immigrants, then, had known large, half timbered dwellings, generally with a street-facing gable. Both Frankish and Saxon farmsteads were inward-looking, the former facing its fortress-like courtyard and the latter focused on a central open hearth.

In comparing these ancestral German house types with those built in the new homeland in Central Texas, it will be useful to consider floorplan, wall construction, roofs, heating devices, apertures, and decoration separately. Even a cursory study of Hill Country houses reveals that both Hessians and Saxons departed immediately and radically from their millennia-old floorplan traditions. In the course of twenty years and thousands of miles of field research in the German-settled area of the Texas Hill Country, I have never seen a dwelling even remotely resembling any of the Hessian or Saxon floorplans. Absent is the Frankish courtyard, the Saxon and hill Hessian cohabitation of people and farm animals, the massive dimensions, the inward-looking plan. Instead, I have found British-American floorplans, types rooted in the South and bearing an architectural ancestry traceable to the Delaware Valley and Chesapeake Tidewater, to England, Northern Ireland, Scotland, and Wales.

Perhaps most striking among the Anglo-American floorplans adopted by the Germans was the "dogtrot," a very common southern folk house consisting of two main rooms on either side of a broad open-air passageway (figure 2).[6] The dogtrot plan appears frequently among the Hill Country Germans, who were building them as early as 1846. Most of the passageways are now enclosed as central halls, a modification also typical in Anglo-American areas. Other common Anglo floorplans adopted by the Hill Country Germans include 1) the "single-pen" (one-room) cabin or house and 2) the "Cumberland" or "basic double-pen," formed by two abutting full-sized rooms not separated by a hall or passageway (figures 3 and 4). These styles, among Anglos and transplanted Teutons alike, normally are confined to single-story or story-and-a-half height. Even the somewhat rarer prestige folk dwelling of the southern Anglo—the so-called "I" ("eye") house—was adopted by the Germans. "I" houses are formed by adding a full second story to a dogtrot, central hall, or Cumberland type (figure 5). Anglo, too, were the rear shed rooms and front porches added to most Hill Country German houses (figure 3). However, the Germans often did add a distinctive design element to their shed rooms by elevating them to story-and-a-half height, thereby providing additional storage space. The presence of these shed attics is revealed by the roof profile, which takes on a "saltbox" shape (figure 6).[7] Similar multi-level rear additions are uncommon in Germany but do occur occasionally in the Westerwald, a major Hessian source region of Texas settlers.[8]

Except for the humble single-pen type, these British-inspired folk houses had greater width than depth, a trait apparent still today across the American South and the British Isles. The longer axis of the dwelling, among Anglos and Hill Country Germans, paralleled the road, a direct contrast to the practice in Germany. Only in compact settlements, such as New Braunfels and Fredericksburg, did the Hill Country houses often attain greater depth than width.[9] The cause was likely the shape of the town lots rather than any residual architectural allegiance to Germany.

Another minor departure from Anglo floorplans is seen in the widespread Hill Country German use of gable-end exterior stairs on story-and-a-half houses (figure 7). Perhaps this feature was derived from similar stairs occasionally seen in some Rhineland vineyard districts, but it could just as easily have been inspired by the Anglo custom of locating stairs in the open-air dogtrots.[10]

The Texas-German methods of wall construction present a somewhat more complex picture. As in the case of floorplans, the Germans did immediately upon arrival adopt the prevailing Anglo-American technique—horizontal notched-log construction (figure 2). To be sure, notched-log houses are known in some parts of Germany, in particular the Alps, Silesia, the Ore Mountains, East Prussia, and other southern and eastern parts of the European German realm. But the Hill Country Germans, overwhelmingly, were drawn from districts in the center and west, where log construction was unknown. They can only have learned this technique from neighboring Anglo-Americans.[11] Certain details of construction strongly suggest that the Anglos who instructed them came from the Ohio Valley and Appalachian areas. In any case, log construction was adopted throughout the German Hill Country, and many representative structures survive to the present day as proof. At least as late as the 1880s, the Germans continued to build with logs. A local individuality was added to log construction by some Hill Country Germans, particularly around Fredericksburg in Gillespie County, when they began leaving unusually wide chinks (gaps) between the logs, to be filled with mortared stones.[12] But the Hill Country log technology was, in the main, indistinguishable from that of the Anglo-Americans.

Simultaneous with the adoption of log wall construction from the local hill southerners, the German immigrants also borrowed the picket (or *palisado*) method from the nearby San Antonio Mexicans. Typically, picket walls consisted of cedar poles inserted vertically into shallow trenches and held in place by the weight of the dirt when the trenches were filled. More rarely, the pickets rested on a horizontal sill beam. To make the walls airtight, a mixture of clay and straw was pressed against the pickets, a technique which surely reminded the Germans of their traditional wattle-and-daub. The similarity was extended to plastering the finished wall. Though they never rivaled log construction in popularity among the Germans, picket walls were erected in the Hill Country from the late 1840s to the 1870s. A traveling artist recorded the presence of picket houses in Fredericksburg as early as 1849.[13] Few of these buildings survive today, though similar Mexican picket corral fences remain abundant in the region.

Curiously, at the same time that the Germans were employing notched-log and *palisado* wall construction, they were busily implanting their traditional half-timbering (figure 8). As early as 1846 and 1847, half-timbered buildings were being erected, and over the following two decades numerous such dwellings were built. Notable concentrations survive today in Fredericksburg, Comfort, and New Braunfels. Native oak, cedar, and

German Folk Houses in the Texas Hill Country

Figure 8

Figure 9

cypress all proved suitable for the beams. In the choice of nogging material to fill the interstices, the German immigrants generally departed from their Central European tradition. Only very rarely did the immigrant builders employ Hessian wattle-and-daub or Saxon fired bricks (figure 8). Instead, sun-dried adobe bricks, another obvious borrowing from the local Mexicans, were widely used as the filler (figure 9). Still more common were hewn blocks of native stone, mortared firmly into the interstices, a method very rare in Germany (figure 4). Also counter to German tradition was the practice, adopted very early, of nailing milled weatherboards over the exterior of half-timbered houses, concealing the beams from view and presenting the appearance of typical Anglo frame construction (figure 9). So common was weatherboarding in New Braunfels that it is difficult to find examples of exposed half-timbering there today. More in keeping with German tradition was the Hill Country custom of plastering walls, regardless what type of wall construction material had been employed (figure 7). Significantly, however, the plaster often covered both the nogging and the beams on half-timbered walls, a practice uncommon in Germany (figure 8). In this manner the alien timbering could be concealed from view.

Beginning about 1850, a fourth type of wall construction appeared among the Hill Country Germans and within a decade became dominant: hewn stone masonry (figures 3, 5, 6). Utilizing the abundant native limestone and sandstone, German masons erected hundreds of "rock" houses in the latter half of the nineteenth century and into the first decade of the present century. So numerous are these stone structures today that most casual observers regard them as the typical German houses of the area. The puzzling aspect of the Texas-German preference for hewn stone construction is that there is no clear antecedent. Stonework does occur occasionally on the first-story level beneath a half-timbered superstructure in Germany. Moreover, there are districts in far western Germany where stone construction very similar to that of Texas prevails. An example is the zone of reddish sandstone construction in the Hardt, especially in and around Kaiserslautern. A few stonemasons came to Texas from such districts, including one man who had served an apprenticeship in masonry near Trier, a city with a heritage of hewn stone construction dating to Roman times.[14] There is no question, however, that half-timbering was the preferred building method in the source regions of the large majority of Hill Country Germans.

Another possible source of the rock masonry is Mexican San Antonio, where limestone houses were being built as early as Spanish colonial times. Such an origin is supported by the fact that the quality of German stonemasonry improved markedly after the 1850s, as would be expected if the builders were learning an alien technology.[15] Nor was stone construction absent in the nearby Anglo areas. Burnet and Lampasas counties, in particular, offer some excellent surviving examples of Anglo stonework. Local Hill Country lore attributes the rise of stone construction to an innovation developed by the immigrant builders themselves. Once hewn stone became the preferred nogging for half-timbering, goes the story, the builders quickly realized that the timber beamwork was unnecessary, since the masonry did not require any additional support. Still another possible answer was suggested by cultural geographer Hubert Wilhelm, who maintained that a growing scarcity of oak wood caused the demise of half-timbering in the Texas hills.[16] However, both of these explanations leave unanswered the question of why the builders began employing hewn stone nogging in the first place.

The Hill Country Germans did not hesitate to combine two or more methods of wall construction in the same house. Enlargements were often built of wall material different from the original dwelling (figure 4). One notable house on Schubert Street in Fredericksburg consists of an original single-pen log room, to which was later appended a half-timbered shed room and a multi-story limestone addition.

In sum, the wall construction of Hill Country houses displays profound dissimilarities to Old World German types. Half-timbering does represent a notable survival, but if we take into consideration the tendency of the Texas Germans to conceal half-timbering beneath weatherboarding or plaster, we are left with the inescapable conclusion that the Germans did not make much effort to perpetuate or display in Texas the walls they had known in Europe. While they apparently sought to imbue their houses with greater permanence than was characteristic of the homes of the traditionally mobile Anglo-Americans, they generally created walls that were not visually alien.

The great majority of Hill Country German immigrants had lived beneath thatched, tiled, or slated roofs in Europe. Some of the early, temporary shacks they built in Texas were thatched, probably more out of necessity than any desire to perpetuate old ways.[17] Within less than a decade, however, shingle mills dotted the banks of the Guadalupe and other Hill Country streams, permitting the Germans to adopt, universally, the wooden roofs dominant among Anglo-Americans (figures 6, 7). The later adoption of metal roofing, which seemingly appealed to the Teutonic striving for permanence, was not sufficiently eccentric to label the houses as unusual. In the process of copying the prevalent Anglo roofing material, the Hill Country Germans also copied their roof style. This meant, above all, side-facing gables, in direct opposition to the prevalent German tradition. It also meant a roof devoid of partial gable hipping, and one of much gentler pitch than was common in Europe (figures 3, 8, 9). I cannot agree with Sylvia Cook's claim that Hill Country German houses have steeper roofs than those of the local Anglo-Americans.[18] All in all, the roof of the Hill Country folk house in no way betrayed the Teutonic heritage of the people who lived beneath it.

The chimneyed fireplace is one of the least efficient heating devices ever developed. Most of the heat escapes through the chimney, and a rapid flow of air permits the fuel to be consumed rapidly. Of British origin, fireplaces vented by large, exterior, gable-end chimneys became a basic aspect of southern Anglo-American folk houses. In Germany, by contrast, stoves or open hearths were the rule, either of which was more efficient than the chimneyed fireplace. The average Hill Country German balked at adopting this Anglo architectural feature, though a minority did. Most remained loyal to the German stove, close kin to the so-called "Franklin" stove perfected by the Pennsylvania Germans. As a result, German houses in the Hill Country can usually be detected by the absence of sizable

Figure 10

exterior chimneys (figures 2, 5, 8). One notable exception, the huge chimney attached to the rear shed room of the famous Tatsch house in Fredericksburg, is so unusual as to be freakish.

In the positioning of doors and windows, the Hill Country Germans conformed to Anglo-American patterns from the very first. This often meant multiple front doors, an alignment of front and rear doors, and certain other minor features lacking a clear German antecedent. The Teutonic houses may well have more gable-end windows than are common in Anglo houses, since British tradition restricted such apertures. Typically Teutonic casement windows are common on some of the older Hill Country houses (figure 10). And horizontally split "Dutch" doors occur occasionally, but the majority of houses display typically Anglo sash windows and single-unit doors (figures 3, 5, 8). In Germany, Lower Saxon casement windows open outward, while those in Hesse open inward. In Texas the Saxon type seems to prevail. Shutters are unquestionably more common on the German houses, probably reflecting an Old World influence (figure 4).

The Hill Country German pioneers refrained initially from decorating the exteriors of their houses with inscriptions or designs that might label them as European. Only later, when Victorian gingerbread came into vogue, did the Germans satisfy their suppressed desire for ornamentation. They took to the Victorian era with gusto, hanging an incredible variety of decoration on their existing and new folk houses (figure 10). Traditional German designs, notably the heart motif, found a place in exterior decoration at this time.

The foregoing analysis of floorplans, wall construction, roofing materials and design, heating devices, apertures, and decoration leaves little doubt concerning the intentions and outlook of the immigrant builders. Clearly, the Hill Country Germans preferred to copy the houses of their Anglo neighbors rather than implant in Texas the dwellings of their abandoned Fatherland. The houses speak very precisely for their long-dead builders. "We want to be accepted as Americans, as southerners, as Texans," say these German dogtrot, Cumberland, and "I" houses. "We no longer desire to be Germans and certainly not Hessians or Saxons. We have not crossed the sea to recreate

Germany." If, as August Meitzen suggested, the folk house is truly the embodiment of a people's soul, then the Hill Country immigrant's soul was already American when he started building his first house on Texas soil. Where they saw glaring inefficiencies in the Anglo house, as in the fireplace arrangement, they often retained German features, provided these could be unobtrusive or even invisible. Whenever useful Mexican features, such as adobe brick, were incorporated, they, like the Teutonisms, were often concealed, for the Germans correctly perceived that the socially dominant host culture was Anglo-American rather than Hispanic.

Another element in the decision by the Germans to build Texan houses was no doubt the local physical environment, in particular the climate. Although the immigrants were unprepared for the recurrent drought that is so integral a part of the Hill Country climate, they were aware in advance that the climate was warmer. They realized that smaller houses were more practical since many tasks performed indoors in Germany could be accomplished out-of-doors in Texas. The rarity of snow made steeply pitched roofs unnecessary. Still, the Old-World German house would not have been a handicap in the Texas climate, had the immigrants chosen to build them.

The end result was a folk house which, while distinctively Texas-German, was more nearly British-American than Teutonic. I have yet to see a dwelling in the German Hill Country in which a Britisher or an Anglo southerner would not feel comfortable. The German architectural elements are so rare and subdued that the houses must be regarded as essentially Anglo southern. In Germany, these dwellings would be absurdly out of place.

Interestingly, German immigrants seem to have made similar housing decisions elsewhere in the United States. Even in colonial Pennsylvania, where Germans constituted a third of the total population and dominated a large block of contiguous counties, the houses are dominantly British.[19] The Georgian "four over four" is a favored Pennsylvania "Dutch" folk house. The Germans in Missouri, Wisconsin, Indiana, and other states made similar housing decisions.[20] Almost everywhere abandonment of German plans and adoption of British-inspired substitutes was the rule. In a surprising number of North American settlement areas, the German-Americans paralleled the Texas experience by gravitating to hewn stone construction.[21]

In light of the architectural evidence, I conclude that acculturation was not merely inevitable; it was *desired*. Eventual assimilation was foreseen and favored, even by the immigrant generation. If that desire has subsequently changed, if in the past decade or two some descendants of those immigrants have begun to cling nostalgically to the faded remnants of German culture, then the change in attitude is more than anything else a function of the waning promise of America. Those scholars who believe that the mainstream of eighteenth- and nineteenth-century German immigrants intended to create a "New Germany" overseas are simply not looking at the available evidence provided by material culture. The German-American folk house, at least, is saying loudly and clearly, "Color me Anglo-American."

CHAPTER 5

Views of Texas: German Artists on the Frontier in the Mid-Nineteenth Century

JAMES PATRICK McGUIRE

THERE is a tendency to think of art and artists in nineteenth-century Texas in relation to wider fields and schools. American art of the past century was in a process of forming from convergent threads of European Classical and Romantic art of the eighteenth and nineteenth centuries. An overview of European influences on American art during that period brings to mind a handful of notable Germans or Swiss-Germans whose collective contribution focused on the westward movement, the Great Plains, the American Indian, and the majesty of mountainous barriers which blocked trails to the Pacific Ocean. Among those whose drawing pads and finished canvases contained this vast frontier were the Swiss artists Peter Rindisbacher (1806–1834), Carl Bodmer (1809–1893), and Friedrich Kurz. Three great German recorders were Karl Wimer (1828–1862), Balduin Möllhausen (1825–1905), and Albert Bierstadt (1803–1902). Their contributions to American art have been recognized by art historians. They accompanied history *in the making*, the expeditions of exploration into the American West. The results of their European training left America a priceless heritage of art—of unspoiled land, of Indians who roamed the plains, and a legacy of pioneers who began to fill and tame the land. They were catalysts of an embryonic American national myth. Did immigrant German artists on the Texas frontier play their part in this process? Was there any unifying element throughout their careers in terms of choice of subjects, values, social statement or the lack thereof, or development of a significant artistic identity as a group? An investigation of four major German-Texan artists will seek answers to these questions.

Men and women, some trained in the art academies in Berlin, Dresden, and Düsseldorf, accompanied the thousands of immigrants who began arriving in Texas after 1844 as the result of the Adelsverein's colonial efforts. Their presence in Texas resulted from a variety of reasons which were personal, political, or economic in nature. The art they produced in this new land has become part of a regional and national art tradition, but one not unique to America by any means since this "American" art had its counterpart in Europe as well. Surviving paintings, drawings, watercolors, engravings, lithographs, and other graphics witness their presence, observation, artistic outpouring, and sheer endurance. It was not easy. Most experienced war, famine, epidemics, Indian threats, and perhaps most devasting, the indifference of the vast majority of their contemporaries on the Southwest frontier.

Like all others, the German artists in Texas faced an uphill fight for recognition, appreciation, patronage, and economic security. Until the decades after the Civil War, central and western Texas was subject to invasion, war, and Indian raids, as well as the havoc caused by nature and economic recessions that periodically dried up capital. Therefore, when we examine the often sketchy stories of four, perhaps foolhardy German painters, we must picture the odds against their survival and success.

In talking about German artists in Texas, we must also remember that they were mostly schooled in the Northern Romantic tradition. Once in Texas, they worked in almost total artistic isolation and against great economic odds. Whether their efforts produced a new school or pattern of art or not, their creative talents and outpouring formed the first important group of state and regional art and contributed to a transatlantic migration of ideas which paralleled the development of North German Romanticism.

Four individuals concern us here. The first was Carl G. von Iwonski (1830–1912), who was born in Silesia. He came to

Texas in 1845 as a teenager with his parents and settled at the new German colony of New Braunfels. The others were Hermann Lungkwitz (1813–1891), Richard Petri (1824–1857), and Louise Wueste (1805–1874). They are representatives of a score or more of other Germans whose record forms such a large part of the nineteenth-century Texas art collection.*

* Almost twenty German artists in mid-nineteenth-century Texas, in addition to the four major Texas-German painters, should be mentioned. Carl Rohrdorf (d. 1847), a Swiss-German landscapist, was among the very first. He came to New Braunfels about 1845 as an employee of the Adelsverein, taught art in the new German colony, and produced the first panorama of the village in 1847. It was lithographed in Berlin four years later as a promotional illustration for German immigration to Texas.

Others of the 1840s and 1850s included Carl Nebel, whose lithographs of the Mexican War battles have been discussed in works by Ron Tyler. Carl Schuchard (1827–1883) was a mining engineer who accompanied the Gray Survey of 1854 as a topographer. He produced thirty-two drawings of the wildlife and landmarks of West Texas on the 32nd parallel route for the Texas Western Railroad. Erhard Pentenrieder (1830–1875), a native of Bavaria, became a San Antonio merchant and produced two lithographed letterheads of Main Plaza. One contains a group of camels in front of San Fernando Cathedral, reminding us of the famous U.S. Army experiment in camel transportation in West Texas just before the Civil War. Wilhelm C. A. Thielepape, famous as the Reconstruction mayor of San Antonio, was a surveyor, architect, artist, musician, and politician. Other Central Texas German artists included Augustus Koch (active in Texas during the 1870s and 1880s), who prepared careful and accurate bird's-eye views of many Texas towns. Hermann Brossius (active in Texas in the 1870s) also left panoramas of such places as New Braunfels, Waco, Jefferson, and Victoria. Two other artists, John Beckmann and Ida Weisselberg Hadra (1861–1885), were born in Texas of German parents and pursued art careers in San Antonio during the last part of the century.

Texas's main port city, Galveston, attracted the attention of a handful of itinerant artists: C. O. Bahr (active in Texas ca. 1856), William Neuser (1837–1902), Augustus Behne (1828–1895), and the Reverend Peter A. Moelling (active in Texas during the 1860s). Helmut Holtz (active in Texas in 1860), a German sailor, drew

Iwonski's first thirteen years in Texas were spent in New Braunfels, where he opened a studio about 1856. His early art training is unknown, although it would be reasonable to assume that he had contact with Lungkwitz and Petri after their arrival in Texas in 1851. One scrap of supporting evidence was Iwonski's sketch of the old Altgelt Mill at Comfort, identical to one drawn and later lithographed by Lungkwitz.

Iwonski might be considered within the German Biedermeier tradition because of the concentration of "domestic" subjects relating to the daily and cultural life of his contemporaries. One early village scene included a group of men playing Skat and conversing in a tavern. Another was of the New Braunfels *Germania Gesangverein* (lithograph, 1857), Texas's first German singing society. Iwonski's profusion of detail and choice subjects point to a Biedermeier identity in his New Braunfels works, an expression of comfort, prosperity, and appreciation for mundane daily life. They certainly convey the energy and optimism, however, of the immigrant spirit in the new Texas homeland.

Surviving examples of Iwonski's work during the last three years in New Braunfels, 1855–58, illustrate a variety of cultural interests and a mastery of technique all the more surprising in

---

pictures of Matagorda and Indianola, and Theodore Lehmann (active in Texas in 1839) chose Houston for his studio. He was known as an artist of reputation and standing, in whose portraits one could see, said a local paper, "the lips speaking, the eyes of beauty flashing and the form heaving with emotion from the canvas." The Reverend Moelling, a clergyman first and foremost, painted heroic canvases of Civil War encounters such as the Battle of Galveston and the capture of the *Harriet Lane*, which he witnessed in Galveston. He reportedly had to carry the huge paintings around in a wagon for exhibitions in Houston, Huntsville, Chappell Hill, Independence, Washington-on-the-Brazos, Hempstead, and Richmond on his lecture tour.

Very little is known about Louis Hoppe (active in the 1860s), whose primitive watercolors were often done on stationery. Only four examples of his work, from Columbus and Fayette County, have been located. Two are floral scenes and the remainder are of farm houses. All are now on exhibit in the Witte Museum in San Antonio.

Views of Texas: German Artists on the Frontier

The Log Cabin
by Carl G. von Iwonski

Courtesy of Daughters of the Republic of Texas Library at the Alamo

New Braunfels, 1857
Carl G. von Iwonski
Courtesy of San Antonio Museum Association

Theatrical Sketch
Carl G. von Iwonski
Kabale und Liebe, 1856
Courtesy of Sophienburg Memorial Museum

Elise Haseloff, 1869
Carl G. von Iwonski

Courtesy of Mrs. Murray Brooks

Carl G. von Iwonski, ca. 1865–70

Courtesy of James P. McGuire

light of his lack of known formal training. Among his first sketches were scenes along the Guadalupe River such as a shingle-maker's hut, a grist mill at Comfort, a group of travelers at his father's inn across the river from New Braunfels, and a much-publicized panorama of the little town.

Although his reputation was later to rest mainly on his fine portraiture, Iwonski's first large grouping of sketches dealt with an amateur theater group, founded to collect funds for a local public school. Seventeen theatrical sketches have survived and have been verified from contemporary newspaper reviews of plays which appeared in Ferdinand Lindheimer's *Neu-Braunfelser Zeitung*. The sketches clearly illustrated not only the cultural endeavors of the German colonists, but the artist's skill with pen and pencil. They witness the desire of the immigrants to preserve their German heritage. Now part of the permanent collection of the Sophienburg Memorial Museum, they complement Iwonski's early lithograph of the local *Germania Gesangverein* and other Biedermeier genre scenes of the colonists' life.

Few portraits of local citizens can be traced from the New Braunfels period before the artist moved to San Antonio about 1858. For the next fifteen years thereafter, Iwonski's artistry blossomed steadily, as shown in portraits of local merchants, their families, and various other political and military figures. One of the most beautiful and emotional portraits was that of Elise Haseloff, a foster child in the home of Iwonski's parents in San Antonio. Painted in 1869, it became a wedding gift to the young woman, who spurned the artist's own proposal. Like so many of his canvases, it too has been passed down in family hands and has rarely been exhibited.

Iwonski was forced to seek fields other than art in order to make a living. In 1858, he became associated with William DeRyee in photography, a profession to which he returned shortly after the Civil War. Then, with Hermann Lungkwitz, he operated a photographic studio in the Alamo City from 1865 until 1870, when Lungkwitz removed to Austin to accept a patronage post in the state government. In addition Iwonski taught drawing at the German English School from 1860 until 1870, and held the appointed position of city tax collector during the Reconstruction regime of Mayor Wilhelm C. A. Thielepape, also an artist of some talent and sensitivity.

In San Antonio, Iwonski concentrated on German endeavors: on the amateur theater of the Casino Club (the elite German social club of the city) and in support of German-American Republican politicians. Perhaps most unusual among his efforts in the service of politics in post–Civil War San Antonio were three works. The first was a political cartoon photographed and pasted to each copy of the *San Antonio Express* on February 8, 1868, to remind German voters of their hardships in Texas during the Civil War. The Republicans won the election, though no one has attributed that victory specifically to Iwonski's drawing. From newspaper accounts, we know that he also drew other propaganda sheets for the Republicans during his San Antonio days. Alone among these artists, Iwonski sought to make a social comment and to influence his fellow citizens.

Iwonski's second unusual product was a clay bust of Baron Alexander von Humboldt, sculpted from pictures, again with no apparent training. The editor of the *Freie Presse für Texas* in San Antonio judged the likeness excellent, and it was displayed in 1869, first at the Casino Hall and then at a large German gathering during centennial celebrations of Humboldt's birth.

The third unusual item was a giant painting (said to have been ten feet square) of the German general staff, seen in a field tent, planning the capture of Paris during the Franco-Prussian War. The large painting was hastily executed for a raffle held at the Casino Hall in January 1871, and included likenesses of the Prussian king, his sons, Bismarck, and the most prominent German generals. A local citizen won the painting, which was then donated to the Casino Association, where it hung in the billiard parlor for many years. It has since completely disappeared and is known only from newspaper descriptions and from one damaged photograph given to the San Antonio Museum Association by Major Anna Schelper.

One result of Iwonski's immersion in the San Antonio German cultural, political, and intellectual milieu was his ensuing decision to study art and sculpture in Berlin in 1871. Returning to San Antonio later that year, he completed a small number of exceedingly refined portraits which reflect his Berlin training. Then again in 1873, Iwonski and his widowed mother, Marie von Kalinowski-Tschirski von Iwonski, returned to Breslau. Until his death there in 1912, Iwonski continued painting and exhibited in shows sponsored by the Silesian and Breslau art guilds.

For a generation or two after leaving Texas, Iwonski's reputation as a frontier artist was virtually ignored. Then, along with renewed interest in other local and regional artists on the Southwest frontier, his contributions attracted attention and were catalogued, and examples of his work were added to local art museums. More than those of his contemporaries, Iwonski's paintings reflect the prevailing Biedermeier taste of the period, although Iwonski himself was probably more versatile in choice of subjects than his contemporary German artists in Texas.

The second of these pioneer painters was a woman. Louise Heuser Wueste, a native of Gummersbach on the Rhine, was already middle-aged before she voyaged to Texas in 1858 to join two married daughters and a son. Born into a cultivated family with many connections to the art world, Louise Wueste was influenced by two brothers-in-law, Karl Friedrich Lessing (1808–1880) and Adolph Schroedter (1805–1875), both of whom were artists. Lessing was a landscapist and historical painter in the Düsseldorf art academy before becoming *Galeriedirektor* in Karlsruhe. One of Schroedter's sons-in-law, Anton von Werner, was director of the Academy of Art (*Kunstakademie*) in Berlin. Von Werner was attached to the headquarters of Crown Prince Friedrich Wilhelm during the Franco-Prussian War and accompanied him to Versailles as official artist for the German delegation (*Zeichnerischer Chronist*). Louise Wueste also received training at the Düsseldorf art academy in portraiture and was influenced by August Wilhelm Sohn (1829–1899).

Following the early death of her physician husband, Dr. Peter W. L. Wueste, Louise returned to her father's home to raise her three small children and to continue her art studies. There, as in later years in San Antonio and on the Rio Grande, she continued painting, first sketching and then completing portraits of family members and of friends who gave her a commission. She lived periodically with her married daughters in San Antonio and Pleasanton and, later, with her son Daniel, a merchant on the Rio Grande.

Wueste's art was more personal—what she saw within herself—and it was done mainly for her immediate family. She is best known in Texas for her portraits, yet surviving drawings and watercolors of floral arrangements, butterflys, book illustrations, as well as landscape sketches and paintings reflect her similar response to the prevailing Biedermeier sensibility. Her landscapes of Mexican huts and yucca plants lack evidence of formal training and Romantic influence, while her pencil portraits and folk illustrations reflect a skilled craftswoman at work. In short, subjects she had painted in Europe were rendered in the same style she had been taught there; subjects new to her, or those outside her Old-World experience, were depicted with much more originality and freedom. To help support herself, she gave lessons and sold paintings when she could. In 1860 she opened a studio in San Antonio but was forced also to teach sewing classes at the local German-English School. The Civil War, however, complicated this otherwise genteel grandmother's life as she tried to earn a living to help her growing family. One daughter's husband, Ferdinand Schlikum, was forced to flee to Mexico because of his political leanings.

At the height of the war, in 1863, Wueste observed in a letter to her daughter, Emma Schlikum, that

painting is a queer art here in America where only commerce is recognized. All the world strives for profit. That seems the main aim in this America.

She went on to say in the same letter, "I have had very little or no work.... At present, there are no commissions to be had here [in Piedras Negras] for an artist." A year later, she wrote again, from San Antonio:

I have been getting along nicely, had much work, made money, and saved some for hard times which are here and devour my savings. My art, as you can surmise, now brings me small returns, and I wish daily to be far away [from San Antonio] where I could better practice it.

Following the end of the hostilities, Wueste set out for New Orleans to join the Schlikums, but upon reaching Galveston she found that they had moved to Brownsville. From Galveston she wrote to them: "I decided to sell everything [in San Antonio] and with my paintings would go to New Orleans where I hoped to have a better chance to sell them." While in Galveston, she occupied herself for a time giving art lessons at the home of a German cigar merchant named Baer, while debating whether to join the Schlikums in Brownsville. In writing to them she remarked,

My opinion is that I would have no chance to sell my paintings there nor could I paint there, and as everyone in this world must do what he feels is his calling ... I have again felt in Staffel's home [in San Antonio] how little I can stand any exertion in this hot climate and would rather give lessons in art or paint to make a living.

One gets a picture of a proper and portly German gentlewoman crisscrossing hot Texas in a coach to join her various family members, with trunks of paintings in tow. In 1869, she complained of this to relatives in Germany.

You lucky ones who live in our German fatherland surrounded by art treasures.... Life here in America is very difficult, so harrassed with everyone thinking of means to earn money for a return trip to Germany. You may imagine that poetry and art are of little importance here. Only music sometimes provides a little satisfaction and harmony, to make you feel like being in Germany.

Severe eye problems brought Wueste to the brink of blindness in 1869, causing her to seek a successful treatment from Dr. Ferdinand Herff. She wrote to relatives in Germany this time that she was not allowed to paint anymore, a fact she regretted. Now she was afraid of going blind permanently. In the same letter, however, she revealed her sensitive appreciation of the Texas landscape which she so often found intolerable.

Just now I am looking through the door at the wonderful green, which this year is so lush. We had a great deal of rain, which means abundance in Texas. Everybody rejoices at the amount of fruit and flowers. I have never seen the like since I have been here. There are roses so beautiful and aromatic and so many of them that you will see them in every house and garden. Indeed, it is a blessed year. The farmers ought to grow rich.

Waxing even more poetic, she continued,

Oh, what a beautiful country, what fine ranges of hills I saw on my way to the Rio Grande! Vast distances where no farm, no sound to be heard, only this profound stillness impresses the lonely traveler in a foreign country. . . .

but then added, as if to bring herself to her senses, that she was "conscious every moment of possible attack by hostile Indians."

Wueste's reputation rests largely on surviving portraits, mainly in the possession of her descendants. Only a few are now in local museums. Her scarce Texas landscapes, floral and butterfly watercolors, and book illustrations have been preserved for the most part by descendants. Her perceptions of Texas were basically of a hostile, malevolent landscape, and if anything, her art is her attempt to gentle that environment. The last years of her life were spent in Eagle Pass with her son's family. There she sketched the quiet life: Mexican ladies, homes and interiors, carts, and even the army camp at Fort Duncan, as well as the low-bluffed Rio Grande and its border towns.

On a brief visit to a daughter in San Antonio in August 1874, Wueste noted, "I have painted a picture in Eagle Pass of a Mexican girl of the Rio Grande. . . . It will be on exhibition here." A few months later, following a painful stage ride back to Eagle Pass, Louise Wueste died and was buried in the old military cemetery.

The third and most prolific collection of Texas frontier art was produced by a man who spent only six years here, mainly near Fredericksburg. Richard Petri, at his finest in pencil and watercolor portraits, left hundreds of small sketches of pioneer folk life and of various Indian visitors to Fredericksburg before his death by drowning in the Pedernales in 1857.

Petri entered the Academy of Fine Arts in his native Dresden at the age of fourteen in 1838. His teachers there, notably Adrian Ludwig Richter (1803–1884) and Julius Hübner (1806–1882), influenced his work, chiefly in the choice of Romantic themes relating to the Bible and to German legends. Petri's excellence as an artist and craftsman was attested to by six awards he received at the academy.

The roots of his training in what Robert Rosenblum defines as the Northern Romantic tradition can be traced in part to Caspar David Friedrich (1774–1840), the founder of a school in which explicit religious associations, overpowering mystery, and morbid melancholy were conveyed through landscapes imbued with qualities of the supernatural. The relation of nature to the supernatural pervaded each landscape. Ludwig Richter, a late Romantic and Petri and Lungkwitz's teacher, opposed Friedrich's direction and sought to restore a belief in the magic and poetry of human existence in his landscape idylls as well as in his illustrations of folklife. Much of Petri's early European work centered on biblical themes. Later, in America, he drew everyday scenes from family life and frontier experiences. Petri rarely attempted landscape painting, in which the synthesis of realism and poetic interpretation of the Romantic school found its most popular expression. Perhaps he feared revealing his inner feelings through this choice of subject. Had Petri remained in Europe, the young student might have rivaled his teacher Richter as an illustrator.

Little primary material on Petri is now available, family traditions aside. He left Dresden in 1850 with his sister Elise, her husband, Hermann Lungkwitz, and other relatives. In Texas he lived entirely within the circle of the Lungkwitz family near Fredericksburg and may not have traveled much farther afield than central Texas. His personality can only be conjectured from family traditions among the Lungkwitz descendants and through interpretation of his art.

This sensitive, tubercular, lifelong bachelor has been characterized as sympathetic and introspective, yet the color and vigor of his paintings and drawings in Texas testify more to a

Indian Maid
by Richard Petri

Courtesy of Mrs. Hunter P. Harris

persevering, observant personality. Surrounded by what he perceived as pristine wilderness, the young artist worked best in portraits and sketches of daily life and Indians.

With meticulous care, Petri made his small drawings on any paper available, including the flyleaves of books when his supplies ran out. Some genre scenes have been reproduced, including those of the Lungkwitz family going visiting in their ox wagon and of the family women milking their cows. Other rustic sketches show the men flailing grain, husking corn, and attending to various mundane farm duties—duties very different from those to which a Dresden-trained artist was accustomed. A great many other sketches and paintings show the small Lungkwitz children who were born in Texas. Petri's last work was an unfinished painting of the soldiers at Fort Martin Scott near Fredericksburg in 1857. Physical infirmity, economic hardships, and even the necessity of using paints made from native plants and soil did not diminish his delight in drawing what he observed around him. Certainly, Petri's must be the richest visual record of the German colonial experience in Texas.

An excellent craftsman, schooled in the Romantic traditions of the Dresden academy, Petri can be considered the most brilliant and innovative of the transplanted German artists in Texas. Had he lived past his thirty-six years, his reputation might have become more than regional, and his influence greater, for his drawings of the sun-drenched Texas frontier are equal to those of any better-known artists of the American West. Certainly Petri's true-to-life renderings of the Comanches, Lipans, and Delawares, and of the German experience in Texas serve as accurate historical documents as well as art treasures.

Hermann Lungkwitz, a native of Halle on the Saale, was the fourth important German artist on the Southwest frontier. His works form an interesting and significant contrast with the painting of the others because he focused on landscapes and towns. Trained, like his younger brother-in-law Richard Petri, in the Northern Romantic tradition at the Academy of Fine Arts in Dresden, Lungkwitz studied under Richter, won certificates from the academy, and made sketching trips through the Tyrol and Alpine country as well as his native Saxony. Under Richter, his painting teacher in Dresden, Lungkwitz became quite proficient, as shown in accurate landscape painting technique, choice of warm earth colors (although a few of Lungkwitz's later paintings from the 1880s appear almost monochromatic in treatment), and in composition. Richter's *Der Watzmann* (1824), *Genoveva in der Waldeinsamkeit* (1841), and *Spring Evening* (1844) contain the same elements as any of a large number of Lungkwitz's Texas landscapes from the 1870s and 1880s. Both included distant hills or mountains, rushing streams or quiet pools of water, lush forest foliage or stark, gnarled trees, and every size and shape of boulders. In terms of composition as well as Romantic treatment, Lungkwitz's *Swenson's Ruin* had its forerunner in Friedrich's *Ruins of Abbey at Eldena* (ca. 1824).

Lungkwitz was already an accomplished landscapist before events of the Revolution of 1848 (which saw Lungkwitz fighting at the barricades in Dresden) caused his migration to America. Arriving via New York, Virginia, and New Orleans, he brought his new bride, Elise Petri, his aging mother, his brother-in-law Richard Petri, and a few other relatives with him to Texas. This little company first sought a permanent home in New Braunfels in 1851, but soon moved to a farm on Live Oak Creek near Fredericksburg, where they were to remain until 1864. Then, harsh and unpleasant events brought on by the Civil War caused him and his family to sequester themselves in the relative safety of San Antonio. The family, including six children born in Texas, remained in San Antonio until 1870, when he was appointed official photographer in the General Land Office in Austin for the next five years. After the death of his wife in 1881, the aging artist shuttled from one child's home to another, staying for varying lengths of time in Austin, Galveston, and on a ranch near Johnson City. He died in Austin in 1891.

A quiet, peace-loving individual, Lungkwitz almost lost his desire and ability to create and paint in Texas. His large and growing family required financial support, and farming and ranching at Fredericksburg during his first fourteen years in the state became the primary goal. Pioneer life was strange and hard for all, especially for this cultivated and educated family. The women had to learn to milk, and the men to plow,

Views of Texas: German Artists on the Frontier

San Antonio de Bexar
by Hermann Lungkwitz, 1857

Paggi's Mill on Barton Creek, Austin, Texas
Hermann Lungkwitz, 1876

Courtesy of Mrs. Arthur Grenier

plant, and harvest. Lungkwitz soon recognized that Texas was no promised land for one of his profession.

Yet, some of his early sketches and paintings of the 1850s, especially views such as those of Fredericksburg and of Crockett Street in San Antonio, were made into lithographs to be sold. Although the original oil has been lost, his *Friedrichsburg* lithograph (1850s) is a Romantic pastoral idyll, with shepherd boys in the foreground gazing out over the wide Pedernales valley and the tiny farming village of Fredericksburg. The valley is peaceful, a place for hope and certain prosperity. It also has a quality of nostalgia for a past which many German immigrants felt they had left behind.

He visited the old Spanish missions during the early 1850s and included beautiful scenes of them and other San Antonio spots in the famous lithograph *San Antonio de Bexar*. *Crockett Street,* the original oil painting for this lithograph, brought into focus for the first time in his Texas career the profusely lighted southern view full of bright warming colors and the Texas noonday sky.

Despite the shock of frontier conditions, Lungkwitz made a valiant effort to maintain his art career prior to the Civil War. Visits to New Braunfels, Sisterdale, San Antonio, and Austin can be documented from contemporary newspaper accounts and from surviving works like a lithograph of Dr. Ernst Kapp's water cure sanatorium at Sisterdale during the mid-1850s.

About 1858 Lungkwitz turned to photography, a profession which was to assist him in supporting his large family for a decade. Soon after the Civil War ended, he and Carl von Iwonski opened a studio in the Alamo City which lasted until 1870, when Lungkwitz moved to Austin to become chief photographer at the General Land Office. The end of Reconstruction four years later brought this career to a close.

Teaching art, likewise, was another means for supporting his family. Lungkwitz taught in German schools, first in San Antonio and later in Austin, nearly until the end of his life. He also gave art lessons wherever he lived.

Let us turn to his Texas paintings which form the beginning of nineteenth-century landscape painting in the Lone Star State.

Views of Texas: German Artists on the Frontier

We have already spoken of his drawings, paintings, and lithographs in Fredericksburg, San Antonio, and other towns prior to the war. The complete picture of his productivity during that period is only now beginning to be known. Since 1969, through the efforts of the staff of the Texas Memorial Museum in Austin, a systematic cataloging of over 270 extant works has been carried on, and continues today in a joint project with the Institute of Texan Cultures in San Antonio. Lungkwitz painted Shoal Creek, Mount Bonnell, Texas Military Institute, and other familiar scenes of Austin. The documentation they offer of a still-unspoiled Texas town and its surroundings shows a nostalgic view of the state's capital a century ago. Other paintings show Barton Creek, lime kilns, and grist mills of that area.

With the death of his wife in 1881, the artist went to live periodically on a married daughter's ranch near Johnson City. Perhaps grief brought the man back to his first love, painting. Traveling through the hills and valleys to Fredericksburg, where his brother Adolph lived, Lungkwitz executed a series of finely detailed landscape drawings of the Pedernales and surrounding countryside. The 1880s marked the final blossoming of his genius to capture the rushing streams, quiet pools of clear water, jagged boulders, and twisted cedar and oak trees of that region on his canvases. He painted for the love of painting, and now, freed from family demands, he poured out his soul in the solitary wilderness of the Texas hills. From pencil sketches, his finished paintings reflected painstaking care in execution and in use of color as well as in the single-mindedness of his concentration. One has only to study these landscapes to recognize Lungkwitz's basic personality of serenity and harmony with his new homeland. Some scenes, such as Enchanted Rock near Fredericksburg and of the Pedernales and Guadalupe rivers, were painted many times and in many sizes, as if returning again and again both to the refuge he found in painting a scene and perhaps to "finish out" unresolved or only partially resolved technicalities through a series of works on the same subject. One of these technicalities was the problem of lighting. His early works were, for the most part, drenched with lighting and luminosity, almost as if

Lungkwitz imbued nature with a supernatural essence or religious quality. However, his post–Civil War landscapes became desolate, brooding panoramas with infrequent use of luminous, radiant lighting but still suggestive of this supernaturalism. Throughout his works there was an increasing tendency toward monochromaticism and synthesis. In these respects, Lungkwitz's development as an artist parallels, a half-century later, the development of the Northern Romantics.

Taken collectively, these four German artists' record of Texas in the nineteenth century forms a chronicle of local settlement and cultural life limited mainly to their immediate environment and related to their personal experiences. Iwonski, Wueste, Petri, and Lungkwitz comprise an informal "big four," a grouping of the most productive German immigrant painters in central Texas. Portraits of family members, friends, Indians, and a few commissioned likenesses are typical of Iwonski, Petri, and Wueste. Biedermeier influence can clearly be found in the variety of Iwonski's subjects in New Braunfels and San Antonio, and North German Romanticism made its first Texas foothold in the frontier illustrations and religious subjects chosen by Petri, as well as in Lungkwitz's searching, brooding landscapes in the newly civilized Texas Hill Country.

Today, yellowing and damaged drawings and cracked, darkened oil paintings testify to those pioneering experiences detailed by other German settlers in histories, journals, newspaper accounts, and personal letters. This early body of Texas art reminds us that the work of these men and women was as much in the mainstream of American and German art as that of nationally known German-American artists. Their contribution to nineteenth-century American art was strictly regional. On the other hand, Bodmer, Bierstadt, Möllhausen, and other immigrant German artists who traveled farther afield and selected more varied and majestic subjects are better known today.

The works of Petri, Lungkwitz, Wueste, and Iwonski were compassionate, understanding, and sensitive perceptions of the Texas subjects which they chose and painted. They communicate to us not only a point in time but the spirit of the immigrants' lives. This body of art has firm experiential roots in the total immigration story.

One wonders why these immigrant artists formed no art clubs

to further their mutual profession. Certainly they were all acquainted with each other, with the exception of Wueste, who arrived after Petri's death. Texas's first art association came into being in San Antonio and Austin through the efforts of others in the 1870s and 1880s. Only Lungkwitz assisted in the formation of an art group in Austin. Other artists lived and worked in central Texas, yet there is little evidence that the German "big four" associated with them. Was it a sense of superiority based on education or culture? Did Iwonski, Wueste, and Lungkwitz even know Theodore Gentilz, the Paris-trained immigrant who concentrated on Mexican cultural themes in San Antonio? No evidence exists today to answer this puzzling question.

Iwonski, Lungkwitz, and Wueste—disoriented, perhaps, and disillusioned by their American experience—were forced to supplement their incomes in a variety of ways, including teaching. Yet none produced a successor in their tradition. Lungkwitz actually discouraged his children from art careers because of his own devastating experiences. It must have seemed simple to each of them: art did not put bread on the table. Only Wueste passed on her talent and taught her grandchildren to paint, but then again only in the sense of a dilettante.

Finally, we must recognize that nothing new came of their Texas experience. It was as if their physical isolation in central Texas ossified their art. They kept doing what they had always done, painting in the styles of Germany, Biedermeier, and Northern Romanticism.

Public taste changed, and new generations of Texas artists forgot these German Romantic pioneers whose works were jealously guarded within the family fold, to be passed on to each succeeding generation. Since their students were few and, at best, mediocre, Iwonski, Wueste, Petri, and Lungkwitz were only faint memories to the public by the turn of the century. Now their art is being studied, catalogued, and shown as examples of the visual record of the Texas frontier of the mid-nineteenth century. In that sense, their achievements are important to us. As pioneers, their art should be analyzed to see how they interpreted their environment and how their new homeland affected their art and perceptions.

CHAPTER 6

The German Woman in Frontier Texas

CRYSTAL SASSE RAGSDALE

WOMAN'S place in the nineteenth century, by contrast with that of the previous century, was based on a philosophic as well as physical commitment to her family. Her days were spent in a continuing and lively participation in the affairs of her husband, children, and relatives and in the care of her household. She was portrayed both by writers of popular literature and painters of the time in the supportive mother-sister role of the Victorian period, a role that was almost an about-face from the female stance of the latter eighteenth century, when the educated woman enjoyed an active, outgoing wife-lover role. At this time, however, woman's life in an expanding nineteenth-century United States often demanded several roles of her, when she traveled west on the robust tide of frontier that crossed the Mississippi River in the half-century after American independence. The new land imposed the same harsh living patterns which had characterized the earlier East Coast settlement experience with a reenactment of the initial practice of occupying raw land by clearing fields for farming and at the same time making some kind of living arrangements with but few creature comforts.

The immigrant German woman in Texas met with many of the same conditions which had confronted Daniel Boone's wife, Rebecca, in colonial Kentucky. One German woman's reaction to her change in worlds was expressed by Mrs. Mathilde Herff a few weeks after she arrived in Texas in 1850, when in a moment of self-pity she chided her husband, Dr. Ferdinand

The German Woman in Frontier Texas

Herff, that he had not told her of everything as it was in Texas. Herff, who had already lived several years in the German-Texas colonies, replied prosaically that "when one in Germany tells of great privation and hardships, it is generally taken for granted, thought little of; but when privation and hardship strike the individual, then it seems unbearable."[1]

The German woman came upon a bewildering confluence of civilizations and time periods when she landed in Texas during the years of settlement. She came to the frontier without a word in her native language that adequately expressed the nuances of meaning in the American word "frontier." The new land was vast, and land holdings were inconceivably large. Life there meant few roads, almost no bridges, great distances, and few population centers. Some of the immigrants who pushed on to the western frontier met with the threat of Indian depredations.

What ideas the educated German woman may have had of the Indian were probably influenced to some extent by Rousseau's romantic "noble savage" and by readings in translation of Cooper's *Leatherstocking Tales*, then popular in Germany. The contrast between this romantic ideal and the brutal reality fell hard, for example, on the Latin colony of Sisterdale, built on the edge of civilization and scattered amid small clearings on the Sister creeks on the upper Guadalupe. The contrast is evident when one reads the diaries and letters of these settlers.

During the summers, the settlers worked in the cool mornings and on the warm afternoons gathered for intellectual discussions. At one such time, early in the colony's existence, Ida Kapp read aloud from *The Song of Hiawatha*, Longfellow's poetic characterization of the Indian.[2] What an impractical interpretation this was, in harsh contrast to the cruelty of Indian thievery and murder these idealistic families were to experience! Practical Ernst Kapp must have planned the architecture of their house with the threat of the hostile neighbors in mind. The front door, facing east, was built in the medieval manner of double layers of thick timbers held together with heavy metal bolts. The back of the house to the west was almost solid, with no large window openings onto the wilderness, where the Indian was master.

Yet even in the relatively settled areas the educated German woman must have felt the lack of what had been an integral part of life in Europe—her enjoyment and participation in the fine arts of music, theatricals, dancing, painting and drawing, and of reading the classics in German as well as in French. This is not to say that the average German émigrée knew or missed these elements of German society, for the majority were from the craftsman or agricultural class and knew little of these cultural patterns. She depended on them hardly at all. The milieu of the educated woman and her friends (in town or in the country) was where the men of the family were lawyers, engineers, architects, artists, university professors, merchants, and bankers by training, even if for a while they played at being farmers.

To counteract the backwoods cultural climate in which she lived, she must early on have decided to add another dimension to her life and arrived at a way to cope mentally and aesthetically with her frontier environment. While she fulfilled her Victorian role of dedication to children, church, and kitchen (*Kinder, Kirche, und Küche,* in the German vernacular formula which was a favorite expression of Nazi propagandists), at the same time she chose to foster *Kultur* in whatever way she could by drawing from her European training and heritage.

Perhaps the earliest record of the German woman's interest over and above frontier necessities was of Valeska von Roeder's decision to have her piano brought to Texas. She arrived on the Texas frontier in 1833 with her three brothers and a manservant as a part of the scouting party for the large von Roeder family which was to follow. However, the frontier defeated Valeska and she and her brother Joachim and the manservant, Franz Pollhart, died of malnutrition in their camp at Cat Spring. When her piano arrived later with the tons of luggage the von Roeders brought, Valeska's sister Rosa Kleberg inherited the boxes of sheet music and the piano, and she played for the young people's dancing in Harrisburg in 1835.[3]

Valeska's piano, which had given so much pleasure, was burned in 1836 during the Texas Revolution but another piano brought to Texas by a German girl a decade later to Cat Spring did become an important part of the life in the community. It belonged to Caroline Bauch, who soon after coming to Texas had to sell it when she moved to California. The Hermann Amthor family bought the piano, and after that the entire community shared in the pleasure of having music to sing by and listen to and "frequently a musical afternoon and evening was arranged at the Amthor's."[4]

Training in the cultural arts came in good stead when necessity forced the newly arrived German woman to earn her living. In 1840 the English traveler Francis Sheridan wrote in his diary of a social gathering in Velasco where he had met a "dear little German woman named Seffield," who was dancing mistress there. Frau Seffield's singing "in good voice" evidently helped ease the trying experience of listening to the other, untrained soloist on the program.[5]

Emilie Schuetze was another German woman who helped earn a living by the arts, when in the spring of 1854 she joined her brothers Louis, Adolf, and Julius to form a traveling troupe to sing in quartet and solo to the accompaniment of the guitar. However, after audiences poor both in money and in attendance in Yorktown, Indianola, Goliad, and Hallettsville, the young people decided that there was not enough interest in music in mid-nineteenth century Texas to guarantee a living for them.[6] For a time the young men turned to agriculture and freighting between the Coast and San Antonio, where Emilie settled and found employment in teaching music to young Germans.

Germans often turned to their love of music as a way of raising money for community projects, and when the New Braunfels newspaper, the *Neu-Braunfelser Zeitung*, was established in 1852, a musical concert was decided on to raise money to pay for the printing press waiting to be brought up from Indianola. Dr. Adolf Douai, who later worked on the paper, arranged a performance of male singers, but whether the community was too busy to attend, or knew of the men's limited talents, was not related. Whatever the reason, the audience did not contribute enough money for the necessary payment. Douai then proposed another musical program, this time advertising that his wife, Agnes von Beust, would be singing. That event was well received, and within days the press was paid for and the German colonists of New Braunfels were soon reading their own weekly newspaper.[7]

The traditional German love for instrumental and vocal music equaled their fondness for dancing, and the frontier German woman must have been an exuberant partner. Although the Germans and their Anglo-American neighbors at times attended the same dances and balls, Rosa Kleberg's comment on the Anglo-American dances must have expressed the sentiments of some of the Germans when she commented that "reels and squares were the favorite dances," all led by "loud prompting which is not customary in Germany."[8]

Before the advent of the spacious open *Schuetzenverein* halls which were scattered over the countryside like great white pavilions, dances were held in small homes. In Comfort during the summer months, space for dancing was made on "a grassy spot under the live oaks" in the center of the village, while Herr Schimmelpfennig, the music master, sat on a low limb and played his violin.[9] To have a ballroom in the community was the greatest of rare pleasures, and so it was with satisfaction and pride that the George Willrichs added a large room, or *Saal*, to their home, "Mt. Elise," in the Bluff Settlement on the west bank of the Colorado River above La Grange in the late 1850s. The long (17' by 30') room was built with a raised area at one end which had three openings so that stage directions for amateur plays could be followed.[10]

The Willrichs and their Latin scholar neighbors who lived on farms scattered along the road to Schulenburg were then able to enjoy local musical, dramatic, and literary entertainment in the new room, and at times traveling groups gave performances which contributed greatly to the intellectual life of Fayette County Germans of the area. Among the most enthusiastic gatherings that used the *Saal* was the young people's literary society, the *Prairie-Blume*, whose members met on regular occasions to read compositions which they had written at home. Assembled here in intellectual equality the young Germans, boys and girls, read their thoughts in prose and poetry and exchanged critical ideas on the papers. Later they played charades or danced the rollicking *Schottische, Polonaise,* and the slow waltz of the *Laendler.*

The German Woman in Frontier Texas

While we know a great deal about the German woman in Texas from her treasures of letters, diaries, and reminiscences, we can also know, with few exceptions, what she looked like and what she wore. If an unusually large number of young women and matrons look out at us from canvas, sketches, ambrotypes, ferrotypes, and carte de visites photographs, it is probably because the Germans were familiar with the European portrait tradition. They had paintings, etchings, and drawings in Germany, and among the prized objects from the homeland that were displayed in their new homes were family likenesses, as well as landscapes and copies of classic religious works. Frederick Law Olmsted, visiting a German farm above Sisterdale in the early 1850s after the owner's family had been established there for about two months, observed that displayed on the newly plastered walls of the two-room log cabin were "a very excellent old line engraving of a painting in the Dresden gallery, two lithographs, and a pencil sketch all glazed, and framed in oak."[11]

As an old woman Rosa von Roeder Kleberg bemoaned the fact that the unpacked art collection her family had left stored in Harrisburg had been destroyed when the Mexicans set fire to the town on their way to San Jacinto, and in Central Texas years later while Hermann Lungkwitz was painting the scene of her home at Cypress Mill Creek, Ottilie Fuchs Goeth remarked that she wished she had the money to buy the finished work. The von Meusebach–von Coreth families in the 1960s still displayed the evocative watercolors of room interiors of their early nineteenth-century homes in Germany.

Sometimes the German woman was the unpaid model for an artist husband or brother in Texas. Furthermore, a number of wealthy Germans paid to have portraits made during the years of growing prosperity in the 1850s and later in the 1870s after the Civil War. The *Mädchen, Fräulein,* and *Frauen* of New Braunfels, Fredericksburg, and San Antonio were recorded for time by the bachelor artist Carl G. von Iwonski, during the twenty years he worked as an artist in Texas from 1853 to 1873. One of his early portraits, painted in 1857, is of Hulda and Thekla Moureau, the young Texas-born daughters of Franz and Alwine vom Stein Moureau of New Braunfels. Later in

San Antonio, he painted the two Schenck sisters, young ladies in elaborate party dresses, teasing each other over a valentine.

In an Iwonski drawing of 1864 Mrs. Dorothea Wilhelmine Pape Guenther, wife of the prominent San Antonio businessman

The Pioneer Cowpen
by Richard Petri

Courtesy of Texas Memorial Museum, Austin

Carl Hilmer Guenther, sits beside her husband, hands clasped primly in her lap, looking solemnly but gently at the artist. Seven years later Iwonski returned to Berlin for a year's study. His subsequent, formal oil portrait of Mrs. Guenther, after his return to Texas, shows an elegantly attired young matron, hands crossed casually in her lap, regarding the painter with a sophisticated half-smile. One must always wonder who changed more in those seven years, Mrs. Gunther or the artist her husband paid to do the portrait? Whatever contemporary German paintings Iwonski may have seen during his foreign study, Mrs. Guenther's likeness, as he painted it the second time in 1873, seems caught in the realistic photographic style of portraiture, popular in Germany beginning in the mid-1840s.[12]

Although many paintings were of the German woman who lived in town, two rare, genre watercolors show her on a farm in Gillespie County in the 1850s.[13] The first, by Dresden artist Richard Petri, shows his two sisters Marie and Teresa in their impractical, trailing dresses milking long-horned cows in a log corral. In the cow lot with them is a pictorial inventory of the Texas farm animals the German family had acquired since their establishment of country life. A cat sits comfortably on the long skirt of one of the sisters, while in close range are chickens and ducks and cows with calves. Guineas cluster in one corner, the warning clatter of their voices silenced by the artist's brush more than a hundred years ago! There are surely few other Texas paintings that capture the pure *joie de vivre* more than Petri's companion picture, *Going Visiting* (ca. 1855). It is a rare scene of pioneer elegance and delight. Seated on an oxen-drawn, rug-draped wagon bed are the three Petri sisters, Marie and Teresa in back and Elisabeth with her artist husband, Hermann Lungkwitz, in front. The ladies, in stylish European dresses, with veils over their ribbon-tied hats, are holding small butterflylike parasols as protection against the Hill Country sun, while barely visible amid the swirl of skirts, petticoats, and shawls are the customary European gifts of flower bouquet and basket of food.

The German woman, as no other in nineteenth-century Texas, was portrayed as actress in local theatrical productions. The accepted practice among the Germans of a woman's taking part in and attending amateur theatricals is shown in two Iwonski paintings and a drawing which he made at the Old Casino Club in San Antonio sometime in the late 1850s. Women make up a large part of the well-dressed audience and several women are in the cast onstage. Fortunately for historical record the artist brought along his sketch book to rehearsals in San Antonio and New Braunfels, where his detailed drawings of scenes from the plays show them in the costume productions.[14] Surely the women members of the groups must have not only acted but also contributed their knowledge on matters of proper period costumes and on furnishings for the stage sets. They may also have taken part in selections.

For the Germans in New Braunfels and in the surrounding settlements, October 1856 was a special time because that was when Texas-German singers gathered for their fourth *Staats-Sängerfest* (state song fest), one of the largest on record. Part of the entertainment was a presentation of a five-act comedy by the little theater group which must have been both energetic and ambitious since it was in almost continuous rehearsal. During the following Christmas season that year, the group also presented a series of three new plays to the community.

With few exceptions, comedies were the usual presentations. However, in 1857, the group chose an abbreviated form of Schiller's *Kabale und Liebe* (Intrigue and Love), which had recently enjoyed a successful revival in Munich in 1854. Despite its European popularity in Munich, that center of German taste, the classic tragedy was poorly received by the New Braunfels audience, far removed as it was from the historic conflicts of old Germany. However, the play must have appealed to the spirit of the female members of the audience and of the acting group for the central character of the drama is Louise Miller, the victim of a stratified social system caught between the bourgeoisie and the aristocracy, in the context of the corrupt political practices of eighteenth-century German nobility. Ferdinand Lindheimer wrote in his *Neu-Braunfelser Zeitung* editorial that the choice of the play was perhaps a poor one, but he did congratulate the players on their production, saying that they provided cultural entertainment that "gave witness to the heights attained by civilized pursuits of the German border towns of Texas."[15] Did he say that with some irony?

By the early twentieth century the tradition of presenting plays seems to have become an expected part of entertainment at special festivities, and the Texas-German woman had a personal commitment to amateur stage productions in many rural communities. A rare recollection of one such community's observances is told about the farming center of Clear Spring, east of New Braunfels.[16] Stage productions were planned for the celebration of Thanksgiving, Christmas, and Independence Day. In the months before each holiday, a committee of women would select and order a German play or operetta. During the weeks preceding the holiday, they faithfully attended rehearsals, made costumes, and assembled stage properties. Speaking parts and singing roles were memorized and practiced at home and then rehearsed on Saturdays and Sundays in the community house. Members of the cast who lived on farms came to the community center by buggy or wagon from miles away over unpaved rural roads—bundled in quilts and coats against winter northers and rain or shaded in summer by umbrellas, hats, or wide-hooded cotton bonnets.

Early on the chosen day or on the day before, the men cut cedar boughs to frame the stage and the women brought potted plants and flowers as colorful decoration. Members of the local band began the festivities with music, when they led the crowd from the church to the community house. After the stage show, the crowd followed the band first to the picnic grounds and later to the place where an evening and night of dancing ended the full day's schedule. The women of the community also provided great quantities of food—cakes and pies, beef roasts, sausages and fried chicken, bread and butter, pickles and chow chow, head cheese, cream cheese, jellies and preserves, fresh vegetables and fruits, and gallons of hot coffee for what was to many, as often as not, the best part of the holiday enjoyment.

These periodic dramatic productions by the Texas-German woman brought a touch of fantasy or imagination into the lives of farm children far from urban centers of entertainment. In these seasonal festivals of the arts, traditional German songs

Very young Texas Germans take part in the annual New Braunfels Children's Masquerade, or *Kindermaskenball*. No masks are required, but costumes inspired by early day settlers' dress are popular.

Courtesy of New Braunfels Herald: *Chancy Lewis, photographer*

and poems alternated with exciting stories where costumes of other times and other places brought magic before the eyes of the enchanted young who sat in the audience, wrapped in a cloak of special wonder that remained for many of them a lifelong remembrance.

Another community event that could not have survived without the support of the German woman who came to Texas was the *Kindermaskenball*.[17] In New Braunfels this annual masquerade ball and parade of younger children was started by schoolmaster Hermann Seele in 1865 during the early years of settlement, and for over a century this Old-World celebration has been a community tradition in the lives of the New Braunfels woman and her children. During the colony's first years, much ingenuity and improvising must have gone into the creation of each young performer's costume. One New Braunfels woman recalled of her first-grade class in the early 1900s that all the boys and girls were dressed as little George and Martha Washingtons in a youthful show of patriotism.[18] Since then, Indians and pioneers have been favorites, as well as animals and flowers and story-book characters, to which have been added those from the movies and television. Even costumed babies ride in wagons or carts pulled by older sisters or brothers.

Each year in New Braunfels in early May, hearkening back to European May celebrations, children eleven years old and under gather on the announced day dressed in their chosen costumes. The highly informal parade of laughing and talking characters, accompanied by a marching band, weaves its way through the downtown streets past the judges' stand. The prize awards made later are an important part of the festivities and after that is over some of the little paraders linger in town with their mothers, reluctant to forsake the excitement of the *Kindermaskenball*. These celebrations for young people have been popular throughout both parts of the German belt— in the area around La Grange and Brenham in the east, as well as west of New Braunfels in the German Hill Country.

In the vigorous settlement years before the American western frontier closed in Texas, the German immigrant woman of education made a remarkable contribution to the appreciation and enjoyment of the cultural arts in the areas where she came to live. At the same time that she followed her family-centered role of the nineteenth century she managed to maintain something of an eighteenth-century woman's intellectual and social qualities. She encouraged her husband's and children's participation in cultural activities while at the same time she also took an active and imaginative part. She brought with her the training of the intellectual class to which she had belonged in Germany, and, although her surroundings were for the most part in an unlettered society, she drew on her background to enrich her new living environment, fostering the treasures of the mind. Olmsted might well have been describing the quality of the spirit and character of this especial German woman in Texas when he made this observation of the Sisterdale Latin scholars: "The dinner was Texan, of corn-bread and frijoles, with coffee, served in tin cups but the salt was Attic, and the talk worthy of golden goblets."[19]

CHAPTER 7

The Function of the German Literary Heritage

HUBERT P. HEINEN

THIS essay should have as its proper, typically German title some such phrase as "prolegomena toward a sociocultural history of the Texas Germans with respect to the importance successive generations placed on their German literary heritage." Preliminary research into the extent to which early German immigrants to Texas and their descendants derived a sense of ethnic pride and self-definition from the accomplishments of their native or ancestral country's poets has indicated that the topic deserves consideration, but much remains to be done. My observations may serve as a focus or catalyst for further, more informed and authoritative research and conclusions.

A German immigrant who became a leading industrialist and civic leader in San Antonio comments in his memoirs only once about the importance his German literary heritage had for him, and the nature of the comment is revealing. Max Krueger was a justice of the peace in a rural area when

William Haas... came to me one day with his bride to be married. Both were of German descent, and I tried to make the ceremony particularly solemn and impressive, and for the occasion I composed a nice address in German teeming with eloquent passages from German authors. I quoted Schiller's beautiful lines: "honor to woman! To her it is given to garland the earth with the roses of heaven." I committed it to memory and it made a deep impression on the couple, the bride being moved to tears, as she had never before heard anything so beautiful. Naturally I expected an extra fee for this effort, but after the ceremony Haas came to me and said rather bashfully that as everything had been so solemn and beautiful, he would not insult me by offering me the customary five-dollar fee, but that he and his wife would reward me with their undying gratitude instead. Needless to remark that after this experience I conscientiously adhered to the simple marriage ceremony provided for in the statutes.[1]

The jocular tone of Krueger's remarks should not prevent us from making some generalizations based on them which we can then examine more closely. An interest in literature in primitive circumstances was not practical—it did not put meat on the table and even tended to interfere with one's earning a livelihood. However, as a rare treat, key phrases from the German classics could lend dignity to such events as a wedding, a dedication, or a funeral. The classics could provide moral sentiments and appeal, in brief quotation, to the emotions. We may surmise, on the basis of scattered hints and scraps of evidence, that German literature played such a minimal role—to the extent that it played any role at all—in the lives of most immigrants and their descendants. However, for some immigrants and for some of their descendants, literature was and is very important indeed.

It is misleading to speak of immigrants as if all were alike in origin, education, and motives, and as if all reacted to Texas in the same way. Their economic circumstances varied immensely, even if most suffered unexpected deprivation. The settlers of Austin County faced somewhat different problems than the colonists who came to New Braunfels and Fredericksburg. The Texas Revolution, the Mexican War, the Civil War, and the Indian raids along the frontier all caused hardships for groups of colonists, but their effects were not felt equally by all. George Bernard Erath, for example, who came to Texas to escape Austrian and German reactionary tyranny, became assimilated through his service as a soldier at San Jacinto and during the Civil War and his subsequent service as a Texas ranger.[2] For all extents and purposes, he was not a Texas German, but rather a Texan of German (Austrian) birth who apparently did not associate with his former countrymen.

Most immigrants congregated in predominantly German communities, or at least maintained their contacts with fellow immigrants. The importance given to literature was determined by several factors. If the cultivation of literature had been important for the individuals and families before they left Europe, there was generally an attempt made to retain their heritage and even remain abreast of newer literary developments. This tendency was strongest among the immigrants of aristocratic and patrician origin, and among the typically highly educated Freethinkers, for whom a cultivation of literature in a broad sense served as a surrogate for religion. Conversely, a strong religious fervor tended to displace an interest in secular writings, as can be seen most clearly among the German Methodists, e.g., in the memoirs of Carl Urbantke.[3] Among those immigrants who did not arrive in Texas with an interest in literature there was rarely enough leisure or the proper opportunity to acquire an interest.[4]

During the calm before the storm, during that short period of time after they recovered from the rigors of crossing the ocean and settling in a virtual wilderness and before they were driven to flight by Santa Anna's army, a remarkable group of immigrants gathered in Austin County and took up life much as they had left it—in crude log cabins rather than in mansions.[5] Caroline Louise Sacks von Roeder wrote back to Germany:

Be sure to bring all the sheet music that you can collect. My piano is in excellent condition.... And do not fail to bring the complete works of Goethe. Day before yesterday, the third anniversary of the poet's death, we all assembled and read aloud many of his poems. Ludwig read the beautiful poem "Warte nur, balde ruhest Du auch."... All of us wept. Robert Kleberg began to sob and went out under the trees.[6]

The same letter contains several references to Shakespeare. The book of Goethe's poems may have been among those Rosa Kleberg mentions when she recounts that "we had buried our books, but the place had been found and they were torn to pieces. We had to begin anew, and with less than we had when we started."[7]

Ottilie Fuchs Goeth, who wrote one of the most polished memoirs by a Texas German pioneer, draws a poignant picture of her family's arrival in Cat Spring in 1846. Pastor Adolph Fuchs was determined to become a farmer, but

> how he must have suffered, this intellectual behind the plow; how clumsy and difficult it all was for the hands better suited to the use of violin bow or at most a pair of light garden shears. But these oxen, this plow! All of the geometry, the six languages and the logarithms he knew were of no help; it seemed impossible.[8]

Despite the difficulties, the family and others, such as the Romberg family, which settled nearby in 1847, scraped out an existence. As Adolph Fuchs wrote in a letter to Germany,

> our houses are cabins, our clothes are poor, our beds are hard, our hands often dirty—but our hearts are free and gay! Incidentally, we have decided to do more for our comfort than is customary by the local German settlers and particularly by those who are former German scholars.[9]

Pastor Fuchs had to supplement his farm income with music lessons and, a bit later, a teaching position at Baylor College in Independence until he moved with his family to Burnet County.[10] The family of Johannes Romberg moved about the same time to a farm near La Grange, close to what developed into a "Latin" settlement, one of the many created throughout the Middle West and down into Texas by the immigration of university-educated scholars turned farmers. This constellation of families became a center for German literary culture in Texas.[11]

Growing up in families for whom literature was a necessity, not a luxury, two young women developed their love of literature despite the rigors of their existence. Louise Romberg Fuchs recollects that

> often after hard work in the field chopping cotton . . . we lay still, enjoying the noon rest and reading. Poems gave me great pleasure, and I liked to memorize them and later recite them at my work

The Function of the German Literary Heritage 161

in the field, so that I would not forget them. For me it was a pleasure to rejoice in their beauty while I was working. In our long book-shelf we had such a nice selection of books we could read and study.[12]

Ottilie Fuchs Goeth remembers that she had no inclination to marry early, stating among other things that

I had been busily reading Schiller.... My mind was probably so occupied with a Posa, Karlos, a Max Piccolomini that I would scarcely have lent an ear to any cavalier of lesser rank.[13]

When Louise married Ottilie's brother William in 1861, Pastor Fuchs officiated. In his sermon

he said that in hard times it was especially necessary to protect the family, and in developing the theme he referred to Goethe's *Hermann und Dorothea*. This book, as well as the other works of Goethe, we received as a wedding present from brother-in-law Louis Franke.[14]

A reference to Goethe's idyll, with its overtones of a search for peace in the midst of strife, was particularly appropriate.

Other immigrants compared their situations to those of the characters in Goethe's works and derived inspiration from them. John O. Meusebach, as he chose to be known, sought to emulate the Faustian ideal of personal and social fulfillment—it is not surprising that he frequently quoted such lines from *Faust* as

> Only he earns freedom as well as life
> Who must win them anew each day...
> I'd like to see such a boisterous throng,
> To stand on free soil with a free people.[15]

He doubtless thought of his own work rescuing whatever could be rescued of the colonization project of the Adelsverein when he quoted these lines. His daughter remarks,

These words move me deeply, for as I say them I recall vividly my father's fervor as he repeated them to me. Goethe's idea of freedom never left him. In his old age, he penned the quotation, almost as a kind of valedictory of his life's work, for me on the fly-leaf of the account of his work as a colonizer.[16]

Ernst Kapp probably had the same verses in mind when he wrote, "I leave Germany, exchanging comfort for toil, the familiar pen for the unfamiliar spade, but I will be a free man in a free earth."[17]

Ottilie Fuchs Goeth and Louise Romberg Fuchs were children when their families came from Germany. So was Clara Schlecht when she arrived a decade later. Nevertheless, the pattern of concern with literature was established within the family. In Clara's case, this interest was reinforced by her marriage to Arnold Matthei, who did not immigrate until 1860 when he was twenty-four and whose intellectual interests were therefore already developed. The mixture of drudgery and literary inspiration which characterized their young married life can be surmised from two brief entries in Clara's diary.

In the afternoon Arnold went to Constant to mail the lottery letter. . . . He brought along a bottle of kerosene and Schiller's poems. [Six days later, on March 9, 1868:] Arnold is brewing—he is not feeling well. I made him tea of camomile, he got better soon. . . . In the evening . . . Arnold read to me.[18]

In addition to the classics which they bought or brought with them—and these were not restricted to German writers—the early settlers received newspapers and new publications from home. Ottilie Fuchs Goeth mentions that

even the cultured people of Mecklenburg speak *Plattdeutsch* when they feel relaxed. With the publication of the delightful books of Reuter, we soon discovered how poetic this semi-barbaric language can be. Soon after publication, these books were also brought to Texas, and it seems doubtful that any family found greater joy in them than ours, particularly as my cousins Heinrich and Otto Fuchs were playmates of the great humorist.[19]

Reuter's major works were not published until the late 1850s and the 1860s, and Ottilie may be referring here to a time after the Civil War. During the Civil War communications were cut off.

> The harbors were blocked, nothing was coming in, not even newspapers.... One turned again to the classics, Goethe, Lessing, Schiller, Shakespeare, as well as Jean Paul. People borrowed literature from one another. The German families traded books. What the one did not have, the other probably had. It was impossible for me to read Schiller during this war period, having read him so avidly as a young girl, and not wishing to destroy these impressions.[20]

Another comment by Ottilie can serve to place the former two in perspective. In reflecting on the limited opportunities, which her children and her brother's children made the most of, she observes that

> as I had little time in later life for literature, I was glad that, under Father's promptings, I had well utilized the time of my youth to become familiar with its golden treasures. These continued to sustain me while carrying out the taxing duties of a young mother and housewife.[21]

To be sure, some of the immigrants simply took the time to devote themselves to reading. We can find a number of statements such as "Robert Kloss was a jeweler and gold smith by trade, but farmed by proxy in this country. He loved to read and preferred doing this to following the plow."[22] His brother Emil Kloss

> was a highly educated man and very talented in the finer arts of music and painting.... Life with all its hardships in Texas did not prove altogether satisfactory and they [he and his wife] returned to Europe.[23]

About another immigrant, Frederick William Schnerr, we are told that

> having never learned to work, he could neither fence a field nor tend their cattle; he could only hire help. Instead of adjusting to pioneer life, he retreated into a world of books. In the issues of *Die Gartenlaube*, an illustrated, literary magazine from Germany,

Music Festival Poster
by Richard Petri

Courtesy of Texas Memorial Museum, Austin

he lived vicariously back at home. He read the periodical to the children and taught them to value it.[24]

This account tells us more, perhaps, about the values of its author than about Schnerr, but it certainly suggests that for some people German literature may not have been a source of strength and inspiration to meet the challenges of life in Texas but rather an escape. Though Conrad Wehmeyer, as a tradesman, did not need to know how to fence a field, otherwise the account of his activities sounds much the same, but the tone is different.

[Conrad] was a great reader. In the *Stube* where the family gathered evenings to work or play, he read aloud to them from German periodicals, and from books of fiction, travel, history and religion.[25]

Not only was it difficult to find leisure time in which to read, it was difficult for many settlers to find books. The library of classics which the Sisterdale "Latin" colonists established and drew on for their learned discussions burned with the building that housed it.[26] Other family libraries were destroyed as those who had assembled them passed away.[27] Some libraries, to be sure, survived more or less intact into the middle of the twentieth century, and some perhaps are still extant. A survey of these libraries could be revealing. In a letter to me dated 1 February 1978, Minetta Altgelt Goyne, the great-granddaughter of Ernst and Emma Altgelt, lists the German books she inherited from her mother, Agnes Coreth, who married the son of Hermann and Ottilie Coreth Altgelt.[28]

To an extent, reading societies were formed and provided access to literature, but many of these were short-lived. Ferdinand H. Lohmann reports that the *Comforter Leseverein* (1869–83) made the works of Fritz Reuter and numerous periodicals, among them *Die Gartenlaube* and *Zickels Novellenschatz*, available to its members.[29] Interest flagged, the club disbanded, and a new club founded several years later apparently had more modest literary aspirations.[30] Not until 1903, a time in which Lohmann was complaining bitterly about the inaccessibility of German books,[31] did the Comfort area have an association dedicated, among other things, to the nurture of interest in and discussion of German literature, the Cypress Creek *Damenleseverein*, with sufficient internal structural stability that it survived the demise of the immigrants for whom such materials were a link with their native land.[32]

In an interview with Vera Flach, Annie Holekamp gives an account which is based on family tradition and reflects a modern understanding of the conditions of the past, but which probably presents an accurate assessment of what happened to many settlers' love of literature.

My husband's grandfather had ... expected to be a gentleman farmer with men to work for him. Instead, he had to become a real farmer, too tired at night to read the many books he and his wife had brought with them. Many another German was similarly disappointed. Give them credit. They buckled down and did what had to be done.[33]

I have not tapped what should prove to be an important source of information about attitudes toward literature, the German newspapers in Texas. The correspondence, memoirs, and diaries of their editors, to the extent that they can still be located, as well as, of course, the issues themselves have never been systematically studied.[34] In addition, though a number of writings of the first settlers are becoming available—and hopefully more will be published—the papers of their descendants are largely inaccessible. At most, we have brief sketches, memorials, and obituaries. Fortunately, there are enough exceptions to this rule that a few observations can be made.

My research failed to unearth much information about the children of the early settlers, those born in Texas in the 1850s and 1860s. Although there is doubtless much more material to be found and evaluated, a few sparse comments must suffice here. John Oswald Wendel was, to be sure, born in Germany, but he came to Texas in 1859 at age one and thus can be considered together with Peter Jordan, who was born in Fredericksburg in 1852, and Emma von Donop Jordan, born in the Upper Willow Creek settlement in 1859. A descendant reports that John, although he had little formal education, ... became a well-educated man through reading along lines of his varied interests. He was especially interested in literature, history and geography. He instilled his own interests in his children.[35]

Emma, the daughter of "one of the early school teachers at the Upper Willow school," where she and Peter received their education, married Peter in 1877. Since both she and Peter were Methodists, it is somewhat doubtful that her father, Otto von Donop, "who had been a student at the prestigious University of Berlin,"[36] endowed her with the respect for the German classics as a virtual surrogate for religion which many of his fellow students felt and taught their children. Thus it is quite likely they were reading the Bible, religious writings, and/or one or the other of the German (or English) Methodist newspapers, when, as a descendant relates,

in their later years, Peter and Emma enjoyed sitting on the porch holding hands. They were a peaceful picture as they sat there—white haired Peter, with his pipe in his mouth, listening to Emma reading aloud to him.[37]

The German Methodists probably did not have the same reverence for German as the language of religion and for the Luther Bible as did many German Lutherans. Even the latter did not necessarily look to German literature for inspiration, but to the extent that religious ties strengthened ethnic bonding, Methodist, Lutheran, and Catholic German communities may have created a linguistic basis for a continued or newly awakened interest in literature. The numerous published and unpublished histories of churches in Texas with German-speaking congregations, and especially further investigation of the papers of their prominent members, might be another source of information.

The sponsors, teachers, and students of the schools where German was the dominant language certainly stressed the importance of literature in a number of attested cases. A systematic study of the schools and their influence would be rewarding, even if my specific topic were not furthered. For example, a number of leading citizens of San Antonio were interested in and supported the German-English School. Frederick C. Chabot mentions John Conrad Beckmann, Friedrich Groos, Frederick Jacob Waelder, and Carl Griesenbeck in connection with the school, as well as Albert Steves, who both attended the school and later served as a director, and Dr. Rudolph Menger, who served as "vice-president of the 'Texas Museum, Scientific and Literary Association'" in 1884, some years after having attended the school.[38] These and other German Texans in San Antonio, and their counterparts in Houston, Austin, and Dallas, may well have contributed to a furtherance of interest in German literature which has escaped my attention. The usual forum for light dramatic, musical, and intellectual entertainments was the Casino Club, which spread in one form or another throughout the German-speaking areas of Texas, and a study of this institution and its sponsors should be profitable.

One institution which has served to preserve German culture is the singing societies. They may be only a shadow now of their former selves, but they do persist. The strongly sentimental songs which characterize their repertoire have been the touchstone of German literary quality for most Texas Germans for at least a century. The symbiosis of songs, societies, and indigenous poets such as Ferdinand H. Lohmann and his (short-term) pupil Hulda Walter deserves further study.[39] The function of the singing societies was and still is primarily social and musical, but at times, certainly, the content and literary style of the songs was as important to some of the members as the musical setting. Patriotism, nostalgia for Germany, praise of German customs and ideals, and, perhaps most frequently, the excellence of German song and singing are recurrent themes. The importance of the societies for a cultural history of the Texas Germans has been recognized, but the topic still awaits a definitive treatment.[40]

For one German Texan, born in 1872, whose parents had come to Texas with their parents, singing and the singing societies played an important role, especially when he was in his twenties and thirties. His introduction to and concept of literature, however, were derived from other sources. He describes, some seventy years later, his first encounter with German literature as follows:

In the Comfort School were several dozen little German library books of about the size as later on the "Harvard Classics." Each contained a—for me—fascinating story, designed for children, religious, and with a good *Moral*. We could read three of them for a nickel—and since Grandmother enjoyed reading them as well as I did—they were printed in large German type—she provided me with the necessary nickels; often from the proceeds of the eggs I delivered to Ingenhuett's Hotel at perhaps 10¢ a dozen.—Little did those ancient German writers dream that their stories should play such an important part in moulding the character of a little waif in the far-away frontiers of Texas![41]

After three years of school in Comfort and one year in a private (ranch) school at Bear Creek being taught by Emil Habecker, this ranch boy, my grandfather, was sent out to herd sheep, an occupation he detested.

The only reading I had access to was the *Freie Presse für Texas*, a German weekly published in San Antonio, which, besides current news and correspondence, carried one or more serials of novels (*Romane*); also volumes of German magazines, such as *Die Gartenlaube*, in carefully preserved *Jahrgänge* (one-year volumes containing fascinating *Romane* and short novels) were passed from one family to the other, and, naturally, I fell for reading these stories. Having lots of time on hand, I acquired the habit of "slow-reading" (not overcome to this day), but absorbed all and lived with and through the whole story. Meanwhile, as I was thus absorbed in reading, the sheep would drift apart in all directions, and I had to spend hours trying to get them together again. . . .

But there might have been some compensation—I acquired a fair knowledge and vocabulary of the German language, and most of the stories dealt with the life of the German nobility, clean and moral. Personal honor was played up almost to extremes, and I remember that whenever someone insulted me, my first impulse was to challenge him to a duel, as the noblemen in my stories had done. Thus, I believe, these readings helped to develop in me . . . such traits as honesty, a keen sense of honor, ambition and perseverance.[42]

His knowledge of the German classics was apparently acquired during the almost forty years he taught school—he especially loved Schiller.

Another Comfort-area German Texan, also born in 1872, though to native Texans, a grandchild of the same Fritz Holekamp referred to above, may have had a slightly more direct introduction to German literature, but as the oldest of eight children growing up on a farm in the Cypress Creek community she would scarcely have had more leisure than my grandfather. She was a charter member of the Cypress Creek *Damenleseverein*.[43] For some time she was "a private schoolteacher for the Real family on Turtle Creek," as we learn from interview notes made by Glenn G. Gilbert, who interviewed Ida Holekamp in Comfort in 1966. He notes further that she

still possesses various G[erman] books, such as *Schillers Werke*... still reads G books and newspapers; she wrote a book about her family in G, she also formerly wrote numerous G letters; her father subscribed to the *Freie Presse fuer Texas*; she subscribed to the *Neu-Braunfelser Zeitung*.[44]

Among the several second-generation descendants of German immigrants to Texas born in the last quarter of the nineteenth century about whom information is available, one couple is especially interesting, since both John R. (Hans) Fuchs and Patty Wenmohs Fuchs descended from Pastor Fuchs. John writes:

In both the homes of her grandparents [Goeth and Wenmohs] you would find, for that day and time, in this comparatively new land, wonderful libraries... [with] the classics in both the English and German languages. At the firesides in these homes, these inmates, even though weary from the daily toil, found time to read aloud and discuss the classics. These discussions, of course, took place in the family circles, and there much of the teachings and philosophies of the great authors were handed down to and absorbed by the children.[45]

A Husband's Tribute to His Wife portrays Patty as vitally

interested in literature and music, communicating her enthusiasm both to her family and, through her gift of public speaking, to wider audiences. An excerpt from a paper she delivered to the New Braunfels Study Club can exemplify this attitude.

> The people of New Braunfels can be proud of their heritage. The compliment paid them applies to all the pioneers of German extraction. It is well deserved. While they were fighting for their very existence, they at the same time did not forget the spiritual side of life. Music, art, education, and all things to develop the inner man were cultivated.... It is incumbent upon the present and future generations to maintain these things. Let us do our part.[46]

While a student at the University of Texas, John was a charter member, along with twenty-four other "Germans," of an organization which did not survive the First World War—just as so many other institutions designed to promote German culture did not.

> On October 23, 1907, a new organization was brought into existence. This was the *Germania,* a German literary society, which has for its object the fostering of the German language, literature, and ideals in this University. Such an organization has long been a need, and when the idea was first advanced it found universal favor among the Germans both of the Faculty and of the student body. Although still in its infancy, the *Germania* has made some advance toward the attainment of its ideals. The German students have been drawn together and have become better acquainted with each other; a German library has been started. All exercises are conducted in German.[47]

For the "Americans" there was a German Club—separate but equal.

The ravages of the First World War on attitudes and efforts to use one's German cultural heritage are well known and well documented. Another descendant of Pastor Fuchs, the capable translator of Ottilie Fuchs Goeth's memoirs, Irma Goeth Guenther, has mentioned to me how she was taunted and pestered because of her background while she was a school girl in San Antonio in 1918. My father had fewer problems, since there were not that many *Ausländer*, i.e., "foreigners," non-Germans, in Comfort in those days, but regular German instruction in the schools of Texas was interrupted and in many cases discontinued altogether. Economic developments after the war tended to encourage children to leave the Texas-German communities and thus marry outside their ethnic group. All these factors help explain why an unbroken tradition of interest in German literature, such as can be seen among some of the Fuchs descendants, is rare.

Approximately 300 informants were interviewed for the *Linguistic Atlas of Texas German* (281 interviews, some with more than one informant, in the early to mid-1960s).[48] There is no specific information about the German reading habits of the informants given in the sociolinguistic notes on some 206 interviews. Since no information is given about the reading habits of a prominent Comal County historian, Oscar Haas, who has read and translated numerous German documents and newspaper articles, we cannot automatically assume that a lack of information indicates that these informants no longer read or have never read German.[49] Still, if the reading of German literature was important to the informant, this fact would most likely have been noted. To be sure, at least one person interviewed, my grandfather, who read fairly extensively in German and for whom German literature was very important, was excluded from the study because he talked like the schoolteacher he had been and thus was not representative of Texas Germans.[50]

Only five informants explicitly state that they read German frequently, although at least two more certainly do so. Nineteen read occasionally; seventeen report they once read but no longer do so. Only a few, some six, expressly mention that they never learned to read German.

One informant, we are told, born in 1887, is

a housewife on a ranch; she has a 10th grade education and took a "special primary course" at Baylor University; reads and writes G very well and frequently; this inf. is a very intelligent and alert person; she subscribes to the periodical *Die Hausfrau* from Chicago

The Function of the German Literary Heritage

... she has read Goethe and Schiller in the original and has a fine library of old books that she still reads.[51]

About a couple, born in 1884 and 1886, we learn that their

library includes G works by Schiller, Goethe, Lenau, Boerne, and Heine; "I got them from my parents" [Mrs. K. I.] ... both inf. completed the 4th grade; "we children had to read to father, he had trouble with his eyes," says Mrs. K. I. ... Mr. K. I. can read G but does not do so any more, Mrs. K. I. still reads G books and magazines. ... Mr. K. I.'s father subscribed to *Texas Vorwärts* and the *Friedrichsburger Wochenblatt*.[52]

Another informant, born in 1886 or 1889,

either had considerable schooling or was an autodidact; his G tends toward the standard language and betrays a wide reading vocabulary; the inf. lives alone in a small house with walls lined with books; his attitude toward the world seems to alternate between benevolence and embitterment.[53]

Yet another informant, born in 1901, is

a farmer and rancher with a 6th grade education; G is always spoken in the household; inf. reads G often and fluently; this was one of the most Germanophile of all the inf.s; he prides himself on his correct speech; he regularly writes letters to relatives in Germany and has several bookshelves of G books and periodicals.[54]

A granddaughter of Caroline von Hinueber, born in 1912, was interviewed and apparently no longer reads German; two grandsons of Ottomar von Behr were interviewed, one of whom (born in 1889) no longer, the other of whom (born in 1914) barely, reads German, though the latter's wife "still reads *Die Hausfrau*."[55] Another informant, born in 1919, one of the most highly educated,

finished high school and completed law school at the Univ. of Texas in 3 yrs.; he studied "G area studies" for 9 months at Cornell Univ. and spent 18 months in Germany just after World War II ...

reads... very little G now... has an extremely wide G vocabulary but does little reading.⁵⁶

The evidence of the *Linguistic Atlas* sociolinguistic notes, as fragmentary and imperfect as it understandably is—the notes are not intended as source material for cultural history—suggests strongly that the German literary heritage is no longer a significant part of Texas-German ethnic identification. Texans who not only treasure but also read any German literature in the original are increasingly rare and isolated. A more thorough study of the question will of necessity be historical, rather than sociological.

It is, perhaps, instructive to examine one case which is exceptional, an instance in which German literature is still alive for a Texas German. In an interview with me, Irma Goeth Guenther (born in 1909) outlined her background, mentioning that she remembers vividly being read the Grimms' fairy tales, Wilhelm Busch, and *Struwwelpeter* by her grandmother Hedwig Klappenbach Schroeter (who had come to Texas at the age of four), a highly literate woman who wrote poetry and novels for the newspapers.⁵⁷ Irma Guenther also recollects singing the songs from which she, starting at the age of four, was taught to play music, a collection of *Kinderlieder*. From cousins she has heard how her grandparents Carl and Ottilie Fuchs Goeth would read to the grandchildren, but she remembers only how impressive the bookshelves filled with books were. She learned to read German from her mother, who taught the children of friends and relatives in Marble Falls, from the wife of the principal of the Thomas School in San Antonio, and from Mrs. Richter in Brackenridge High School (in the late 1920s). She remembers, however, that she and other Texas Germans found the German literature they were expected to read in high school childish, dull, and boring. She does not recollect much of what she read as a young woman, only that she did read a lot. One incident sticks in her mind. An Austrian visiting San Antonio in the 1920s was struck to find her reading Nietzsche in the original. She feels that her contacts with literate and cultivated Texas Germans and her consciousness of her intellectual heritage, informed by such sources as her grandmother's memoirs, were

The Function of the German Literary Heritage

more important to her as a source of ethnic pride than German literature. Indeed, she does not remember that she paid much attention whether she was reading German or English. During the Second World War she worked for the U.S. Army as a translator in San Antonio. From 1945 to 1964 she worked for the army as a translator in Germany, where her second son, John, was born. She returned to Texas in 1967 and has kept up an interest in German literature which was rekindled in Germany. John, who is very interested in German literature, reads widely and enthusiastically, but, since he grew up in Germany with a German father and a German-speaking mother, he is essentially a recent German immigrant, not, in the sense the term is used here, a Texas German.

Many descendants of German immigrants have intensified their acquaintance with German literature through academic study—and some have had to learn German, as I did, to do so. The revival of interest in one's roots may yet stimulate a renewed interest in the source of the ideals, opinions, and thought patterns of many of our ancestors, in their literary heritage.

CHAPTER 8

German Cultural Heritage in the Hill Country of Texas

GILBERT J. JORDAN

MANY unique traditions, all deeply rooted in European folklore and practices, were brought to the Texas Hill Country by the mid-nineteenth-century German colonists, and some of these customs have lived on to the present day. The most striking are the Christmas and Easter customs, but much additional *Kulturerbe* (cultural heritage) was perpetuated by the German settlers in Texas, such as the practices pertaining to holidays, greeting cards and memory albums, weddings, proverbs, godparents, handshaking, children's songs, poems and prayers, family reunions and genealogical studies, homeopathic remedies, folk beliefs, nature and weather signs, water witching, faith healing, pranks and spooks.

As is well known, many of our American Christmas customs can be traced back to northern Europe, especially to Germany and Holland, as for example the Santa Claus (*Sankt Nikolaus*), Kris Kringle (*Christkindlein*), and the Christmas tree (*Tannenbaum*). Several favorite Christmas songs, like *Stille Nacht, heilige Nacht* (Silent Night, Holy Night), *O Tannenbaum* (Oh Christmas Tree), *Der schönste Baum* (The Fairest Tree), and *O du fröhliche, O du selige* (Oh, Thou Joyous, Oh, Thou

---

This essay is adapted from *Yesterday in the Texas Hill Country*, by Gilbert J. Jordan. The editors and author acknowledge the kind permission of Texas A&M University Press to reprint this article.

Blesséd), were brought over by the Germans; and some, like the first two above, were translated into English and merged with the Anglo culture; but others, like the last two listed above, were never transcribed adequately. They lived on in the Texas Hill Country and elsewhere in German neighborhoods in their German versions, along with other songs and customs.

In most German-Texan settlements the religious element of Christmas was perpetuated in a *Gottesdienst* (Divine service) in church on Christmas day. A very unusual activity was the children's program, also held in the church several evenings before Christmas. In addition to the reading of the Christmas story from the Bible, short speeches by the pastor and the Sunday-school superintendent, and singing of songs, a program was presented by and for the children. Songs like *Alle Jahre wieder, kommt das Christuskind* (Every Year Again Comes the Christ Child) and *Morgen kommt der Weihnachtsmann* (Tomorrow Comes Santa Claus) were sung by the children, and they recited poems, such as:

> Der Weihnachtsmann ist ein guter Mann;
> Er bringt den Kleinen, was er kann.
> Die Grossen lässt er laufen;
> Die könn'n sich selbst was kaufen.
>
> (Santa Claus is a good old man;
> He brings the children all he can.
> The grown-ups he will leave alone;
> They buy their presents on their own.)*

The highlights of the evening were the large Christmas tree and the big paper bags filled with fruit and sweets that were passed out after the program.

One of the most enjoyable pre-Christmas activities at home was the baking of cookies in the shapes of stars, doughnuts, birds, chickens, ducks, horses, Santa Clauses, trees, and toys. The entire family then gathered around the dining table and

---

* All translations are by Gilbert J. Jordan.

decorated the cookies. On some evenings between December 6 and Christmas a stern *St. Nikolaus* came and checked up on the children, and he had them say their prayers to prove that they were good children. On such occasions many a child recited a well-known prayer:

> Ich bin klein,
> Mein Herz mach' rein;
> Soll niemand drin wohnen,
> Als Jesus allein.
>
> (I am small,
> My heart make pure;
> Shall none there dwell
> But Jesus for sure.)

The Christmas tree was usually decorated secretly by the parents or the older children on the afternoon of December 24. Then after supper a little bell was rung or the children were told that the *Weihnachtsmann* had come and had prepared a tree and left presents for them. This was the long-awaited moment, and the whole family walked to the Christmas room together. Before the children could touch the unwrapped presents under the tree, they had to stand and sing some Christmas songs, such as:

> Der Christbaum ist der schönste Baum,
> den wir auf Erden kennen.
> Im Garten klein, im engsten Raum,
> wie lieblich blüht der Wunderbaum,
> wenn seine Blümlein brennen,
> wenn seine Blümlein brennen,
> ja, brennen.
>
> (The Christ-tree is the fairest tree
> That we on earth can know.
> In smallest rooms our eyes can see
> How lovely blooms the wondrous tree
> With its fiery blossoms glowing,
> With its fiery blossoms glowing,
> Yes, glowing.)

The children also found a table or a bench with plates or boxes filled with goodies (*die Bescherung*) and some fireworks near the tree. The presents all stood or lay under the tree. The children rarely ever saw the *Weihnachtsmann,* and some of the older ones repeated disrespectful verses about him:

> Ich bin klein, du bist gross;
> Der Weihnachtsmann hat ein Loch in der Hos'.
>
> (I am small, you are big;
> Santa Claus has a hole in his pants.)

The old German custom of setting aside December 26 as second Christmas was followed everywhere in the Texas Hill Country, and it was a day for visiting relatives and friends. Then, several days later on New Year's Eve, *Sylvester,* the young people held Watchnight parties and religious programs at church.

The Good Friday and Easter activities were not as elaborate as the Christmas celebrations. The religious element was again in the foreground, from the somber *Karfreitag* (Good Friday) services to the joyous Easter-morning celebration, both held in the church.

On Saturday before Easter the children went out to the fields and pastures with play wagons and baskets to gather wildflowers and grass for their Easter nests, which they then built on the front porch, where the Easter rabbit could find them and fill them with brightly colored eggs. Here the children found them on Easter morning. The day after Easter was *zweite Ostern* (second Easter) and it, like second Christmas, was set aside for visiting.

Thanksgiving Day was called *Danksagungstag* (Thanks-saying-day) by the Germans in the Hill Country, and it was celebrated in a manner similar to the American holiday, but the tradition of stuffed turkey dinners with cranberry sauce and pumpkin pie was introduced and accepted only gradually. There seem to have been some vestiges of the North German *Erntedankfest* (day of harvest thanks) celebrated in Germany on the Sunday after September 29; of course, without the

Erntebier (harvest beer). Again the religious element was prominent. In Texas, as in Germany, the people sang *Nun danket alle Gott* (Now Thank We All Our God).

A number of German games were introduced in Texas. Among these we should mention *Mühle* (mill), played on a homemade board with buttons or grains of corn of different colors, and *Sautreiben* (sow driving), also called *Mummela*. The latter game was played with three-foot sticks and a vicious crushed can, the sow. The player who was "it" had to drive the mean sow into the pen, which was a hole in the ground within a circle of holes defended by other players. Smashed shins and feet were the usual consequences.

Memory books or albums were well known in Anglo and German communities alike. In German-speaking communities these books took on a German flavor by the use of certain verses, such as:

> Dem kleinen Veilchen gleich,
> Das im Verborgnen blüht,
> Sei immer fromm und gut,
> Auch wenn dich niemand sieht.
>
> (Like a little violet
> That blooms in secrecy,
> Be pious and be good,
> Though unseen you may be.)

Some of these verses, especially English ones, appeared also on the *Stammbuchblümchen*, the flowery and lacy overlays, on friendship cards that were exchanged among friends around the turn of the century. One of the chief contributions of the Germans in the Hill Country to the popular card-sending craze were the "vinegar valentines." Some of the practical jokers and pranksters had a great talent for inventing derogatory verses and caricatures, which they sent for mischief to friend and foe alike.

Weddings usually were large, all-day affairs to which hundreds of people were invited and came. The proverbial fatted calf was killed and all the people were fed two big meals in the style of the German peasant *Hochzeit*. The wedding ceremony was in the morning, and among the members of the southern branch of the Methodist Church, for example, the bride plighted her troth to the bridegroom by giving a positive answer to these words: *Willst du ihm gehorsam sein, ihm dienen, ihn lieben und ehren, ihn pflegen in Krankheit und Gesundheit,* ... (Wilt thou obey him, serve him, love, honor, and keep him, in sickness and in health, ...). The Anglo custom of a chivaree, called *Katzenmusik* (cat music, or caterwauling) in German, and related to the rural German *Polterabend*, a noisy, wedding-eve party, was common in the Hill Country. In true Texas style, men and boys came on horseback, riding like wild Indians, shouting, yelling, dragging tin cans, beating on old washtubs, ringing cowbells, and blowing horns. This was a much wilder affair than the tame German *Polterabend*, during which pots, pans, and old dishes were thrown against the front door of the newlyweds.

Sprichwörter, or proverbs, were an ever ready source of folk wisdom and they tended to preserve a basically conservative outlook on life among German families, as Curt Schmidt has pointed out in his book *Oma and Opa: German-Texan Pioneers*. There were literally hundreds of these sayings current in the Hill Country, and they are typical of German proverbs everywhere. I will quote only a few here:

1. Arbeit macht das Leben süss
    (Work makes life sweet),
2. Der Klügste gibt nach
    (The wisest one gives in),
3. Hunger ist der beste Koch
    (Hunger is the best cook),
4. Wenn die Maus satt ist, schmeckt das Mehl bitter
    (When the mouse is full, the flour tastes bitter).

There are various customs, also well known elsewhere, some even in Anglo circles, that were especially prominent among the Hill Country German Texans. The people placed more emphasis on the activities of godparents (German *Paten* or *Taufzeugen*) than Anglo families did at the time. The godparents were supposed to be guardian angels, so to speak, for the godchild. They stood in at the baptizing, often gave presents, and continued to follow the child's development with something of a parental interest.

Handshaking was far more prominent in the German communities than in the Anglo settlements. Whenever people met or took leave from each other, there was a big handshaking ceremony. Most people gave their greeting by saying, "*Guten Tag, wie geht's bei euch?*" (Good day, how are you all?), or perhaps with a slight dig at the complainers who mistook a greeting for an inquiry about their health, "*Sonst geht's gut*" (Otherwise everything goes well). The German expression *Wie geht's* means literally, "How goes it?" but the verb *gehen* also means "to walk," so you not only said, "How goes it?" but also, "How do you walk?" This sometimes called forth the facetious reply, "*Auf zwei Beinen, wie eine Gans*" (On two legs, like a goose).

Many of the better German children's songs, poems, and prayers were kept alive in the Hill Country. When the parents bounced their children on their knees or let them ride on a swaying foot, they pretended to drop the child as though he were falling from a horse, while they spoke or sang:

>Hopp, hopp, hopp!
>Pferdchen, lauf Galopp,
>Über Stock und über Steinchen,
>Pferdchen, brich dir nur kein Beinchen!
>Hopp, hopp, hopp, hopp, hopp,
>Pferdchen, lauf Galopp!
>
>(Trot, trot, trot!
>Horsie, run a lot,
>Over sticks and over stonies,
>Do not fall and break your bonies.
>Trot, trot, trot, trot, trot!
>Horsie run a lot!)

While English and American parents sang: "Patty cake, patty cake, baker's man" and patted the children's hands together, the German Texans said or sang:

German Cultural Heritage...

> Backe, backe, Kuchen!
> Der Bäcker hat gerufen:
> Wer will guten Kuchen backen,
> Der muss haben sieben Sachen:
> Eier und Schmalz, Zucker und Salz,
> Milch und Mehl,
> Safran macht den Kuchen gehl (gelb).
> Schieb in den Ofen 'nein!
>
> (Baking, baking, cookie!
> The baker man is calling:
> Who will bake a tasty cake,
> Seven things he has to take:
> Eggs and lard, sugar and salt,
> Milk and flour,
> Safran makes the cake turn yellow.
> Shove it through the oven door.)

A lovely custom used when a child fell or got an injury in some way was to kiss and blow on the sore spot and say or sing:

> Heile, heile, Segen,
> Drei Tage Regen;
> Drei Tage Dreck,
> Und jetzt ist alles weg.
>
> (Healing, healing, blessing,
> Three days of rain;
> Three days of mud,
> And now there's no more pain.)

The favorite prayer taught to the children in the German Texas Hill Country is similar to the English "Now I lay me down to sleep, I pray the Lord my soul to keep." The German prayer is the well-known poem by Luise Hensel, which has the following lines, among others:

> Müde bin ich, geh' zur Ruh',
> Schliesse meine Äuglein zu;
> Vater, lass die Augen Dein

Über meinem Bette sein.
Hab' ich Unrecht heut' getan,
Sieh's, mein lieber Gott, nicht an!

(Tired am I, go to bed,
Close my eyes, lay down my head;
Father, let the eyes of Thine
O'er my resting place incline.
If I've done some wrong today,
Take, dear Lord, my guilt away.)

The best-known table prayers or blessings are:

Segne, Vater, diese Speise,
Uns zur Kraft und Dir zum Preise!

(Bless, our Father, this our food,
For thy glory and our good);

and

Komm, Herr Jesu, sei unser Gast
Und segne, was Du uns bescheret hast.

(Come, Lord Jesus, be our guest
And let the food you gave be blest.)

The children in the German Texas communities memorized dozens of poems in school, such as:

A, B, C [pronounce: Ah, Bay, Tsay],
Die Katze lief im Schnee [pronounce: Schnay].
Und als sie wieder 'raus kam,
Da hatt' sie weisse Zeh' [pronounce: Tsay].

With some alphabetical license we might translate this verse as follows:

M, N, O,
The cat ran in the snow:
And when she came out again,
She had a white toe.

There were literally dozens of such ditties, too many to enumerate here, and many other German poems, riddles, tongue twisters, counting-out, rope-jumping, and nonsensical ditties, as for example the following:

> Fischers Fritz fischt frische Fische;
> Frische Fische fischt Fischers Fritz.

This tongue twister is just about as hard in English as in German:

> Fisher's Fritz fishes fresh fish;
> Fresh fish fishes Fisher's Fritz.

One of the better-known, apparently nonsensical ditties goes as follows:

> Fritz, Stiegelitz, dein Vogel ist tot;
> Liegt unter dem Baum und frisst kein Brot.
>
> (Fritz, Stiegelitz, your birdie is dead;
> Lies under the tree and eats no bread.)

Family reunions began as birthday celebrations for grandparents, and they have continued to the present day and have multiplied and grown in number and magnitude. The side effects of the reunions are genealogical research and family histories. This writing of family histories is characteristic of the outlook of German-Texan families of the Hill Country.

Many specimens of folk beliefs can be found among the German Texans, some harmless and interesting, others sheer superstition. The people used to say that good and talented children will die early because the Lord will take them to Himself. When I was a child, I was fond of singing and I sang at the drop of a pin, both English and German songs. When one of my aunts heard me sing, she said to my mother, "You won't keep him long; the good Lord will take him from you." I am sure, if this aunt had heard me sing after I was grown, she surely would have recanted.

Homeopathic remedies played a big role. The best cure for a sore throat was to sip heated honey mixed with vinegar. Tobacco juice or a chaw of freshly chewed tobacco was applied to stings and insect bites. A harmless cure for rheumatism was to steal a small potato and carry it in one's pocket until it wrinkled and dried. If this pet potato rotted, the results were negative. A strange practice was to treat the thorn or splinter, as well as the wound it inflicted. The usual remedy for this was lard and turpentine. Asafetida was used for the prevention of contagious diseases by hanging small bags of the vile stuff around the children's necks. Actually this was quite effective because it kept all disease carriers at a proper distance from you as a consequence of the stench. Some animal doctoring was strictly quackery. Blackleg in cattle was treated by inserting asafetida under the skin, sick cows were bled by cutting gashes in the roof of their mouths, holes were drilled in horns to cure "hollow horn," and swinney (German, *Schwinne*) was treated by inserting a coin under the skin of a horse's shoulder. For distemper, horses were made to breathe the vapor from some boiling and stinking preparation.

Weather signs and sayings played a large role in everyday life. When both horns of the new moon point upward, they will hold up the water, and it will not rain; but when the moon has a halo (German, *Hof*), there will be rain within three days. Everybody knew the saying:

> Abendrot, gut Wetter droht;
> Morgenrot, schlecht Wetter droht.
>
> (Evening red, good weather ahead;
> Morning red, bad weather ahead.)

This same weather prediction is found in several English versions, as for example:

> Red at night, sailors' delight;
> Red in the morn, sailors' alarm.

There were also the familiar signs about the waxing and waning of the moon, prescribing the best time for planting seeds, setting out plants, cutting fence posts, and branding calves.

Water witching has a long history in both Anglo and German traditions. Well witchers are called *Brunnenschmöcker* in some German-Texas settlements, and the believers would stake their eternal salvation on the reliability of the forked sticks, or divining rods. Some people claimed to have such well-trained sticks that they could easily find the water veins and tell how deep they were.

The most spurious folkloric practice is the so-called faith healing. It is hard to get any true believers to divulge all they know about exorcising worms and evil spirits, and the secrets can be unfurled only by a woman to a man or by a man to a woman. A person has to lay three sticks in a triangular position and call upon the Holy Trinity to rid him or his livestock of worms and evil spirits, and on top of that he has to indulge in all manner of hogwash, hocus-pocus, and mumbo-jumbo. All this reminds one of the old German *Wurmsegen* and other charms used in ancient times to cure worms and other ailments.

Rural German Texans were inveterate pranksters. Every boy had to be subjected to a snipe hunt, which is probably an Anglo prank. The more original pranks of the Hill Country folks were mostly practical jokes that required considerable ingenuity and some manpower. When a boyfriend became a regular caller at a girl's home, he might discover that his saddle was reversed on the horse or even missing, or the stirrups were tied together under the horse. If he came in a buggy, he probably found one of the large, rear wheels in front and the smaller wheel in the back, or better still the reins might be crisscrossed, so that the horse turned left when the driver pulled the right rein. Gates were tied up tight with barbed wire, and this was effective for horseback riders and buggy riders alike. Later the car courters fared no better, what with deflated tires, crossed wires on the spark plugs, or drained radiators and gasoline tanks. Halloween time always called forth pranks, like overturning or removing outhouses, or tying a milch cow to a bell rope in church or school. Minor pranks were: sewing up pants or shirts or tying hard knots in sleeves, putting gravel or pebbles in shoes, and the like.

Some of the Hill Country German Texans were quite susceptible to spooks (German *Gespenster*) and they believed their houses were hexed. They said, "*Es spukt bei uns*" (There are spooks in our house). And sometimes they were right because mischievous boys knew how to encourage this spooky business by making weird sounds and ghostly noises around the homes of the spook addicts.

Much of the Texas-German heritage has survived for nearly a century and a half now, and it can still be collected, preserved, and presented, as many are now doing. These traditions live on primarily in the precious memories of the elderly people, but such treasures will be lost with the passing of the older generations, unless we preserve them carefully for the future. This has been the chief purpose of the present essay on the cultural heritage of the Texas Hill Country.

Part III

The Crisis of Ethnicity

CHAPTER 9

Ethnicity and Politics in Texas

JOE B. FRANTZ

WHEN they made their first impact on Texas politics, the Germans were newcomers. But then, everyone else except Indians and Mexicans were comparative newcomers, and most groups had not yet arrived.

The Germans had emigrated in part because they chafed under the authoritarianism of Prussia, Hesse, or some other principality. They had wanted freedom, they had found freedom, and they cherished their freedom. And all of this advance had come about under the flag of the United States. Pursuing freedom had not been easy, and many of the Germans had teetered on the ragged edge of starvation while they learned to make their peace with the land. But they had persevered, and a decade later they safely had their roots down.

But now it was 1854, and Texas was coming apart like the other Southern states. Abolitionists were everywhere, as common as Communists during the late, unlamented Senator Joe McCarthy's days. Suspicion was rife that life in the South had degenerated into a Yankee plot to undermine the institution of slavery. If the free soilers persisted, Texas would have little recourse but to depart the United States.

In San Antonio, where the Germans were gathered innocently enough for their annual *Staats-Saengerfest* (State Song Fest) in mid-May, various politically minded Germans began to talk about doing more than singing. Already organized into local political clubs dedicated to looking after their local interests, they fused this scattered bent toward organization into a com-

Answer of the Germans to the Above
cartoon by Carl G. von Iwonski, 1868 [*San Antonio Express*]

Courtesy of Miss Mary Vance Green

"THE ANSWER OF THE GERMANS TO THE ABOVE."

"On our first page we print a picture, executed by Mr. *Iwonski*, which is a complete answer to the appeal to the Germans by the murderers' apologist.

"The picture represents [Judge] Devine appealing to a German to join hands with him in putting down the Union party; old Maverick stands by watching the effect of Devine's appeal; [Col. George H.] Sweet of the Herald is attempting to draw the curtain over the past, but does not succeed. The Union-loving German points to the past—represented by the hanging and shooting of loyal Germans, and to our loyal fellow-townsman, Mr. Simon, lingering in the dungeon in which he has been cast by the arch-traitor Devine. The picture is a perfect study. The figure representing the German will be readily recognised [*sic*] as 'Michel [*sic*].'

"The picture speaks for itself, and needs no more explanation." p. 3.

SAN ANTONIO EXPRESS

San Antonio, Texas, Saturday, Feb. 8, 1868.

Vol. II   No. 45

"To Our German Fellow-Citizens"

Are you in favor of disfranchising your own country, and the "white race" generally, and enfranchising unqualifiedly the ignorant negro who does not know the first letter of the English alphabet? If not, vote the whiteman's ticket.

Are you in favor of sending these ignorant negroes, to frame the organic laws of a people constituting the largest State in the American Union? If not then vote for your own race and kindred, who are opposed to [words missing] vagabonds of the "carpet bag" estates, who favor negro supremacy for the sake of the spoils, and who if it does not work well on trial, can and will leave the country, fleeing to California, or Canada; while those left behind are a ruined wreck of their former selves.

Do you wish to convert Texas into a second San Domingo, where all industry and material prosperity has dried up like a withered leaf, crisped by a December frost? If not, vote for the candidates of the Conservative Union Reconstruction party.

Shall our State be so placed under the ban of ignorant Africans, and worse whitemen, as to jeopardize capital, and drive away from us all railroad, telegraphic and manufacturing investments? If not, then vote for the friends of moderation and good government.

Do you wish to expel and stay from emigration to Texas, the free born white men of the North, and all [word missing]? If not, then vote against radicalism.

Do you wish Texas restored to one Union—to her normal condition; that peace and harmony may prevail, capital find security, and industry prosper, and the "negro supremacy" question settled forever? Then vote against negro suffrage, as the hundreds of thousands of white men voted in the Northern States last Fall and as they will vote with doubled majorities next Fall.

bined statement for freedom for all mankind. In short, they declared for the American Declaration of Independence, which periodically has proved a dangerous, radical stand to take, for we don't really believe that "all men are created free and equal, and are endowed by their Maker with certain unalienable rights." Rather, we frequently believe, like the creatures on George Orwell's farm, that all animals are equal, but, in his terms, pigs are more equal than others.

Nonetheless the Germans stuck out their political necks. Slavery, they declared, was not only evil, it was an unnecessary evil. This was a forthright statement of treason for someone in the South to make. It advocated abolition by everything but name. And everyone knew that hanging was too good for abolitionists.

The Germans went further. Abolition, they said, was a state's right. A thrifty, pragmatic people, they recognized that abolition might break most planters economically. Therefore they called for an alliance between the states and the federal government. If states would abolish slavery, the federal government would pay for the loss of the slaves. No one would be hurt, except the taxpayer. But the burden would be spread amongst all the people who had allowed this tarnish to develop on the shield of freedom.

If Henry Wallace's plan for paying farmers to plow under cotton and to kill little pigs provoked a storm in the 1930s, you can imagine the average Texan's reaction to this plan in the 1850s. Not only would the federal government pay for property not sold, but it would be subsidizing the privileged class, not an unknown procedure, certainly, though never a popular one. As a class the Anglo-Texans were outraged.

In vain the Germans tried to allay their neighbors' suspicions, to make them understand that they were trying to be rational and reasonable, to persuade them to believe in the freedom that all of them espoused. And the Germans had people who were good at explaining, heavily accented though their English might be. One of the more notable was Ferdinand Jacob Lindheimer, who after studying law had fled his native Frankfurt in 1833 after participating in the abortive Frankfurter Putsch. Three years later Lindheimer arrived in Texas, like Davy Crockett, to "fight for his rights." He had then settled down in New Braunfels to become a noted botanist, the first such person to organize the flora of Texas into a system. Many plants that he discovered would be named after him, carrying the tag *Lindheimeriana* along with their regular botanical names. For the past two years he had been editor of the *Neu-Braunfelser Zeitung*, a post he held for more than two decades.

But the Anglo-Texans were not about to listen to men like Lindheimer, no matter how impressive their credentials. They would as soon have given credence to Lindheimer's arguments as Mississippi rednecks would heed Hodding Carter's pleas for racial progress a hundred years later.

The slavery issue alone set the Germans apart as a separate people, an ethnic group not to be trusted. As the years succeeded each other and the South's mood approached hysteria, the position of the Germans became increasingly difficult. Instances of persecution abound. Out in Burnet County, for instance, in the middle of a cactus-strewn pasture lies a sink called locally Dead Man's Hole. Near there Adolf Hoppe was clearing cedar posts from a flat rock area when two men rode up and took him away. A Texas Ranger was with them. The ranger later testified that the pair accused Hoppe of having attended a Union meeting, which he denied. They finally appeared to accept his protests and rode off in one direction while the ranger rode in an opposite one. The ranger, the only witness of any kind, said he had gone some distance when he heard a shot. He hurried back, but found neither Hoppe nor his accusers in the heavy cedar brakes.

When Hoppe failed to come home, his anxious wife organized a search party. It turned up neither Hoppe nor clues. A year passed, and Hoppe's widow knew only that he had gone out to work one day and had never come back. She had to think that he had met some sort of foul play, for the team had come home, cut free from its harness. Finally some men stumbled onto Dead Man's Hole. Peering down into the dark, they discerned some harness fragments hanging on a limestone ledge.

They lowered a lantern into the Hole to burn out any poisonous air, and then dropped one man on a rope. He found a skeleton wearing Hoppe's shoes, as well as several other piles of human bones. Hoppe's widow and two children never heard anything more, and no one was ever arrested or prosecuted. More than a century later Hoppe's descendants still believe that Southern sympathizers waylaid him and dumped him there as punishment for his belief in black freedom.

Most people with any knowledge of Civil War Texas know what happened next. With the advent of the fratricide the Germans were observed almost as warily as were the Japanese-Americans on the Pacific Coast during World War II. A cadre of sixty-five fled for Mexico, only to be intercepted in the Battle of the Nueces on August 10, 1862. The Germans were taken by complete surprise, for they had camped about twenty miles from Fort Clark without bothering to post sentries. The Confederates massacred them in one of the ethnic tragedies that too frequently dot Texas history.

Small wonder, then, that when the Civil War was over, the Germans joined with the newly freed slaves to support the Republican party. The Democrats had shown them no mercy—that is, if you oversimplify and use the terms Democrat and Confederate interchangeably. As the years proceeded and the Republicans receded from power, the Germans continued to vote as solidly for the G.O.P. as some brass-collar Democrat for his party's ticket. As the blacks lost their franchise, the Germans became the backbone of the Republican party in Texas.

The best-known case of the Germans' Republican consistency surfaces in the person of Harry M. Wurzbach, a San Antonio and Seguin lawyer. In Seguin, a heavily German town, Wurzbach, a Republican, served as county attorney and for four terms as county judge. In 1920 Wurzbach was elected to the United States Congress from the 14th Texas District, the first native Texas Republican to be a Republican representative. The Germans in the San Antonio-Seguin area combined with San Antonio's military to continue to elect him for four terms, again the first Republican from Texas to be elected for more than two terms. The Germans voted as automatically for him as Boston's Irish voted for James M. Curley. In many ways Wurzbach proved to be more than the 14th District's representative; he was the congressman for every German-descended Texan in the state.

Politicians running for statewide office have long talked of the "German counties" as a separate bloc. As the years passed and increasing immigrants have moved to Texas, the solidity of the German vote—if ever there was such a thing—has undoubtedly been diluted. Nonetheless a German vote did exist. Gillespie, Kendall, and Kerr counties regularly gave a heavy vote to Republican candidates, particularly in the presidential election years. Comal, DeWitt, Guadalupe, Mason, and Washington counties also gave heavier than usual Republican percentages. Standing as exception to this rule, however, are seven other counties with large German populations—Austin, Calhoun, Colorado, Goliad, Lavaca, Lee, and Victoria, each of which showed about as little variation from the norm as any other Texas county.

Undoubtedly the appeal to the Germans had to be made on different bases. The fundamentalist minister preaching against the evils of alcoholic beverages would find approbation only from those German families who might have been embarrassed by the presence of a family alcoholic or the Mennonites among them. As a group the German counties never did approve of the national Prohibition movement and probably never observed it privately. Especially is this true with beer, which was as natural a drink to them as coffee to a Brazilian. They gave scant attention to those "dry" candidates who spoke in evangelical tones of prohibiting the manufacture and sale of beer.

Texas never did approve of statewide Prohibition until after the 18th Amendment to the federal Constitution was sent out for ratification. When, for instance, the question was raised in 1909, the legislature defeated the prohibitionists by only two votes. The German vote easily provided the difference. Two years later the issue was submitted to the voters. Again the drys lost, 231,000 to 237,000. In a contest that close the almost solid wet vote of the Germans insured the margin for defeat.

On the whole the Germans were better educated than the average Texan. Not infrequently the first ones who came had the equivalent of high-school educations, while a surprising number had attended a university. Nineteenth-century Germany prided itself as a nation of thinkers and poets, and its people were highly literate. Unlike many other Texans, the German Texans read. And they studied, most notably biology and botany. John Meusebach was attracted as much by the prospect of learning about the exotic flora of Texas in its transitional position between the temperate and tropical zones, as he was by land. The Adelsverein granted him a $2,000 allowance to purchase and take scientific equipment and a technical library. Meusebach had attended universities at Bonn and Halle; Lindheimer, at Jena; Felix von Blücher, at Berlin; Ferdinand Herff, at Bonn and Berlin; and so on.

Like a modern corporation executive Prince Solms recruited directly from the universities. In company with Hermann Spiess, he made speeches in 1846 at Heidelberg and Giessen that set the students aglow. Germany, he declared, held no opportunity for professional men with their university training. But Texas, raw and empty but developing, did. It was such a group, forty young professionals from Darmstadt, that resolved to emigrate to Texas and found the colony of Bettina.

Such men were dedicated to cultural uplift, and still are. Later generations, including today's, had a high regard for formal education, so that an outsize number have sent their children to college.

Now universities may not make an irrational person any more rational, but in their training universities do place a certain emphasis on fact-gathering as a prelude to careful decision-making. The Texas Germans were therefore less likely to fall for the bombastic sloganeers who so often win elections. Instead, they preferred the more sober-sided candidates who promised less but likely would deliver more. As a rule they favored the more conservative, conventional candidate. Pappy O'Daniel, running for governor of Texas on string music and the Ten Commandments, would be too bizarre for their tastes.

In the earlier days the fact that the Germans were led by men of such stature as Prince Carl of Solms-Braunfels—men who did not stampede easily, would have undoubtedly inhibited the Germans from chasing after fly-by-night office-seekers. Although few of them came from even the minor nobility, they did derive from a nation that stressed respect for authority and would have had a tendency to vote with their leadership unless their personal rights were endangered. This argument cannot be pursued too far, however, for we are dealing with many Germans who in part came to Texas because of their discontent with authoritarianism. The mere fact of their coming constituted a break with authority and tradition. But having once fractured the mold, they were more likely to take pains to maintain their freedom of decision.

But the Germans are among the more disciplined, hard-working people of the world. Indeed, they make a fetish of discipline. The German educational system was predicated on an unquestioning respect for authority; Germany's soldiers were prepared to march to hell at a commander's orders, and never look back. Undoubtedly some of that disciplinary inoculation followed them to the New World.

Such a background would thus produce a people who tended to be more "liberal"—and that adjective has to be put into quotation marks because of its changing nuances through the generations—than the Anglo-Texans all around them. They would be more liberal intellectually and philosophically, but with the contradiction that inheres in the German psyche, they would also be more conservative and more vigilant politically. Admiring industriousness for its own sake, they would look askance at the spread of social welfare measures from the 1930s onward for fear they might reward laziness and poor planning. They believed in liberty, but not in equality.

After all, their rationale could cite perfect examples for their contradictory nature at almost any stage back in the *Vaterland*. Germany's longtime chancellor-political architect, Count Otto von Bismarck, comes down to us as the Iron Chancellor, the embodiment of Prussian authoritarianism, nationalism, and conservatism. Yet in the 1880s under Bismarck Germany gave its workers such social gains as health insurance, old-age and dependent-children support, and social security. In the supposedly more relaxed United States we were still arguing those issues without passing enabling legislation fifty to eighty years later. If the German is conservative, he tends also to be somewhat enlightened and socially conscious in his conservatism. Again, he examines issues rather than following a course of knee-jerk acceptance, whether on the liberal or the conservative side.

As any observer knows, the Germans placed great store in their diverse *Vereine*. They liked to get together to discuss issues and ideas, just as they congregated for *Saengerfeste* and for chamber music. The poet Sidney Lanier settled in San Antonio in the latter nineteenth century because of the high cultural tone set by the Germans there; he enjoyed playing flute to their violins and talking about all sorts of subjects. Evidently he found frontier San Antonio as intellectually and culturally stimulating as he had Baltimore, a much larger city. Although Lanier's forte was not politics, his experience indicates that ideas were thoroughly aired before action, if any, was taken. San Antonio at one time in the 1850s was two-fifths German, and by Lanier's time the Germans still would likely have been the largest minority group there. San Antonio was no town in which to practice hayseed, backwoods politicking.

And though life was necessarily cruder on the frontier, yet even here the cultural comforts were not unknown. We have already seen that Meusebach carried his books and scientific instruments to the low hills around New Braunfels. And the chroniclers of travel in Texas at that time—Duke Paul of Württemberg, John Russell Bartlett, and Frederick Law Olmsted—tell of visiting Ottomar von Behr on the banks of the Guadalupe in Comal County and finding in his log and *Fachwerk* cabin books, paintings, and a harpsichord. And what was von Behr doing? He was crossbreeding German and Mexican sheep, running a lending library (perhaps the first in Texas), serving as justice of the peace and postmaster, and in his spare time practicing as a meteorologist and naturalist.

Texas Germans have been consistently property-minded. True, they did establish their communal colonies, such as Bettina, but these were more intellectually than economically based. They remind one of such experiments as Brook Farm during New England's literary golden age—"high thinking with plain living." But the mere fact of Bettina testifies to the higher educational and cultural level of the German immigrants. Named for Bettina von Arnim, a nineteenth-century German feminist, it included among its first settlers scholars from the universities of Heidelberg and Giessen. For their motto they espoused "Friendship, freedom, and equality." Like most such experiments Bettina faded away, but again it gives insight into the German penchant for translating intellectual ideas into a style of living.

But most Germans did not favor a communistic style of living. They believed in free private enterprise, in enjoying the fruits of their extraordinarily effective labors. Consequently they disdained those candidates who promised a pie-in-the-sky existence. Though not against social welfare, they wanted such programs based on work instead of giveaways. Economically they believed in a judgment day.

In Austin and Waller counties in 1880, for instance, 86 percent of the German-born farmers owned their land, against 62 percent of the Southern whites and 25 percent of the Negroes. The latter, of course, were short on opportunity. Many Germans, coming from parts of Germany where single inheritance was the general rule, did not split the land among their children, thereby sending the uninherited northward and southward, where they too became tidy landholders.

Finally the Germans believed in the sanctity of their word. The best example is the Meusebach-Comanche Treaty in 1847, negotiated between John Meusebach and Buffalo Hump, Santana, and Old Owl. In fact, the Indians developed such respect for Meusebach that they nicknamed him *El Sol Colorado* — Red Sun. The Germans never broke their word to the Comanches, and were so sure of the integrity of the Comanches that they went into the Indians' territory alone and unharmed in search of new farm sites. And the Comanches measured up to the Germans' faith, so that we have that most unusual of treaties in American-Indian relationships—a treaty that was never broken by either side.

Such a people would naturally expect any politician to practice the same strict observance of any agreement he had made, whether tacit or spelled out. Naturally the conservative candidate is going to make the fewest promises, because he will want the least change and he will more likely avoid getting out on limbs. Consequently too, he will be the more pleasing candidate for the average German Texan to support, for in his disdain for change he will be dependable to a high degree.

The influence of the ethnic German in politics then lies in his reasoned, innate conservatism and in his keeping alive a white Republican toehold during the long succession of decades when political fashion dictated general adherence to the Democratic party. The German became a cornerstone of the two-party system in Texas, the loyal opposition to the Democratic party's overwhelming ascendancy. As the black faded from Texas Republicanism with the onset of the 1930s, the G.O.P. conceivably could have retreated in complete disarray. But the German held on to the party, thinking through his votes and his attitudes, and thereby provided the glue that held the Republicans together until their modern resurrection began in the 1950s. The fact that the Germans have never been identified with the extreme right wing of Republican sentiment in Texas likewise testifies to their ability to approach most issues rationally and to arrive at decisions on the basis of merit rather than emotion.

CHAPTER 10

Deutschtum *in Texas: A Look at Texas-German Folklore*

FRANCIS EDWARD ABERNETHY

IN addition to the herding instinct, people's folklore is the bond which holds that group together as a cooperating, working, and surviving society. A band of people sing the same songs and know the same dances; they dress alike and observe the same customs and have the same manners; they worship the same gods in the same way; and they survive as a result of the strength of these common bonds. During the easy times the bonds are loose. The old gods are forgotten. Each in his prosperity drifts through the community, increasing his separateness and individuality. But when hard times come, from trouble within or enemies without, the old lore and the old laws are again remembered and used to shore up the group's defenses against adversity and disintegration.

The folklore of Texas is the weaving together of the many skeins of traditions brought by the many nationalities that settled this land. One group didn't have to come to Texas. The Indians were already here, but under the full tide of settlement in the nineteenth century they suffered the same

This essay is a revision of "Texas Folklore and German Culture" that appeared in *Rice University Studies* 63(3). The editors and author acknowledge the kind permission of Katherine Fischer Drew to reprint this article.

fate that the Canaanites felt with the invasion of the Jews or that King Arthur and the Celts felt before the onslaught of the Anglo-Saxons. The Spanish were the first to come to this land and were the true conquerors for God and king, and their invasion on horses and in armor and with guns was almost as terrifying as their penchant for establishing permanent towns and proselytizing for Catholicism. Early French landings in Texas did little except spur the Spanish into creating more solid settlements. The Mexican population of Texas which grew out of the Spanish settlement comprises about 20 percent of the whole and is the major seasoning in a dominant Anglo-Saxon culture. Besides the Mexican, the Negro has had the greatest influence on Anglo-Texan customs and ways.

Except for the Anglos, the Mexicans, and the black culture, the most noticeable ethnic group from early colonial days to present-day Texas has been the Germans. The importance of the German element in Texas society is marked by the fact that the governor's message and the secession convention reports of 1861 were sent out in three languages: English, Spanish, and German; and a hundred years later in the 1960 census 500,000 Texans listed their direct ancestry as German.

Germans had wandered through Texas before the 1800s, but noticeable German colonization did not begin until 1832, when Friedrich Ernst (Texas's Father of German Immigration) claimed his league of land in the rich river bottoms of the Brazos and Colorado. Friedrich Ernst's town of Industry became a commercial center, as did the settlement of Cat Spring established by Robert Kleberg. The Germans of this era of settlement occupied most of Austin, Fayette, and Washington counties.

The most significant pre–Civil War influx of German settlers came in the 1840s, most of them sponsored by the Adelsverein. The beginnings were inauspicious. Those Germans who were promoting the venture were aristocratic, well intentioned, and naive and were cheated at every turn. They lost thousands of dollars in bad land investments. In the end they purchased rights to settle on what was known as the Fisher-Miller grant between the Llano and the Colorado. They weren't told by Fisher and Miller (originally Heinrich Fischer and Burchard

A Look at Texas-German Folklore

Mueller) that the Comanches considered that area as their own particular and favorite hunting ground. Subsequently, Prince Carl von Solms-Braunfels, the first commissioner-general of the Adelsverein, bought land on Matagorda Bay and established a debarkation port at Carlshafen, later known as Indianola. Another path of German settlement began then as these settlers moved from Indianola northwest along the Guadalupe River toward the Fisher-Miller grant.

One area of German concentration that resulted from the Guadalupe migration occurred around DeWitt County in the settlements of Runge, Nordheim, and Yorktown. The major area, though, centered on New Braunfels, founded by Prince Carl in 1845 as a way station on the route to the Fisher-Miller grant. Prince Carl later told that he awoke one morning with snow in his tent but that by noon it had all melted. He took this as a good omen for founding the new town. Baron Ottfried Hans von Meusebach led colonists farther on toward the Fisher-Miller lands in 1846, founded Fredericksburg, another way station, and negotiated a treaty with the Comanches that opened the Fisher-Miller lands to German settlers. By 1860 German settlement had reached the grant lands around Mason to the Northwest and had moved southwest to extend its sphere of influence to absorb the Alsatians at Castroville, just as other Germans had begun to absorb the Wends of Lee County. San Antonio was a German town in the 1860s.

German immigration slowed considerably during the Civil War years but continued after the war in ever increasing numbers. In a typical five-year period from 1881 through 1885, over 6,000 sailed from Bremen to Galveston alone. The main promoters of immigration were the railroads, which were selling right-of-way and state-grant lands to colonists. The German areas expanded as a result of this steady flow of settlers, and these spheres of influence expanded again as prospering second- and third-generation Germans bought out the more nomadic Anglos, who were still wandering in the spirit of the western movement. New German settlement islands appeared in the north and northwest of the state and followed the break-up of the big Texas ranches into small farm areas. Agrarian settlement stopped in the 1920s, and German immigration since that time has been to the cities, where it has gone virtually unnoticed, lost within the general population.[1]

Germans left their mother country for many reasons: overpopulation, a rural economic depression, the Romantic revolutionary spirit, the Industrial Revolution, and compulsory military training, to mention a few. They left to rebuild fortunes or to seek new freedoms, or both. The best and the worst came, nobility, artisans, and laborers. Romantic idealists came to form socialist communes at Bettina and Tusculum and intellectual communes where Latin was spoken at Sisterdale, Latium, and Darmstädter Farm. And some came for the great adventure of living in a new land.[2]

Whatever their reasons for coming and whatever attitudes they had about their mother country, they were still Germans when they got here. The songs they sang, the stories they told, and their customs and traditions were still German. They brought cures and curses and recipes that were older than the times of their grandparents. They brought their tools and ways of building houses and fences and furniture that would always tie their styles with the ways of the Old Country. They brought the bondings of their German lives that had been a part of their generations for centuries, and they mixed them with their new Texas environment and experiences. And out of this new German culture they created their own kind of Texas folklore.

One kind of folklore is legend, which is the folk history of a people. Legends tell of the past, not in a scientifically historical sense but in the way that people see themselves. Legends might not catch the letter of the facts but they catch the spirit. Thus in telling the tales of the German migration from the Gulf up the Guadalupe to the promised Fisher-Miller land, the stories deal more with the adventures of that hegira than with the near cultural collapse of parts of the group. The stories they tell illustrate the admirable qualities of these ancestor pioneers as they encountered the frontier and the wild Indians and animals of that strange and frightening new land.

Frank Dobie tells one legend that grew out of this movement of German settlers up the Guadalupe toward the grant lands. It was one of the Pacing White Stallion stories that he used in *The Mustangs*. A little German girl was tied on to the back of an old pack mare that trailed along with the wagon train and carried sacks of corn meal. One afternoon the horse and girl wandered off and were separated from the train. The mare joined a herd of horses led by this magnificent and lordly Pacing White Stallion, which chewed through the ropes, gently lifted the girl off the mare, and left her while he and the mare wandered off for a tryst. Two days later the mare returned along with the stallion and the rest of the herd. The stallion lifted the child back on the mare, and the mare returned with her to the wagon train and her distraught parents. She told this story to her grandchildren and as proof showed scars on her legs where the horses had nipped her getting at the sacks of corn meal.[3]

Very little legendary material developed around Prince Carl von Solms-Braunfels, the first commissioner of the Adelsverein. His particular aristocratic attitudes and his poor leadership did not inspire that sort of feeling which gives rise to legend. He was accused of trying to reinstitute German feudalism among Texas Germans, an accusation he indignantly denied; and his financial naiveté, paid for by the deprivations of his colonists, made him more of a villain than a hero to his people. Frederick Law Olmsted, who visited the German Texans in 1854, passed on the following evaluation of Prince Carl which he must have arrived at from listening to the settlers because the prince had been gone from Texas for nine years. Prince Carl, he said, "...appears to [have been] an amiable fool, aping among the log cabins the nonsense of medieval courts. In the course of a year he was laughed out of the country."[4]

Prince Carl did, however, contribute to one German family's legends. Fritz Ernst (son of Friedrich, the founder of Industry), Prince Carl's guide and translator, is credited with out-hunting the prince's *Jäger* (huntsman) and with singlehandedly freeing the prince's boat from a sandbar off Indianola after all others had given up. In another Ernst family tale, Fritz unceremoniously falls to on a piece of watermelon before the prince had begun to eat his.[5] Prince Carl becomes the epitype of the snobbish Old-World aristocrat to be put in his place by the self-reliant and democratic Germans of the New World.

On the other hand, many stories have survived about John Meusebach, his successor. Ottfried Hans Freiherr von Meusebach, as he was known in the Old Country, was a controversial and legendary character during his own time, who as soon as he boarded ship for the Americas democratically changed his name to John O. Meusebach. As titular head of the Adelsverein colonists, he was in charge of finances and was held responsible when money and supplies were not forthcoming, as was frequently the case. But he gained the reputation of a man who could meet the challenge of the occasion. According to one story he dissuaded a disgruntled settler from doing him violence by challenging him and winning in a two-man *Schützenfest*. He quelled the violent anger of another by maintaining an unruffled calm. Meusebach was a strong-nerved man who could handle physical violence. In one instance, Meusebach was cornered by a group of about 120 unhappy settlers who blamed him because they had not received the land and assistance which they had been promised by the Adelsverein. At one point they were ready to hang him, but again his composure—and a box of cigars which he passed around—calmed the mob and eventually dispersed it. Meusebach continued his leadership of the colony.[6]

The Comanches of the Hill Country referred to Meusebach as *El Sol Colorado*, The Red Sun. The name was given to him by one of the chiefs when during the 1847 treaty meeting Meusebach and his men discharged their guns before meeting with the Indians to show that they had no fear for their safety. In another account of the same episode, Meusebach's party fired their guns at the request of the Comanches, who also fired theirs.[7] According to Meusebach family legend, the chief gave him the name because he was a man to be looked up to, like the sun. Another reason the Comanches called him The Red Sun was that he had a fiery red beard and head of hair. One legend about the man concerns his red hair and his negotiations with the Waco Indians. When Meusebach walked forward into the meeting place on the Comal River, twenty squaws grabbed him, dragged him to the river bank, and tried to wash the red out of his hair. They soon gave up and let him go. According to his biographer, Meusebach remained unperturbed.[8]

Although there are stories of chance encounters with and raids and killings by the Indians, who between 1861 and 1870 killed nine persons and stole two children in Gillespie County, the enduring legend is the epic meeting of the heroic Meusebach with the Comanches on the San Saba and the signing of the treaty, which finally gave the Germans access to the Fisher-Miller lands. This treaty of 1847, which opened up 3,878,000 acres to settlement, was the only major Indian treaty in Texas which was honored by both sides. Much of the success of this was due to the commanding manner of the man Meusebach and the impressive way in which he dealt with the Indians. His imperturbability as he moved among the teepees of the most feared Indians of the Americas and his courage in coming directly to them were qualities the Comanches respected. And even after Meusebach's tenure as head of the Adelsverein, the Germans took pains to stand by their commitments to show hospitality to the Indian and not to invade his hunting ground.

During the negotiations, while the Indians were deliberating over the terms, Meusebach and a small group including Ferdinand Roemer, who was to become the father of Texas geology, made an exploratory trip up the San Saba River. Their purpose was to find the old Spanish mission and fort that even then was the subject of many legends, the main one being that somewhere near there was located what had been New Spain's third-richest silver mine. Meusebach himself had caught the treasure fever from hearing these tales, and he had a faint hope that by finding the mines he could extricate the German colonists and himself from their financial problems. Jim Bowie had followed the same rainbow to the old mission in 1829 and returned in 1832 to look for the treasure again, but as far as we know he found nothing. Meusebach and Roemer found no indications of smelting near the mission site nor did Roemer believe that the geology of the area indicated silver ore. They did, however, find areas that were suitable for farming and colonization.

Meusebach, Roemer, and the explorers returned to the Comanche camp on the lower San Saba and concluded the treaty and returned home.[9] Meusebach continued intermittent associations with the Comanches even after he resigned as head of the Adelsverein. There is the tale of one notable visit to his home at Comanche Springs. The Indians joined him at a very lavish dinner table, laid with linen and fine silver. They were on their way to negotiate with state authorities in Austin. On the return trip, unhappy about their treatment at the state capital and angry at whites generally, they stole all of Meusebach's horses.[10]

A legendary character of less fame and stature than Meusebach was a German hunter whom Frederick Olmsted refers to as "P." The main story was about his killing five bears out of one den. "P." had already gained fame by singlehandedly killing a bear with a knife after the bear, which was wounded, had enfolded him for a final hug. The five-bear story begins when he shot and wounded a bear that later escaped into a deep crawl-way cave. He crawled in after the bear, found him dead, put a rope on him, and dragged him out. While doing this he heard another bear moving about in the cave, so he snaked himself back in, knife between his teeth and pistol in his hand. He fired at the sound of movement and made a hasty withdrawal. He went back into the cave with a torch, found that bear dead, and another which he surmised had died from the smoke of his torch. He removed these bears and returned again with torches. In the depths of the cave he saw two sets of eyes, fired twice, and killed the last two. Olmsted concluded that formal history had no place for "P." but that folklore did.[11]

The legends of the prowess of "P.," the imperturbability of Meusebach, the frontier egalitarianism of Fritz Ernst, and the remarkable adventures of the little girl and the White Stallion are the lengthened shadows of truth. The times and the places and the people were real. The stories that grew out of their experiences transcended reality and became Platonic truth. They were illustrations of ideals of strength and courage and endurance, virtues which could keep the settlers alive on the frontier. The Germans were not always brave and enduring, but their heroes embodied these qualities, and their legends helped them to develop the cultural self-image that was necessary for survival in their new land.

A Look at Texas-German Folklore

The source for much legend was the Germans' suffering during the Civil War, especially the Nueces Massacre, as it was sometimes called by the Germans, or the Battle of the Nueces, as it has gone down in history books.

The German settlers from the time of Texas's annexation had accepted the principles of the Union and had been from the first traditionally opposed to slavery. Few Germans, especially in the Hill Country, owned slaves. Additionally, most of them brought with them from Germany the sense of egalitarianism that was a part of the European eighteenth-century revolutionary movement. This romantic sense of equality was a stated part of Meusebach's treaty with the Comanche, during which time he also formally discussed the possibilities of intermarriage between Germans and Indians.

The Hill Country Germans therefore found themselves in a sensitive position when Texas seceded from the Union. Lacking military protection against Indians, they formed a guard unit which, as the war went into its second year, was pronounced a threat to the Confederacy. The unit was disbanded and sixty-five of the young German Unionists began a march to Mexico, either to join the Union army later or to sit out the war. They were ambushed on the Nueces River by Confederate forces on the early morning of August 10, 1862. The battle lasted several hours, in spite of the fact that the 125 Confederate soldiers had caught the Unionists by surprise. Fritz Tegener, the Unionist leader, was seriously wounded in the first volley. According to German tradition, Emil Schreiner took command with the war cry, *"Lasst uns unser Leben so teuer wie möglich verkaufen"* (Let us sell our lives as dearly as we can).

Of the sixty-five Unionists, nineteen were killed in the battle, nine of the wounded were captured and executed on the spot, eight more were killed in October as they were trying to cross the Rio Grande, and the survivors and their families were persecuted and terrorized for much of the remainder of the war. The families of the victims were afraid to go after the remains until the war was over. The ambush, the slaughter of the prisoners, and the disrespect paid to the slain Unionists were shocks that the Germans felt for years, and perhaps in some cases have never recovered from. After the war the remaining bones were retrieved from the battlefield and buried at Comfort under a monument that reads *"Treue der Union,"* the only so-called Yankee monument in Texas.[12]

The villains of the Nueces River Massacre and the Civil War were long remembered in the tales of the Hill Country. Col. James M. Duff, the leader of the Confederate forces, was held the chief offender at the Nueces Massacre. According to legends and some histories, Duff was a Scot who had come to the States, joined the army, had been dishonorably discharged, and then drifted with others of the lawless breed to Texas. His unsavory and "soulless" past equipped him for his role as enforcer, after the German community was put under martial law in 1862. After the war he returned to Europe and died in Paris, and as D. H. Biggers concludes one version of Duff's tale: "... the land his savage crime had stigmatized was saved the further shame of having its soil polluted with his decaying carcass."[13]

Charles Bergman's (or Burgeman or Bauman) position in history and legend is ambiguous. No one is sure what forces caused him to be the betrayer of his people and lead the Confederates after the departing Germans. One survivor believed that he was an outsider who was a Confederate spy in the Unionists' camp. Another opinion was that he was one of the Unionists who was following a strayed horse and was captured by Duff and, because of his weakness, was forced to give directions to the enemy. Whatever the circumstances, the Unionists needed a scapegoat and he was given an unsympathetic role to play in the legends of the Nueces Massacre. He went to Mexico after the war and reportedly became the leader of a band of outlaws. Bergman's story ends with the tale of his death at the hand of a Seminole Indian Negro (an interesting detail in itself), who threw his corpse into the Rio Grande. D. H. Biggers, an emotionally involved historian of the Germans, concludes the account: "Perhaps his last vision was that of a black face, wild with violence and dead to pity, black as the crime that will ever hover over the spot where the doomed refugees died, and black as the ghost that ever pursued the betrayer."[14]

Another man whose name became a part of the bitter

memories and stories of the Civil War was one Waldrip, who led a band of terrorists during the *Henkerzeit*, or hanging times. It is difficult from remaining accounts to tell whether he was a Confederate enforcer supported by the government or whether he was simply an outlaw preying on the unprotected and continually harassed Germans of the Hill Country. Whatever his credentials, the results of his nocturnal visits were long remembered. His band roamed at will during the war, stealing, burning, and killing twice as many German settlers as the Indians killed during all their depredations. Waldrip ruled the area through force and a spy system that kept the populace in continual fear. After the war and during Reconstruction a Gillespie County grand jury indicted twenty-five of the terrorists, but very few of them were ever jailed or punished. Waldrip, for some reason, returned to Fredericksburg in 1867. He was recognized and tried to escape, but was shot down in front of the Nimitz Hotel. His dying words, "Oh God! Please don't shoot any more," carry the sound of proper poetic justice, as does the report that he was buried in a pauper's grave.[15]

The legends the Texas Germans told among themselves and about themselves tied their culture together through their ancestral community of history and happenings. Their customs tied them together by ways of living and doing things that were as much a part of the present as they were of the past.

The German settlers had one thing in common, their sense of German-ness, their *Deutschtum*, an ethnic bond that both strengthened and isolated them. The German leaders during those early hard days of the 1840s and 1850s, when the settlers were just getting a toehold in the new land, believed that the physical survival of the German immigrants depended on their being bound together by their language, customs, and traditions and cooperating as a result of this bonding and isolation. Prince Carl feared dilution of the German spirit and German ways more than he feared the hardships of the new land. He warned the settlers to stay away from Anglos and directed that all settlements begin with pure German stock.[16] His despair was the bastardization of Germanic traditions of language and life-style in the New World, of Anglicizing names, and of forgetting or renouncing the old customs.

Besides clinging to the old customs for the sake of survival, some of the early German observers of Texas felt that the unsophisticated, frontier Anglos lacked the traditions, which were necessary for an interesting and exciting life. The young German traveler Gustav Dresel was appalled that in Texas in 1839 New Year's Eve was not properly celebrated. At the time he was visiting a Mr. Stoner (formerly Herr Steiner) of Montgomery. Christmas had been disappointing—"Americans allow all these fine festival days to go by uncelebrated...," he lamented—but he was determined to salvage New Year's Eve. That night he purchased a large store of raw whiskey, charged his firearms, and began a tour of homes in the area, first discharging a volley, then offering the aroused farmers a drink, then recruiting them for a continuation of the tour. The party—which finally grew to fifteen—watched 1840 come in with an all-night banquet of ham, maizecake, and eggnog, a celebration that fully satisfied Gustav's romantic and German expectations.[17]

As Dresel had remarked, Christmas was poorly celebrated by the Anglos, but there were good reasons for this lack of traditional spirit. They had been camping too long in the wilderness to maintain many of the civilizing customs, they were generations away from the source of their Old-World customs, and, as a part of a Puritan tradition that had largely abolished the celebration of Christmas in 1644, some of them regarded that sort of celebration as pagan. The Germans of the old and new worlds had a different attitude toward this holy day. German Christmas customs can be traced back to the Roman Saturnalia (December 17–24) with its joy of welcoming the new year and its expression of hope for continuing fertility. The Scandinavian countries added to this the giving of gifts at this time of the winter solstice, and the Germans themselves were responsible for the introduction of the evergreen Christmas tree, a fairly late addition probably not more than two centuries old.[18]

Ferdinand Roemer spent Christmas of 1845 among Anglos in Galveston, where, he says, "The customary manner of celebrating it by decorating a tree and exchanging presents appeared to be unknown." He spent the following Christmas of 1846 among Germans of New Braunfels in the "jolly companionship of the Verein's officers around a richly decorated and illuminated Christmas tree, for which a young cedar was used...."[19] The tree and the fellowship were to Roemer German symbols of happy German family life and an indication of the growing stability of the new German colonies in Texas.

From their earliest days Germans of Texas cultivated and celebrated December as a festival month. Generous Saint Nicholas, the patron saint of children, traditionally comes first on his own holy day of December 6 and brings gifts to children. He keeps coming, leaving fruit and candy through these holy days and observing the children until Christmas Eve, at which time he visits the children when the candles on the tree are lighted. If they have been good they get gifts; if bad he leaves a bundle of switches to be used on them during the following year. Sometimes more than one Saint Nicholas visits the house, and the main event of the evening is the family's visit to the church, where there is another tree with gifts for the children. December's festivities end and the new year is welcomed with a dance. Fredericksburg for a long time had a very fashionable New Year's Ball that was celebrated with a dance, a midnight dinner, and a continuation of the festivities at the old Nimitz Hotel until dawn.

The extremely religious Gillespie County Germans evolved another custom that bespeaks practicality and good common sense. Some of the high holy days—Christmas, Easter, Pentecost—are celebrated very seriously. The day after—"Second Christmas" or "Second Easter"—is for singing and dancing and joyful festivities.[20]

Some of the customs of the Old Country blended with happenings in the new and took on different meanings altogether. In northwestern Germany, around Hanover and Westphalia, for centuries back into pagan times the folk in the spring built fires on the mountains and threw in horses' heads and goats' horns and drove their stock through the flames in order to protect them through the following year. This ritual also celebrated the ancient renewing of the hearth's fires. With the coming of Christianity the ritual became associated with Easter (sometimes with the burning of Judas), and the mountains where the fires were burned were called *Oster-*

berge, or Easter Hills. The fields and houses and people which the fire shone upon would be blessed with fertility in the coming year. The custom was brought to Texas and Fredericksburg and over a period of time was changed to fit a new legend in the new land. In 1847, when Meusebach went to Fisher-Miller lands to make the treaty with the Indians, the Comanches, according to local tradition, camped and built fires around Fredericksburg to see that the Germans were not tricking them. The mothers, to calm the frightened children, told them that Easter rabbits were in the hills dyeing eggs in big wash pots with big fires under them. The Comanche-fires story has now become part of the traditional German Easter customs and legends in spite of the fact that historically Meusebach got back from Comanche territory several weeks before Easter—and whether the Comanches ever built fires around Fredericksburg is still a matter of speculation. But the Germanic Old-World fires and the Old-World fertility symbols of rabbits and eggs blended with the New-World Indians into a modern legend.[21]

In addition to observing the nationally celebrated holidays the Texas Germans have many other traditional occasions for gathering regularly. The *Kinderfest* and *Kindermaskenball* are springtime children's parties and frolics, similar to the Anglos' May Fete. The one at Prairie Hill in Washington County has been observed since the early settlement of this community in the 1870s. Prairie Hill also has long sponsored an annual *Schützenfest*, another German gathering. Those early pioneers took, and still take, great pride in their marksmanship, and today one can still find signs along the roads near the German communities announcing shooting matches. Traditionally the marksmen's prize was a beef. The top four winners got their choices of the quarters according to their rank, and the loser got the hide and tallow.

The Germans brought with them from the Old Country a long tradition of folk music and singing clubs, and established similar clubs in the new communities. The *Liedertafel* (Singing Society) of Comfort in Kendall County has been functioning since its founding in 1870. The purpose of the group is not only to provide music for clubs and public entertainments but also to provide singing for weddings, anniversaries, funerals,

A Look at Texas-German Folklore

and numerous other official functions. In addition, the *Liedertafel* functions as a service club, raising money for worthy causes. It was instrumental in 1881 in forming the *Texanischer Gebirgs Sängerbund* (Texas Hill Country Singing Alliance), which organized singers from nearby communities and sponsored regular *Sängerfeste*. The first recorded formal *Sängerfest* in Texas, the *Deutsch-Texanisches Sängerfest*, was held in New Braunfels on October 17, 1853. In 1933 Comfort created a mixed choir, the *Comforter Gemischter Chor*, which formally integrated their band with the choir. This combination was nothing new in the tradition, and the formalizing of it by creating a club is typical of German custom.

One song that they sang in the Old Country and continued singing in the new was "Muss I Denn." It is a sad farewell song of the same sort as the Anglos' "Gal I Left behind Me," and its sentiment is echoed in an Irish farewell song called "Nora Darling," a popular Texas folksong. Bill Owens, who collected Texas folksongs in the 1940s, discussed this Irish-German kinship and tells about a group of German emigrants who sailed out of Bremen harbor to the tune of "Muss I Denn" and were greeted with the same song when they arrived at the docks in Galveston.[22] It is still a well-known song among Germans in Texas.

The Germans were great gatherers, mixers, and joiners, both as a result of their old traditions and because of their early isolation in the New World. Every town had its organizations and *Vereine*, its granges founded for the improvement of agricultural practices, singing and shooting societies, cultural and debating societies, and regular occasions for dancing. Singing and dancing and declaiming were somewhere near the heart of all their gatherings, whether the meetings were formal, like the three-day *Sängerfeste*, or informal. On the night before the Nueces Massacre the German Unionists took turns delivering speeches and singing German folksongs around the campfire, and Ferdinand Roemer and Meusebach and their companions spent an evening during their exploration of the San Saba River drinking and singing the old songs of the fatherland. Frederick Olmsted tells that the Germans of New Braunfels concluded their serious observation of the Sabbath with a

Muss I Denn

Translated and arranged by Dan Beaty

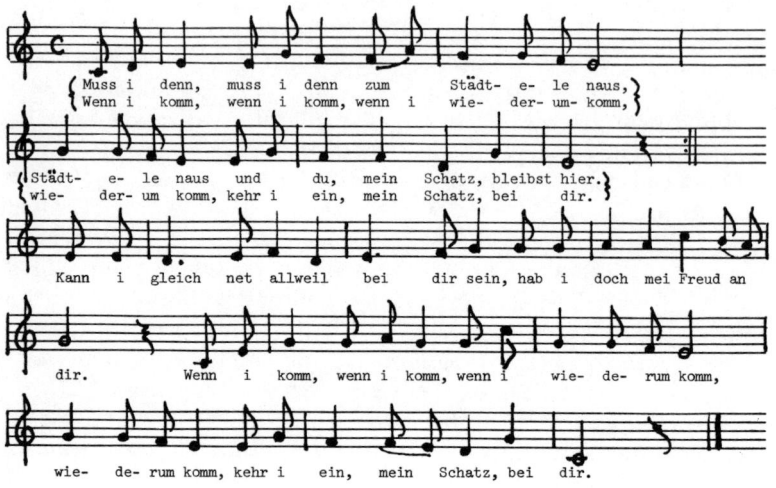

Verse I:
Must I leave, must I leave,
  Must I leave this town,
And you, my dear, stay here.

When I come, when I come,
  When I come back again.
I will stay here with you, my dear.

Chorus:
Even though I cannot be with you,
I still find joy in our love.
When I come, when I come, When I come back again,
I will stay here with you, my dear.

Verse II:
Wie du weinst, wie du weinst, das i wandere muss
wandere muss, wie wenn d'Lieb jetzt wär vorbei.

Sind au drauss, sind au drauss der Mädele viel,
Mädele viel, lieber Schatz, i bleib dir treu.

Chorus:
Denk du net, wenn i en andre seh,
so sei mei Lieb vorbei.
Sind au drauss, sind au drauss der Mädele viel,
Mädele viel, lieber Schatz, i bleib dir treu.

Verse II:
How you cry, how you cry,
  Now that I must go, I must go.
Just as though our love were gone.

Even though there may be
  Other girls where I go, girls where I go,
Dearest, I'll be true to you.

Chorus:
Do not think I'll see another one,
And our love will fade from my heart.
Even if there are many girls over there,
I'll remain true to you, my dear.

festive dance every Sunday night which the Lutheran minister was expected to attend.[23]

Every town had its tavern where the men customarily gathered to talk and sing and play games. Skat and pinochle have been longtime favorite games of Texas Germans. Leon Hale has described two more German games that are regularly played at Wagner's tavern–cafe–grocery store–filling station–and bait stand at Winedale in Fayette County near Round Top. *Mühle* (lit. "flour mill" but called "Trap" in English lore) is a combination of checkers and tic-tac-toe and is played with buttons or grains of corn. Another game, which they played with one die and a homemade board, was *Mensch Ärgere Dich Nicht*, translated as "Friend, don't get upset," which one was likely to do if he played the game.[24]

German women were as gregarious as the men, and every settlement soon had its sewing clubs and study clubs, the *Damen-Lese-Vereine* (ladies' reading clubs), garden and home demonstration clubs, as well as church-associated organizations. Less formal but equally traditional were the home-oriented *Kaffee-Klatschen* and *Kaffee-Kraenzchen*, where the ladies gathered to chat and sew and drink coffee and eat *Schmierkaese* (cheese), *Mandelbrot* (almond bread), *Zimtsterne* (cinnamon stars), *Lebkuchen* (gingerbread), and other fattening foods.

The Anglos, who had pushed off into the wilderness and left their doctors on the East Coast, developed their folk medicine from the Indians, who knew the native plants and molds that had curative powers. The Germans brought their medicine, both scientific and folk, straight from the Old Country. Germans provided Texas with some of its finest doctors and the first of its trained apothecaries. It also put into motion among Germans, Czechs, Wends, and their other neighbors a pattern of folk cures that went back to medieval and Renaissance Europe. A Texas-German cure for extracting a tooth without pain was popular in Brandenburg as far back as 1600: "Boil as many toads as you can catch. The grease will collect on top of the water. Take this congealed fat and anoint the tooth. Then you will be able to pull it without pain." Or for toothache: "Go to an ossuary and remove the same tooth from a skull as the one that is in pain. Rub the gums till they bleed on the old tooth. Replace the old tooth in the skull, but not with bare hands, and pray the Lord's Prayer and one Creed. And you're cured."

Along with the cures were curses. Disappointed lovers attending the wedding of the one they lost could put the curse of barrenness on the couple by snapping shut a lock during the ceremony. This excellent example of imitative magic was called *Nestelknüpfen* (to tie the cord) and worked as long as the lock was hidden. The curse could be forestalled if the bride kept with her during the ceremony a lock with a key in it.

If the rejected lover wanted to cast a spell of impotence on the groom, he attended the wedding with his belt turned inside out and recited magic words, now fortunately lost. Another way to cause impotency in a rival was to throw Saturnus herbs in front of the man as he was about to enter a door. To counteract these curses the groom boiled gentian, sundew, marjoram, and St. John's wort in beer and drank it before breakfast and before going to bed. If that failed, he could resort to the following: "Station a plough against sunrise, take the plough bar out and urinate three times through the hole. You will be helped." Unfortunately the prescriptionist doesn't say "cured."[25]

Country stores in the German areas for years carried *Blitz-Öl* (Lightning Oil); *Heil-Öl* (Healing Oil), for curing wounds; *Schreck-Tee* (Fright Tea) and *Schreck-Kraüter* (Fright Herbs), for tranquilizers; and *Teufels-Dreck* (asafetida), to be used during epidemics of anything. *Lebenswecker* (Life Awakeners), instruments with little needles that were rolled over the skin, were used to cure rheumatism and arthritis and other muscular pains. *Lebenswecker-Öl* was brushed on with a chicken feather.[26]

The most significant aspect of early German culture and lore is its architectural superiority over the early Anglo-Texan building culture. Little investigation is required to see that German building—houses and barns, fences and furniture—is more solidly and sophisticatedly constructed than that of the Anglos. The Anglos had begun their journey from the East Coast of America a hundred years earlier. The generations had moved west, plowing and planting and moving on after they had exhausted their fields. As wanderers, most of them built few things to last, and they carried little with them. Those that made a success out of their lives stayed in Kentucky and Tennessee or Georgia or Alabama; those that didn't moved on to new lands in Texas. Many Texas settlers throughout the century could look back on two or three or more major moves to the west. The Germans, many of them, came straight from the Old Country with the civilized and socialized values—and probably with more capital—of their fatherland. Prince Carl noted the difference: "What with the warm climate and the unaccustomed food, life [for the German settler] is one of privation and hardship. For the Americans it is normal living. To the American settler, who generally does not own more than he actually has on his back, it seems strange that the Germans should burden themselves with so much baggage just to be able to live according to the standard of comfort of their own country."[27] Few Anglo-American settlers' houses in East Texas still stand. The builders required and made very few furnishings. They seldom decorated. On the other hand, many German houses of pre–Civil War days still stand solidly on their foundations. The furniture that the old craftsmen made is still usable and has grown in value over the years. And the artistic touches to both interior and exterior architecture are still the subject of admiration and masters' theses.

The first houses that many of the Germans built when they came to Texas were by necessity very primitive. Caroline von Hinüber, the daughter of Friedrich Ernst, the founder of Industry, tells about her family's first Texas home, which they occupied in 1831–32: "After we had lived on Fordtran's place for six months [Charles Fordtran, a tanner from Westphalia], we moved into our own house. This was a miserable little hut, covered with straw and having six sides, which were made out of moss. The roof was by no means water-proof, and we often held an umbrella over our bed when it rained at night, while the cows came and ate the moss. Of course, we suffered a great deal in the winter. My father had tried to build a chimney and fireplace out of logs and clay, but we were afraid to light a fire because of the extreme combustibility of our dwelling. So we had to shiver."[28]

A Look at Texas-German Folklore

Ferdinand Roemer in 1846 described the temporary structures the Germans built when they first came to New Braunfels as consisting of a variety of makeshift buildings constructed by people who had no experience in building either in the old or new land. There were some log houses, but most were less formally built. Typical was the hovel made of cedar posts set side by side and roofed with an old tent or buffalo hides.[29] Frederick Olmsted described the German settlement of D'Hanis in 1854 as "a most singular spectacle upon the verge of the great American wilderness. It is like one of the smallest and meanest of European peasant hamlets. There are about twenty cottages and hovels, all built in much the same style, the walls being made of poles and logs placed together vertically and made tight with clay mortar, the floors of beaten earth, the windows without glass, and roofs built so as to overhang the four sides and deeply shade them and covered with thatch of fine brown grass laid in a peculiar manner, the ridgeline and apexes being ornamented with knots, tufts, crosses or weathercocks."[30]

As the Texas Germans gained control of their environment they began to build after their own temperament and German traditions, and some of the houses they built in the better times of those early years still stand as monuments to one of the main characteristics of German buildings, the sense of permanence.

German building traditions did not create new house types in Texas, but they did introduce new ways of building. *Fachwerk* was a building method from the Old Country. This half-timbered style consisted of vertical and diagonal wall beams with the intervening spaces filled in with bricks or, as was usually the case in the Hill Country, with limestone. Plastering over this rock filler, or sometimes over other types of walls, was a German custom brought to Texas, as was whitewashing the exterior and interior of houses. The use of casemented windows and shutters was also a German contribution to traditional building ways in Texas.

German building techniques blended with Anglo building styles, and the result was a very solidly built house, one that was constructed for sons and grandsons to live in. Roof lines were lower than they had been in the Old Country because there was little snow in central Texas. Outside staircases and long, open galleries and separately housed kitchens (as well as other out buildings) were adopted from the Anglos because more of their daily lives could be lived outside than was possible in the Old Country. And because these new Texans did not need to bring the stock into the house to protect them from the severity of winter, they were able to get by with smaller houses than those they had built in Germany.

By the 1890s house styles had been modified by acculturation to such an extent that German houses were little different from the houses of their neighbors. Their main distinction was that many were made of stone. Because of their proximity to limestone, Germans became very skilled in stone masonry and were in demand wherever public buildings were being constructed. Lime kilns were commonly run by the Germans in the Hill Country. The old German houses of stone are still prominent features on the Hill Country landscape, and that area is honored by the strength and charm and endurance of that culture's architecture.[31]

Frederick Olmsted contends that a German is responsible for the introduction of outhouses to Texas living, before that the convenience being "the back of a bush or the broad prairie—an indication of a queerly Texan incompleteness in cultivation of manners." One innovative and fastidious German built a privy only to have it wrecked by vandals and to find himself accused of public indecency. The same thing happened to his second privy, but he won with his third, which later became the model for several other outhouses in his town. All was peaceful until the following Christmas when all existing outhouses, now numbering twelve to fifteen, showed up, neatly arranged in a line on the public square.[32]

The survival of German folklore in Texas was the result not only of their traditional—and perhaps inherent—sense of *Deutschtum,* but of their history, of the many things that happened to them in that state. During the times of their troubles and isolation they clung to their old customs for comfort and survival. The trauma of their hardships during their first bad months in Texas in the 1840s caused a temporary breakdown in their social structure. The memories of those ill times were of living in holes in the ground, sick and dying with the pestilence, of family units breaking down, and of panic-stricken flight and fight for survival. The reaction to the chaos and anarchy of those early times was a tightening of traditions and folkways, a solidifying of their familiar German culture in order to get a stable foundation on which the new colonies could survive.

German history in Texas has been punctuated by periods of cultural estrangement and isolation as the nation went through wartime crises and Germans were forced into the role of being not only an ethnic but a political minority. During the Civil War most of the German colonists in Texas were Unionists, and they were isolated by Southern hostility. Although they received some relief during the Reconstruction, anti-German feelings continued for some years afterward. This phase of their separation, which was slowly and happily breaking down by the turn of the century, was revived again during World War I, when German traditions were associated with the Kaiser and with all that was believed to be evil in the world. Pressured by general public opinion and often harassed by the Ku Klux Klan, Texas Germans in some areas were forced to abandon their language in schools, churches, and business. Although this caused the breakdown of one level of their culture, the physical and social abuse many Germans felt during the war times caused them to retreat once more behind the barriers of their own traditions.

Fewer incidents of anti-German hysteria occurred in World War II. Considerable cultural integration had taken place during the ultrademocratic 1930s. The Depression and universal military conscription and training were forces that also ignored and leveled ethnic lines. The anxieties of the war, however, did arouse some latent anti-German sentiments which were frequently based on economic rather than political reasons. One story circulated about an old German farmer near Hermleigh in Scurry County who painted his barn roofs a bright red during the war, convincing his less prosperous Anglo neighbors that they were bright sign posts purposely lined up to direct German aircraft on their way to bomb nearby Camp

Barclay. Reacting to subtle and hostile pressures and remembering the problems of World War I, most Germans kept a low profile for the duration, purposely speaking English rather than German and de-emphasizing their German traditions.

A reaction against the melting-pot philosophy and the cultural leveling that was a part of it began in the 1960s, when the Germans—and everybody else—began to realize that not only ethnic identity but personal identity was being lost in the exploding population and mass urbanization in Texas, the nation, and the world. The Texas-German population, among the many other ethnic groups, is now consciously recovering and taking pride in the old traditions that have given their culture an individual strength that helped it in the past to survive and will give it a singular identity to live by in the future.

A man is remembered for the power of his full personality: the sight of him and his sound; how he moves and talks and walks; what he does that is his and nobody else's. He participates in the sum total of mankind, but because of his difference he is more than the numerator of one over the population of his culture or his country. And that is the way it is with the Germans of Texas. They are an integrated part of a population and a culture of a state, but because of their difference—their own culture's customs and traditions, their own songs and styles and the tales they tell of themselves and their past—because of their folklore they are more than their numbers and their German names and the German-named towns scattered all over the state suggest. Prince Carl had told them before they ever came across the water to "stay together and remain faithful to German culture and habits."[33] They did. They suffered and endured and survived, and they brought a great richness to this land. And they still have their own cultural personality, and they are remembered.

Part IV

Current Dimensions

CHAPTER 11

The German Language in Texas: Some Needed Research

GLENN G. GILBERT

THANKS to the efforts of a small group of dedicated scholars, the last fifteen years have seen a great expansion of our knowledge regarding the German spoken by the descendants of nineteenth-century immigrants in Texas. This includes: 1) the exact geographic origins of the German immigrants (and hence the German dialects they are likely to have spoken); 2) the approximate boundaries of their areas of settlement in Texas; 3) the location of the German dialects that were most probably spoken in the first few decades after arrival in Texas; and 4) the location of communities of dialect speakers that have not yet merged into the Texas German common language (or Texas-German *koiné*).

The koiné has been shown to be based on a Middle German/North German "compromise language" which is considerably closer to Standard German than most of the purely regional dialects which underlie it. It has borrowed massively from English, less so from Spanish.

The great majority of the borrowed words have to do with the new physical and human environment in Texas. Because of the more or less rapid decline in ability to read German, most of the developments in science and technology of the last 100 years, which caused European German to vastly expand its lexicon, had little effect on German in Texas. With some exceptions, the names for these new things were borrowed

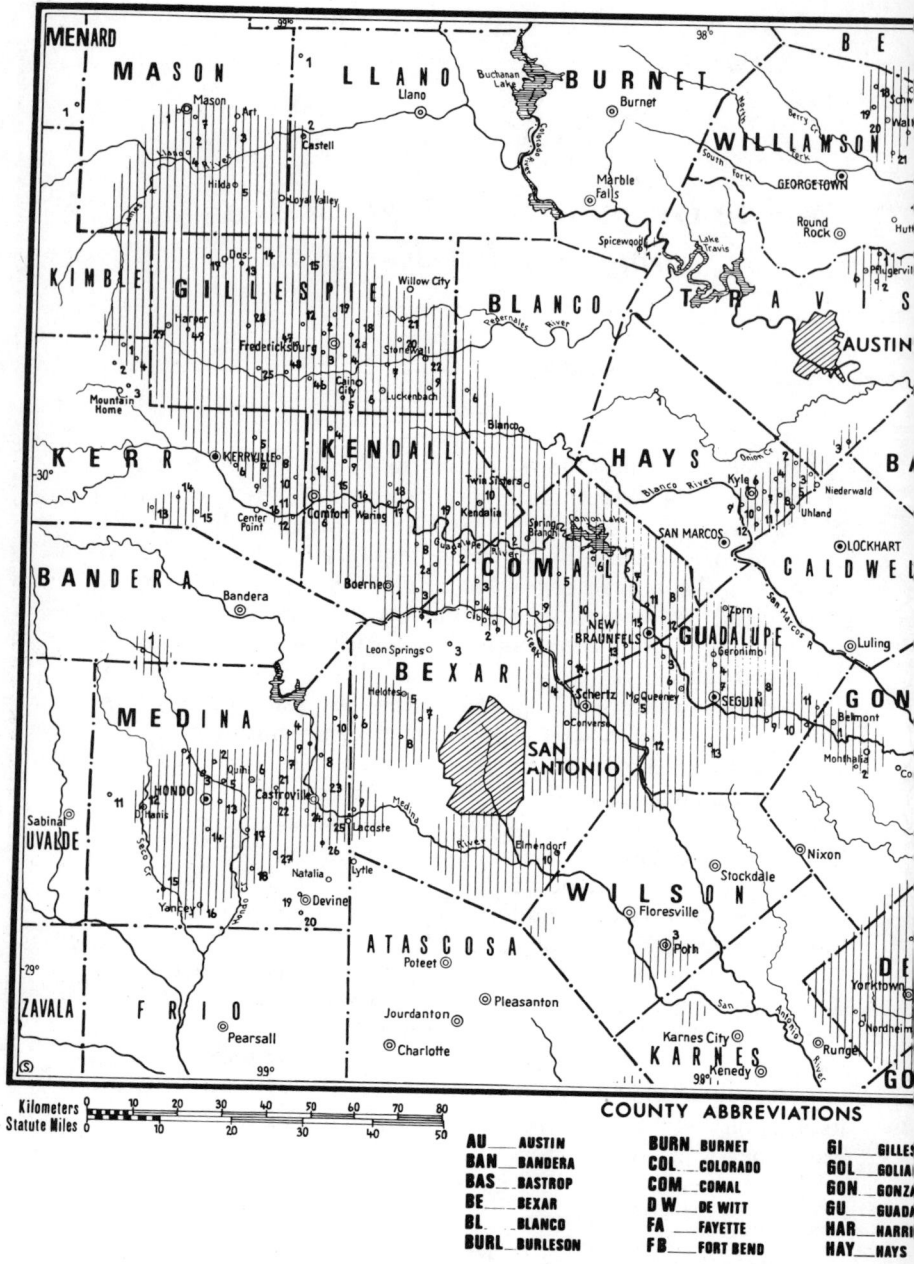

The German Language in Texas

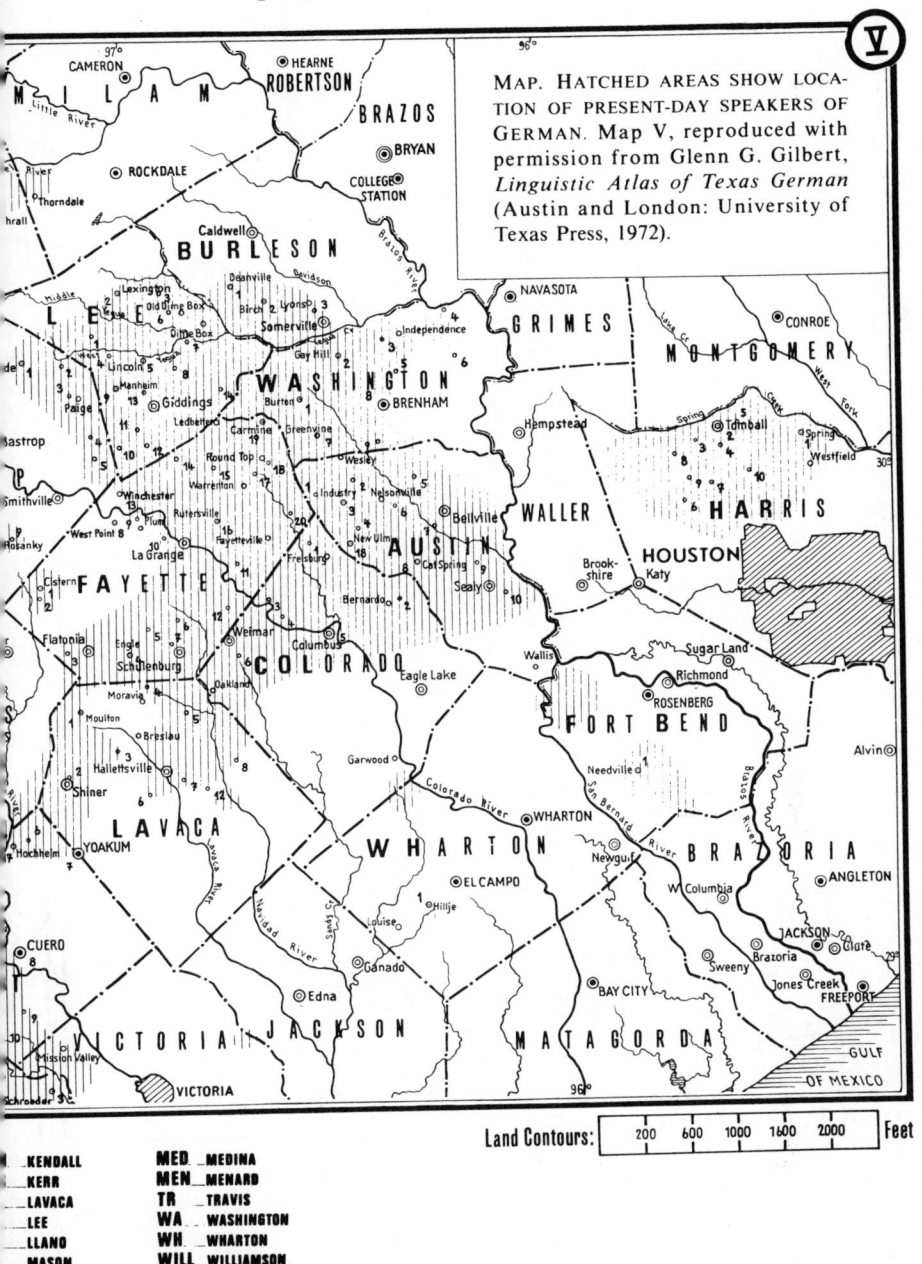

MAP. HATCHED AREAS SHOW LOCATION OF PRESENT-DAY SPEAKERS OF GERMAN. Map V, reproduced with permission from Glenn G. Gilbert, *Linguistic Atlas of Texas German* (Austin and London: University of Texas Press, 1972).

232 GERMAN CULTURE IN TEXAS

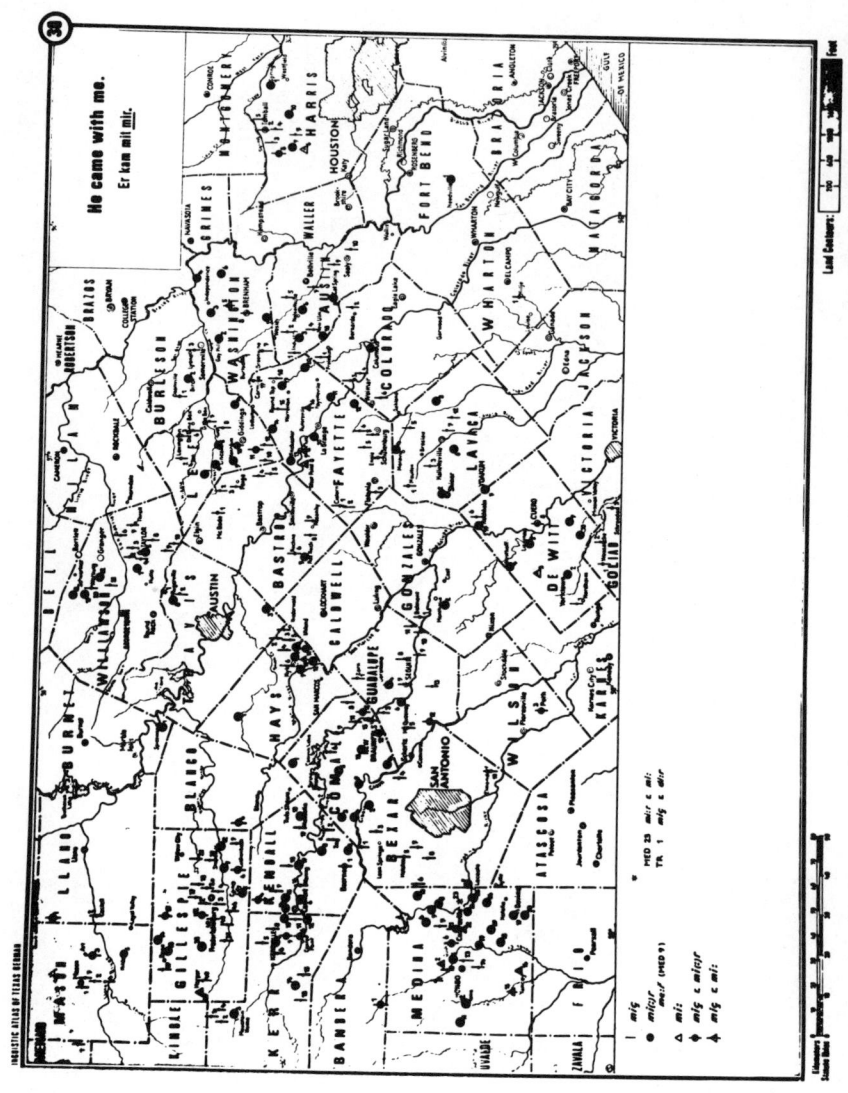

The German Language in Texas

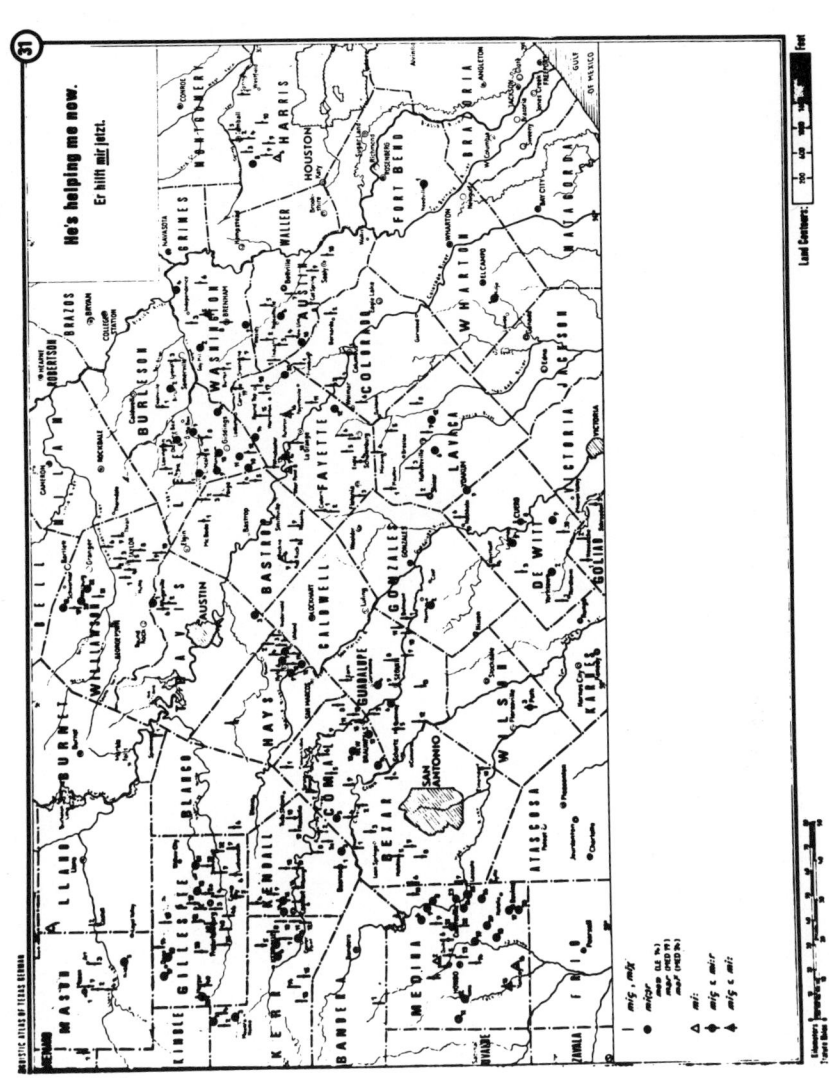

Dative and Accusative Usage by Age

From the *Linguistic Atlas of Texas German*. Dative and accusative forms of the first-person singular pronoun: *mir/mich*

Map 30. He came with me/ Er kam mit *mir* (object of preposition *mit*).

Age Groups	Accusative (mich)	Dative (mir)	Both Accusative and Dative	[mi:]
0 – 19	1			
20 – 29	5			1
30 – 39	12			
40 – 49	18	5	2	1
50 – 59	30	12	4	3
60 – 69	34	31	8	2
70 – 79	30	32	3	
80 – 89	7	12		3
90 –		3		

Map 31. He's helping me now/ Er hilft *mir* jetzt (dative object of *helfen*).

Age Groups	Accusative (mich)	Dative (mir)	Both Accusative and Dative	[mi:]
0 – 19	1			
20 – 29	5			1
30 – 39	11			
40 – 49	23	5		
50 – 59	37	7	1	2
60 – 69	51	23	1	1
70 – 79	45	21		
80 – 89	11	8	1	2
90 –		3		

from English. Thus, it is not at all unnatural to say something like: "Der *sonic boom*, der war gar nicht laut" (That sonic boom, it wasn't loud at all—recorded at Cherry Spring community, Gillespie County, September 11, 1962).

For Northern Europeans, central Texas seemed to have a climate similar to that of Morocco or Algeria. Many descriptive terms were introduced from English for the new climatic conditions (e.g., bevor der *pasture* aufgedeilt gewesen ist [before the pasture was divided up]; die musste *cotton picken* ["she had to pick cotton"]). Although many of the new plants and animals were provided with German names (e.g., Steinesel [donkey]; Stinkkatze [skunk]; die Brennessel [painful nettles], usually a low plant of the genus *Urtica*), others were simply called by their English names (e.g., Heckbeeren [hackberry tree, *Celtis laevigata Willd.*]; ein Zentepied [a centipede]). In some cases the English names had been borrowed from Spanish (e.g., der Armadilo [armadillo]; der Buro [burro]). Occasionally, especially in Medina County, there have been direct borrowings from Spanish (e.g., die Kalavases [wild gourds]; Hormigas [ants]).

These and many other examples can be found in the *Linguistic Atlas of Texas German*.[1]

We can distinguish four main areas of needed research which are likely to provide not only a better knowledge of Texas-German language and culture per se, but may point the way toward improvement in the teaching of Standard German to Texas Germans and may lead to additional insights into the sociolinguistics of immigrant languages generally.

Research Problem #1

What are the boundaries and constraints on language variation in the Texas-German koiné? What are the linguistic and extralinguistic constraints on competing variants? What are speakers' attitudes toward these variants? And are there socially diagnostic variants that can be linked with biologically or socially defined subgroups within Texas German society?

A great deal of data bearing on these questions have already been gathered, and are available in published form and simply await collation and analysis by interested scholars. The *Linguistic Atlas of Texas German*, for example, displays data on linguistic variation which can be linked to geography, age, and sex of the informants, or to purely linguistic factors such as syntactic or phonological environments. A good illustration of such variation is the often-cited coalescence of the dative and accusative case markers. It occurs variably in the definite and indefinite articles, weak and strong adjectival inflections, and pronouns.

Compare LATG Map 30 (*He came with me* / St. Ger. *Er kam mit mir*) and Map 31 (*He's helping me now* / St. Ger. *Er hilft mir jetzt*). Clearly, in the formal translation style of the interviews (Labov's "Style B" or "Style C"), the accusative form *mich* is *not* used exclusively. The Standard German dative form *mir* was used by 95 out of 256 informants as the objects of the preposition *mit*, and by 67 out of 257 informants as the dative object of the verb *helfen*.

This suggests that the occurrence of *mich* is favored when it is the dative object of a verb, and it is disfavored when it is the dative object of a preposition. The frequency of occurrence of the accusative forms thus appears to be variably constrained by their syntactic environment. Note that it is a linguistic tendency which is operating without the corrective of the standard written language.

Extralinguistic constraints also exist. Geographically, there is a relatively uniform mix, although close scrutiny will reveal that the accusative is very much favored in Fredericksburg while the dative is favored in eastern Medina County, the Upper Alsatian dialect area. Generally, the western region is most innovating, followed by the eastern region and the Medina region, in that order. This is probably due to the dialectal origins of the settlers.

The *Atlas* also lists the sex and age of each informant. Although male/female differences in frequency of use of the accusative do not seem significant, there does exist a definite age gradation (see Table 1). People over eighty years old prefer the dative in both syntactic constructions, although even for them, case usage is variable (which indicates that the shift to the accusative must have begun at least by the last quarter of the nineteenth century). The younger the informant, the more the accusative is used. People who were forty years of age or younger had no datives at all.

These interviews were conducted in 1965 and 1966 for the most part. The octogenarians are now in their nineties and the forty-year-olds are fifty-two or fifty-three. The once variable case realization of the first-person singular personal pronoun will soon be categorically accusative.

By charting the variable usage of equal-interval age groups, a technique called "measurement in apparent time," we can uncover the timing, extent, and direction of the change. In this case, it began at least as early as 1875 and was essentially complete by 1925.

Decreasing literacy in German is probably highly correlated with the decreasing use of the dative in the formal oral style. Thus it is no coincidence that the demise of the dative seems to have occurred in the period just after the First World War, a time when all formal instruction in German was prohibited by law.

Research Problem #2

In some areas, trilingualism and even quadrilingualism are quite common. Trilingual Wendish-German-English speakers have admittedly become rather rare; Polish-German-English is more common, as is Czech-German-English. Many speakers in Medina County, immediately west of San Antonio, speak the Texas-German koiné, Alsatian-German, Spanish, and English.

More precise information is needed on: 1) approximate numbers and locations of multilingual speakers in cohesive rural areas, and 2) the languages and dialects spoken.

Research in multilingualism could focus on such problems as: 1) language dominance and language proficiency, 2) mechanisms of triggering and types of transfer, and 3) the nature of language use and of attitudes toward language.

Research Problem #3

In its role as an "immigrant language," German in Texas has been on the defensive since the first days of settlement.[2]

It is true that German has been retained to an unusual extent, at least in comparison with the United States as a whole. The high retention of German in central Texas is due to the following factors: 1) relative isolation with vast distances between settlements, 2) relatively poor public education in English, 3) a strong tradition of German-language education supported by large numbers of Freethinkers and highly trained intellectuals, and 4) the proximity of Latin America which, to some extent, resulted in an increased tolerance by Anglos of languages other than English. Nevertheless, most of the descendants of the original immigrants have eventually become monolingual in English. This process could be termed "deacquisition of German."

It should be noted, however, that there may still be as many as 70,000 speakers of German in central Texas. Although Texas German shows considerable internal variation, it does have a common core of peculiarities of pronunciation, syntax, and vocabulary which identify it unmistakably (See LATG for details). Speakers of European German and speakers of Texas German can still understand each other quite well. Texas German has sloughed off most of the more marked dialectal features that were brought from the Old World and has drifted toward a "colonial koiné," or unified language, which is considerably closer to standard German than any of the local dialects originally brought to the state.

As we have seen, language deacquisition can be studied in apparent time as well as in real time. What written and spoken sources are available for such studies? Can the grammatical dismantlement of Texas German be fruitfully compared with simplified German and pidginized German found in literary sources, i.e., with the way writers of fiction and nonfiction portray the German of American Indians, Africans, South Sea Islanders, etc.? Or can it be compared with the socially structured, broken German still spoken on Samoa, Ali Island, in New Guinea, South West Africa, and elsewhere; or with the broken German of foreign workers in West Germany (*Gastarbeiterdeutsch*)?

And what about parallel grammatical features that have developed in Afrikaans, a Germanic language that has most probably undergone creolization without prior pidginization? One conclusion that might be arrived at is that colonial koinés are fundamentally different from pidginized and creolized languages because of the drastically different social conditions involved in their formation. An opposing point of view would hold that all simplified and leveled languages simply represent points on a continuum with no essential qualitative difference. Almost 100 years ago, Hugo Schuchardt indicated the kind of data that would have to be gathered to solve the problem. But despite his own vast output and that of his successors, the answers still elude us.[3]

Furthermore, does the deacquisition of German shed light on the nature of underlying word order in German (Subject-Verb-Object or Subject-Object-Verb)? Why are certain grammatical distinctions, such as gender, seemingly so tenacious, while others, such as case, are so weak?

Research Problem #4

Fairly precise estimates can now be made of the locations and numbers of: 1) active German speakers in households where German is spoken in preference to English; 2) "passive" German speakers who live in households where German is spoken, but whose own usual language is English; 3) "passive" German speakers who live in households where only English is spoken; and 4) the German ethnic heritage group (persons who are almost totally monolingual in English but who retain a lingering awareness of being of full or part German descent).

One estimate for Texas, 1975, would place these figures at 5,000, 43,000, 117,000, and 534,000, respectively. The first three figures may be as much as 100 percent too low because of the relatively high retention of German in Texas. The last figure, based on statistics issued by the National Center for Educational Statistics, is very conservative. Albert Bernhardt Faust, a writer who did the German element in the United States more justice, gave figures for the 1920s which, when projected onto the 1975 Texas population, would yield an ethnic heritage group of 1,950,000.

When learners in any one of these four groups undertake

the study of Standard German, they obviously do not start with a blank slate. Even monolingual English speakers in the German Ethnic Heritage Group may enjoy motivational advantages as well as perhaps a certain residual knowledge of German.

The question we should now ask is: How can an analytical knowledge of the linguistic structure of the Texas-German dialect and a material knowledge of Texas-German culture be used to assist in better training of teachers and preparation of teaching materials in Texas-German areas?

Is bilingual education still feasible in some localities? Could (or should) German be taught as a second language? Or is it best to treat it everywhere simply as a foreign language?

Innovation in education costs money. How can a convincing case for qualitatively and quantitatively improved instruction in German be presented to local and state governments?

It seems to me that these four research areas would be especially worth pursuing, given the present state of our knowledge of the language situation in Texas.

CHAPTER 12

The Myth of Texas in Contemporary German Writing

A. LESLIE WILLSON

A little less than a year ago Günter Herburger, author of plays, poems, novels, and children's books illustrated by his young son, wrote me: "Ich freue mich [einen aus Austin zu sehen], damit ich endlich einmal einen aus dem sagenhaften Texas kennenlerne, in dessen Universität stets deutsche Dichter verschwinden" (I look forward to seeing someone from Austin, so that I can finally become acquainted with someone from legendary Texas, in whose University German poets keep disappearing). Herburger's hyperbole matches the myth of Texas, a myth of long standing, where Texas is bigger-than-life in size, with braggarts behind every cactus. That myth has in recent years been both heightened and diminished through the program of visiting writers in the Department of Germanic Languages at the University of Texas at Austin and by writers who have found their way to the Lone Star State on lecture tours under the sponsorship of the Goethe Institute of Munich. German writers don't really disappear in Texas, but many of them undergo a kind of sea-change, buffeted between the winds and waves of their expectations and the reality they meet.

Texas is legendary, *sagenhaft*—and the stereotypes in the fervent imaginations of Germans have changed little for almost 150 years. Texas is the land of exotic creatures, broad expanses, a boastful and proud and indomitable people. True, close proximity reveals flaws greedily recorded by some writers, iconoclasts who delight in integrating Texas into their conception of a world-image. Still, the armadillo remains the most elusive and ubiquitous part of the Texas landscape, a creature repeatedly mentioned by German writers who travel on Texas highways.

Since 1967 two dozen writers have been visiting lecturers or have read from their works at the University of Texas at Austin. One of the earliest, the imaginative and reflective Christoph Meckel, in a poem entitled "Talking about Poetry" (that's the title on the German-text poem), muses on the time he spent in the company of his fellow poet Christopher Middleton. The concluding stanza reads:

> Zeit, zu schweigen—
> und unter den Dingen zu sein, wortlos
> hören, wenn sich die Welt unserm Haus nähert, nachts
> mit den Schritten des Gurteltiers,
> unübersetzbar.[1]

> (Time, to be silent
> to be, among the things, wordless,
> listen, when the world comes near to our house, at night
> with the stepping of armadillos,
> untranslatable.[2])

That time of silent communion, communion with objects that are wordless, when the world of nature approaches with the tripping, rustling steps of armadillos, represents only one aspect of a writer's appreciation of Texas nature. More generally, perhaps, the German is struck by the rawness of nature in the vast expanse of Texas. East-German Günter Kunert, whose 1972 fall semester at the University of Texas at Austin spawned a travelogue and subsequent single essays, comments:

Selbst die alltäglichen Wettervorgänge kommen dem europäischen Besucher wie Ausnahmefälle vor. Regen in den Südstaaten (wie etwa in Texas, das auf Sahara-Breitengrad liegt) gibt sich sintflutartig: die drei bis viermal grossmäuligeren Gullys können die Wassermengen nicht schlucken, die Strassen werden zu Flüssen, die Städtebewohner waten bis zu den Waden durch das quirlende Nass, unerschüttert und ohne Aufhebens davon zu machen. Das Pflaster dampft nach solchen Güssen, die gesteigerte Luftfeuchtigkeit verwandelt die Ortschaft in eine Sauna, vor der man an die heimische Klimaanlage flüchtet.[3]

(Even the daily weather forecasts seem to be exceptional cases to European visitors. Rain in the Southern states [such as in Texas, that lies on the latitudinal degree of the Sahara] proves to be a deluge: the three- or fourfold more voracious gullies cannot swallow the torrents, the streets become rivers, the city dwellers wade up to their calves through the swirling wetness, unflustered and without making anything of it. The pavement steams after such downpours, the increased humidity transforms the locality into a sauna from which everybody flees to their indigenous air conditioners.)

Coming from a trimmed and lopped and pruned and manicured natural landscape in Europe, where the climate is mild, Kunert remarks wryly on the nature-loving Texan's ambivalent attempts to get closer to a harsher, hotter, less hospitable nature:

Auf Padre Island, der grössten und südlichsten Insel der USA, im Golf von Mexiko, verharren die Urlauber im Bannkreis der Swimming pools und meiden das Meer, oder man sieht sie in fest geschlossenen Wagen, die Klimaanlage auf Hochtouren, die Damen in Hut und Kostüm auf dem Rücksitz, auf dem Strand entlangfahren, dort wo der Sand feucht ist und trägt; man fährt einmal hin und einmal zurück und hat die Natur im Fenster wie auf einem Bildschirm.[4]

(On Padre Island, the largest and southernmost island of the United States, in the Gulf of Mexico, the vacationers linger in the magic circle of the swimming pools and avoid the sea, or they are seen in tightly closed cars, with air conditioners at maximum speed, ladies in hats and suits on the backseats, driving along the beach, where the sand is damp and supportive; they drive once back and forth and catch nature in their windows as on the TV tube.)

Again exaggeration, extreme—but significant observations by an impressionable writer, who sees the Texan caught between a yearning for, and a flight from, nature.

Kunert again: For a man who comes from a continent with centuries of history, who goes to his bakery to buy bread unsliced and unwrapped, a plaque on The Old Bakery in Austin was a revelation:

Das schmale, einzeln stehende Gebäude ... die Nummer 1006 in der Congress Avenue, ist The Old Bakery, gebaut von Charles Lundberg, einem schwedischen Einwanderer im Jahre 1876, restauriert 1963.
... Das Haus [wurde] erhalten ... weil sich im Parterre, wie eine üppige Stahlgusstafel meldet, die "alte Bäckerei" befand. Ofenwarm erhielten die Kunden das Brot, lesen wir da, und ausserdem sogar "unsliced and unwrapped," ungeschnitten und unverpackt. Legendär schon wie ein öffentliches Schaumahl des hohen Mittelalters, was in der amerikanischen Antike unhygienisch und unvorstellbar stattfand; den erhaben gegossenen und polierten Worten wohnt Verwunderung inne.[5]

(The narrow building standing alone, 1006 Congress Avenue, is The Old Bakery, built in 1876 by Charles Lundberg, a Swedish immigrant, restored in 1963.
... The building was preserved because on the ground floor, as a splendid cast-iron plaque announces, the "Old Bakery" was located. The customers received the bread, we read there, warm from the oven and what is more "unsliced and unwrapped." Already legendary like a feast for the eyes from the High Middle Ages is what took place unhygienically and unimaginably in American antiquity; amazement is inherent in the raised and polished words.)

The visitor from East Germany shares an amazement, astonished that such a common practice should be enshrined on a metal plaque. This is true Texan Gothic. Kunert's memoir is full of bemused comments on Austin, the campus of the university there, Sixth Street, the Texas highways, Lion's Country Safari Park, and the wax figure museum near Dallas, Padre Island, San Antonio. Kunert is particularly annoyed at his experiences in the apartment building where he and his wife, Marianne, lived—but, caught in a snowstorm in Santa Fe, they yearn for home, and they realize with astonishment that they mean Austin. On a return trip in 1976 both the Kunerts were so overcome with nostalgia that they insisted on stopping over for a week in the same apartment building, no longer the butt of jokes but rather the repository of fondest memories.

The cultural shock to which German visiting writers have been exposed lasts in some cases for months. In a number of instances the writer in Texas has tumbled from one plane of shock to another, coming more times than once near the brink, only to find some firm ground underfoot near the end of his five-month stay. Such was the case with Christoph Meckel, who isolated himself for most of his sojourn but who, five years later, on a repeat visit, could write in impetuous bold script: "Texas ist herrlich!" (Texas is magnificent!)

Horst Bienek traveled through Texas in 1973 and almost a year later published his impressions of Austin, the university, the LBJ Library, and of Houston and Rice University:

Ich denke zurück an Houston, an die Rice-University, eine private, immens reiche Universität, die für sehr viel Geld eine Ausstellung von Plastiken von Max Ernst gekauft hat, ich bin dabei, als sie ausgepackt werden.... Nach meinem Vortrag sitzen wir dann noch in der einzigen Studentenkneipe auf der Rice-University, dünnes, bleiches Bier wird ausgeschenkt und Coca-Cola, alkoholische Getränke sind verboten, aber dort hinten, in der Fensternische, sehe ich, geht ein Joint um, die Luft ist heiss und süss, und die Zeit vergeht langsamer, unsere Bewegungen sind schon verzögert, die Worte verhallen....

Als wir zurückgehen, zu unseren Autos, schweigend und fast mechanisch, ruft einer aus: hat jemand schon Vögel sterben gesehn? Niemand erinnert sich, jemals einen Vogel sterben gesehen zu haben. So stellt er sich unter die Bäume am Parkrand der Universität, er klatscht in die Hände und tausend Vögel fliegen auf in der Nacht und einige fallen zu Boden, dumpf ist der Aufschlag, wir stehen da wie erstarrt, gehen dann langsam ein paar Schritte weiter, wo jemand mit der Stablaterne auf den grünen Rasen leuchtet: da liegt ein grosser schwarzer Vogel, die Federn leicht aufgeplustert, reglos, tot, und da noch einer und hier noch einer und dort noch einer. Und wir gehen weiter, zu anderen Bäumen, und wieder klatscht jemand in die Hände, und wieder hören wir die schwarzen Vögel auffliegen (und ich wünschte, die schwarzen Schwingen nähmen mich mit), und wieder stürzen Vögel schwer und dumpf auf die Erde....

Die Studenten hier kennen das, sie probieren das oft aus im Frühjahr, sie klatschen in die Hände. Aber heute lachen sie nicht darüber, sie stehen da, gemeinsam mit uns, und sie schweigen mit uns. Niemand weiss, warum hier in Rice die Vögel tot herunterfallen.[6]

(I think back on Houston, on Rice University, a private, immensely rich University that for a lot of money has bought an exhibition of sculptures by Max Ernst. I am present when they are unpacked. ... After my lecture we sit a while longer in the only student tavern at Rice University, thin, pale beer is poured and Coca Cola, alcoholic drinks are prohibited, but in the back, in the window niche, I see a joint going around, the air is hot and sweet, and time passes more slowly, our movements already protracted, words echo....

When we are going back, to our cars, silently and almost mechanically, someone calls out: Has anyone ever seen birds die? Nobody can remember ever having seen a bird die. So he takes up a position under the trees at the edge of the parking lot at the University, he claps his hands, and a thousand birds fly up in the night and some fall to the ground, the thud is muffled, we stand there as though frozen, then slowly go on a few steps, where somebody is shining a flashlight onto the green grass: There a large black bird is lying, its feathers softly fluffed up, motionless, dead, and there another and here another and there another. And we walk on, to other trees, and again somebody claps his hands, and again we hear the black birds fly up (and I wished the black wings would take me along), and again birds plunge heavy and muffled down to the earth....

The students here know about this, they experiment often in the springtime, they clap their hands. But today they don't laugh about it, they stand there, along with us, and they are silent with us. Nobody knows why here at Rice the birds fall down dead.)

And another Texas myth is born—perhaps not so mythical, but an odd Texas circumstance, bound to a place and time, something to think and wonder about.

Younger writers, such as the Austrian Christian Wallner, were more open to adventurous experience and were more ready to reshape the Texas myth. Wallner's poem "Ausflug nach USA" (Excursion to the USA) contains startled impressions, recognitions, a rock-music happening, and social criticism in a charged commentary:

I
Was ich nicht glaubte: die weite
nach allen schluchten manhattans,
das grün auf der höhe von mauretanien
und das braun von verblichenen fotos
dort, wo man neapel erwartete.
so kam ich ins land der verwitterten stetsons,
mit denen tornados ihr football spielen.
hi friends ohne stiefel und colts!

II
Freundlich blasen die klimaanlagen
in meinen gezuckerten eistee.
so gross wie die steaks sind die freundlichkeiten
der braunen leute in den büros,
bei mc donalds und seven-eleven;
auch der mann mit zigarre im lift, der dich fragt
jeden morgen: wie gehts?
als ob er nur wegen dir schlecht schläft.
und diese frau von der telephone comp.,
die dir von deiner heimat vorschwärmt,
als wärst du identisch mit der.

III
Du fragst dich: wo sind die rüstungsbetriebe
inmitten der parks und bäder und wiesen—
die trusts und konzerne, texaco?
wird nicht von hier die hälfte der welt regiert?
aber auf den zu breiten strassen
bummeln nur freizeitmenschen
in ihren lässigen jeans und teashirts:
die waren in chile? korea?
in vietnam und kambodscha? in laos?
in panama, el salvador?
freilich, man wirbt für die navy,
aber im hintergrund. breit davor, freundlich,
grüsst dich ein longhorn von stadionwänden,
dich, greenhorn in northern american affairs.
doch geht ein mann tief gebückt vorbei.
auf seinem rücken ein zeichen:
chicano power!

IV

a
100.000 lagern im grass rund um die steiner-ranch:
summer farewell, bei 40 Grad. es spielen auf riesiger bühne
chicago, The band und joe cocker woodstock;
100.000 verfolgen mit grossen pupillen
die flüge der frisbees über der menge,
die kreise der geier und helicopter,
bewacht von schwitzenden sherrifs, den colt am gürtel:
no glass containers, no tapes and no cameras.
wir feiern die freiheit des picknicks und summen
unter dem schleier von marihauna.
schmetterlinge umgaukeln tiefschwarze hondas.

b
Aber auch eine grosse ruhe: sechs stunden
standen in endlosen schlangen, in zweierreihe,
die autos am high-way
und keiner hupte.
auf allen dächern im vollmond
knacken die leute die letzten dosen
mit Coke oder Budweiser Beer.
und reden und singen und tauschen
eis gegen zigaretten. noch nie
sah ich bei uns so viele menschen geduldig.
mit denen wäre kein krieg zu gewinnen,
wäre kein krieg zu gewinnen,
gott seis gedankt, nur friedensfeuer
brennen entlang der landstrasse 2002.
(und dass uns um 4 dann am morgen,
als alles losfuhr, der wagen verreckte,
kommt schliesslich auch anderswo vor.)

V

Hier kann man alles kaufen.
die drugstores und drive-ins sind voll
von waren, und jeder ist billiger als der nachbar.
he man: cash & carry,
solang du noch einen dollar hast.
lässig baumeln im kühlenden luftzug
kampfanzüge gleich neben shirts.
und an der kassa bekommst du
die grössten springmesser, die ich je sah.

weiter oben auf dem regal
wartet granatwerfermunition
auf einen kunden, der sie entschärft.

VI
bilder aus filmen: die grossen viertel
ausserhalb auf den hügeln. villen
wie aus prospekten, versteckt in gärten
mit palmen und blumen und schönen hunden.
da geht die sonne nie unter
über dem seltsamsten gras der welt:
hell leuchten die swimmingpools
den gutverdienten mittelklassen.
sie füttern zufrieden die kolibris
in den reklamepausen des kabelfernsehens
und lassen in ihren vierteln
die zwei drei autos noch unversperrt.
(Die neger und texmex und mexicaner
leben im osten der stadt).[7]

(I
What I couldn't believe: the expanse
after all the canyons of manhattan,
the green at the height of Mauretania
and the brown of faded pictures
where one expected Naples.
so I came into the land of weathered stetsons
with which tornados play football.
hi friends without boots and colts!

II
The air conditioners blow amiably
into my sugared ice tea.
as large as the steaks is the friendliness
of the brown people in the offices,
at mcdonalds and seven-eleven;
even the man with the cigar in the elevator, who asks you
every morning: how are you?
as though he doesn't sleep well only because of you.
and this woman from the telephone comp.,
who raves to you about your homeland
as though you were identical with it.

III
You wonder: where are the armament works
in the midst of parks and pools and meadows—
the trusts and concerns, texaco?
isn't half of the world governed from here?
but on the too broad avenues
only leisure-time people stroll
in their loose jeans and T-shirts:
they were in chile? korea?
in vietnam and cambodia? in laos?
in panama, el salvador?
admittedly, there's navy recruiting,
but in the background. broadly in front, friendly,
a longhorn greets you from the stadium walls,
you, greenhorn in north american affairs.
but a man walks past bent far over.
on his back a sign:
chicano power!

IV
a
100,000 camp in the grass around the steiner ranch:
farewell to summer, at 96 degrees. on a gigantic stage
chicago, The band, and joe cocker play woodstock;
100,000 follow with big eyes
the flights of the frisbees over the throng,
the circling of vultures and helicopters,
watched by sweating sheriffs, colts in their belts:
no glass containers, no tapes and no cameras.
we celebrate the freedom of picnics and hum
under the veil of marijuana.
butterflies hover around dark black hondas.
b
But also an immense quiet: for six hours
in endless lines, two abreast,
the cars stood on the highway.
and not one honked.
on all the car roofs under the full moon
the people pop open the last cans
of Cokes or Budweiser Beer.
and talk and sing and trade
ice for cigarettes. not ever

did I see at home so many patient people.
with them no war could be won,
no war could be won,
thank god, only peace fires
burn along ranch road 2002.
[and that at 4 a.m. then,
when everything began to move, our car expired
occurs elsewhere too anyway.]

V
Here you can buy anything.
the drugstores and drive-ins are full
of goods, and each one is cheaper than its neighbor.
Hey man: Cash & carry,
as long as you have another dollar.
casually in the cooling draft of air
army fatigues billow right next to shirts.
and at the cash register you can get
the biggest switchblade I ever saw.
farther up on the shelf
wait grenade-launcher shells
for a customer who can disarm them.

VI
Pictures from the movies: the large neighborhood
outside on the hills. villas
like in prospectuses, hidden in gardens
with palms and flowers and beautiful dogs.
there the sun never sets
over the strangest grass in the world.
brightly the swimming pools illuminate
the prosperous middle classes.
they contentedly feed the hummingbirds
during the ads on the cable television
and leave the two three cars
in their driveways unlocked.
[the Negroes and Tex-Mexes and Mexicans live
in the east part of town.])

The Texas of Wallner is even more in the twentieth century: his friends wear neither boots nor Colts but bluejeans and T-shirts. Like all his countrymen he finds the mixture of air-conditioning and iced tea almost unbearable. But the Texans epitomize friendliness with a cordiality as large as their steaks. The Texans are patient and peaceful, contrary to what one might expect. Wallner might be faulted for believing the grenade-launcher shells he sees in a store are loaded, but he shares the amazement of other visitors at the Texas carpet grass. And like other writers, he uses many American, if not Texan, phrases mixed in casually and precisely in the midst of his German. It's a different world from that of his native Salzburg, but the reader feels Wallner's genuine pleasure, his sometimes open-mouthed wonder (und keiner hupte—and not one honked), and his acceptance of a Texas adventure.

Another young writer, Fred Viebahn, found nostalgia in Austin, an identification with a figure from his own younger, record-listening days. He preserves that feeling, with the inevitable touch of Texas, in his poem "Janis in Austin"; Viebahn begins his poem with a quotation from the biography of Janis Joplin by Myra Friedman, *Buried Alive*: "She sang blues like Bessie Smith, with her notes as open as the Texas sky."

> Neunzehnte Strasse, Ecke Nueces, hat sie gelebt,
> doch meistens war sie im Ghetto, dem Apartment-
> komplex sechs Blocks vom Campus, und probte
> mit ihren Freunden den musikalischen Ernstfall:
> Kinder armer Studenten schrien nach der Mutter.
> Hier, in den renovierten Gebäude der Texas
> Students Union, vor zwei Wochen eröffnet nach
> dreijähriger Umbauzeit, sah ich sie gestern
> abend, sechseinhalb Jahre nach ihrem Tod, rasend
> lebendig, in Pennebakers Monterey-Film; hier
> hat ein dickes Mädchen aus der Provinz manchen
> Sonntag gesungen, trieb ihre Stimme zusätzlich
> Schweiss den nicht allzu vielen, die sie damals
> erkannten in den schwülen Sommernächten von
> Austin.
> Eines Nachts nahm das dicke Mädchen eine
> Überdosis Heroin: längst warn überwunden die
> widrigen Anfänge ihrer Karriere, war sie
> nach San Francisco gegangen mit Blumen im
> Haar, hatte erobert Fans und Titelseiten der

bedeutendsten Magazine, war auf die grössten
Bühnen gesprungen, und ihre wilde Stimme
tobte aus Heimlautsprechern in die Wohnräume
derer, die sie gehasst hatten früher als sie
verriet ihrer Mittelklasse brave Eintönigkeit.
Durch Kopfhörer dröhnte sie jetzt in mir,
"alive"; unter den Schlägen der Konsonanten,
getroffen von den Pfeilen der Vokale, geschüttelt
von der Begleitmusik, unter Strom gesetzt
von der Elektronik zuckt mein Körper im
Schallplattenladen, auf dem Weg vom Campus
zur Neunzehnten Strasse, Ecke Nueces. Ob sie
auch manchmal in der Sonne am Town Lake lag?
Das Haus nebenbei, in dem ich wohne, stand
damals noch nicht: dort war Wiese. So
verschiebt sich das Bild mit den Jahren.
Geblieben ist nur (abgesehen von den starren
Dingen) der texanische Himmel, täuschend
ähnlich unerreichbarer Freiheit.[8]

(Nineteenth Street, corner of Nueces, she lived
but mostly she was in the ghetto, the apartment
complex six blocks from the campus, and with
her friends rehearsed the musical moment of
truth: children of poor students cried for their mothers.
Here, in the renovated building of the Texas
Student Union opened up two weeks ago after
a three-year reconstruction I saw her yesterday
evening, six-and-a-half years after her death,
frantically alive, in Pennebaker's film
"Monterey"; here a fat girl from the sticks
sang on many a Sunday, her voice brought more
perspiration to the not too many who knew
her then in the humid summer nights of
Austin.
One night the fat girl took an overdose of
heroin; long ago the adverse beginnings of
her career were overcome, she had gone to San
Francisco with flowers in her hair, had
conquered fans and the covers of the most
important magazines, had jumped onto the largest
stages, and her wild voice romped from home

loudspeakers in the living rooms of those whom
she had earlier hated, when she betrayed
the nice monotony of her middle class.
Through earphones she now boomed into me,
"alive"; under the blows of the consonants,
struck by the arrows of the vowels, shaken by
the accompaniment, electrocuted by the
electronics my body jerks in the record store,
on the way from the campus to Nineteenth
Street, corner of Nueces. Did she sometimes
lie in the sun at Town Lake? The house nearby,
in which I live, was not standing then:
a meadow was there. So changes the image with
the years. What remains is only the Texas
sky [aside from immovable things], deceptively
similar to unattainable freedom.)

Viebahn is not the first German writer to find some part of himself in Texas, some part of his past, whether it be the legendary Texas of Wild West stories or the mythical Texas of the twentieth century with its wide-open sky and its singer of rock melodies and her sad destiny.

I have not mentioned the Texas connections of Martin Walser, Max Frisch, Rolf Dieter Brinkmann, Friederike Mayröcker, Peter Rühmkorf, Hans Bender, Uwe Johnson—because I have discussed them elsewhere. No doubt there are comments and observations by other German-language travelers in Texas in recent years, almost all of whom winged their way to Texas with visions of cactus and cowboys, and when they landed found that Texas was indeed vast, friendly, informal, and wildly natural, as they expected. But as Texas and Texans make their way into contemporary German writing, the myth of the Lone Star State is undergoing the inevitable change the age demands, with the paradox that the demythologizing of Texas is producing a phoenixlike rebirth of a twentieth-century Texas myth, of a land that is still legendary enough to intrigue and fascinate the German-writing visitor today.

Part of the new myth is the German writer who comes to Texas but does not disappear—not literally, as Herburger puts it—but who returns to his homeland a different person, struck with the magic of Texas and its people, indelibly marked by Texas, and having left the mark of Texas in the German literature of his day.

CHAPTER 13

Appraisal and Outlook

DONA B. REEVES

AN advertised objective of the 1978 Southwest Symposium was the discovery of areas of Texas-German cultural survival. The heavy attendance at the symposium by all age groups would seem to indicate that a genuine concern for such cultural survival exists, that even though the older generation preserves artifacts and language, the younger generation declares its willingness to interpret and retrieve, and that further exploration will provide steady source material for continuing interpretation, combination, recombination, and evaluation.

It is impossible to be impartial about Texas. Travelers who ventured out of Texas from the earliest times until the present can verify that people of all social strata, education, and ages throughout the world have heard of Texas and are eager to affirm its virtues or vices—but seldom both. For many, Texas is an emotion, a psychic and physical reaction to a social, historical, and geographic concept, to the "progression of metaphors" of which it is composed. For others, Texas is "pop culture." It is, if nothing else, a viable and common topic of research for historians, sociologists, naturalists, psychologists, ethnologists, linguists, and an assortment of other scientists. Texas has charisma.

The unexpectedly enthusiastic public response to the symposium at which these essays were presented is explained in part by the myth and the emotion of Texas. In addition, however, its success derives from the same factors which in San Antonio brought 3,000 guests to a "German Christmas" cele-

Appraisal and Outlook

bration at the end of 1977 and over 100,000 to the Texas Folklife Festival in 1978, that is, from what journalists and folklorists variously describe as a search for roots or a quest for self-identification. All ethnic groups share this attraction equally, and more and more, the German-Americans, that is, the German Texans, are being recognized as an ethnic group.[1]

The essays combined that charisma with the role of one ethnic group as a constituent in the larger dynamic progression. In this role, the examination was largely from within the group, the German migrant view, an approach which is subject to the risks of adulation and ethnocentrism. It may well be the task of subsequent research to sort out the "filiopietistic" and to ponder the total view, that is, the "Texan" view of the German migrant.

How diverse the "Texan" and the German perspectives were can best be illustrated by two incidents from the early history of Texas. They are representative of two cultures in collision and serve to summarize the underlying difficulty facing the German arrival in a new, democratic, and frontier environment.

The first event focuses on the second president of the Republic of Texas, the intellectual, aristocratic visionary Mirabeau B. Lamar. On the eve of dispatching Texan troops to establish commercial and diplomatic alliances with the settlements of what is now New Mexico, commonly referred to as the Texan–Santa Fe expedition, Lamar joined the encampment on the banks of Brushy Creek for their last night, roughing it with his volunteers, cooking his own steak over an open fire, and spreading a single blanket on the ground for his overnight stay.[2]

The second incident involves the Texas sojourn of Prince Solms as reported by Rosa von Roeder Kleberg, who already sensed the collision of opposing cultures. She reports a visit by the prince, who arrived dressed in a German military uniform and accompanied by his courtly retinue. After he asked that coffee be made for him, she continues, "he impressed me as a conceited fool. He was unwilling to eat at the same table with the other people—a manner of conduct which, I fancy, did not raise him in the estimation of the American farmers."[3]

Two leaders of men, two illustrious and respected figures,

both destined to contribute in a unique and immeasurable way to the development of the state, reacted to a similar situation in a culturally distinct manner. Every German migrant had, of course, to approach his new environment in his own way; Rosa von Roeder Kleberg recalled the visit of the prince in her later years, with the advantage of having made such an adjustment. Perhaps her adjustment was unusually rapid, but we must wonder if her impression of the prince's conceit was an immediate or an acquired reaction. In the social history of the German in Texas, we read but little about the migrant who could not adjust, who returned to Germany, or who remained and turned to crime or to alcohol as a response to the promise of America. It is probably fitting that we not consider the darker figures in the assimilatory process, for they fall outside the mainstream of interpretation and the direction of the German component of Texan culture. However, the existence of such darker figures proves the difficulty, or the impossibility, of the cultural encounter.

While most of the symposium essays necessarily concentrated on the establishment years of German culture in Texas, namely the years of the Republic of Texas, the nascent Adelsverein colonies, the Forty-Eighters, and the life span of the first immigrants, Lich, Walker, Ragsdale, Heinen, and G. Jordan related the promise and problems of those years to the present with some resulting hypotheses:

1) the Romantic ideal of a "transatlantic Europe," fundamental to the organized emigration attempt of the Giessener Gesellschaft and the Adelsverein, was absorbed by the practical Texan consideration that the prosperity of the group depended on political, social, and economic assimilation;

2) the same ideal which spurred the German migrant to Texas directed him, until 1865, into the ideological frustration of the American Civil War, while the fulfillment of that ideal in 1871 in his old homeland without his participation further isolated him from both cultures;

3) in spite of spirited intellectual beginnings, the utopian venture found itself without substance and directed inward, only to be eclipsed by a myth of the West that yielded a German element largely disassociated with and disinterested in political activism;

Appraisal and Outlook

4) small-town social life in Germany transplanted successfully to the *Vereinsleben* of Texas, generally by means of close-knit family ties and a shared emigration experience;

5) the supportive role of women did not change dramatically in the move to Texas, but contrasted in some degrees with that of the rural Anglo-Texan women;

6) a cultural heritage in the sense of "high" culture was important to the migrant in Texas if it had been important before emigration, but in general, reading was probably considered more important to the German migrant and his children than to the "Texan," and in school, the German "classics" were stressed until the arrival of Sputnik; and

7) traditions associated with year and life celebrations provide the richest area of cultural or folklore survival, very often of linguistic survival as well.

Selected features of the German experience in Texas are best described as points in a continuum, as in the essays of T. Jordan and Sass. The continuing assimilation process is seen in its clearest form in the choices made by the German Texan for his habitat. While some log cabins and *Fachwerk* structures continue to be occupied and restored and studied by descendants of immigrant families, the urge to be regarded as Americans and the availability of cheap lumber led the immigrant to adopt more standard Anglo-American forms of architecture as rapidly as means might afford. Like folk architecture, faith, or its absence, can also be viewed as a continuing force. The influence, or lack of influence, of the transfer of church and religion to the frontier becomes evident in the social patterns and landscapes of the German communities today. In like manner, the contributions of individuals such as Ernst Kapp or John Meusebach, two of what may prove to be an army of wielders and molders, are equally valid from the perspective of their lifetime in Texas as well as from the focus of the present and foreseeable future.

Other uniquely German areas for investigation mentioned by Abernethy are and must be limited to the past; their relevance to the present and future has yet to be discovered. The practice of medicine, where once the German-Texan scientist found himself at the vanguard, has given way to the modern anonymity of a highly regulated profession, save in a few—even more anonymous—*Braucherei* practices in which folk medicine is allowed to follow its ancient patterns. Architecture, once a distinguishing feature of the German immigrant, has assimilated into a corporate image. In these two areas, however, much can be done to preserve the features which still exist.

Two essays were devoted entirely to the present. Gilbert suggests topics for further research in the surviving vestiges of the German language, and Willson describes the continuing adventure of Texas for the German migrant. The twentieth-century intellectual repeats much of the encounter of the free-thinking political émigré of the mid-nineteenth century. Common to both is what Willson calls the "planes of cultural shock," largely conditioned by an awareness of the immensity of nature, here so far less hospitable than in the homeland. Inevitably, acclimatization for the German is a process nearly as complex and as hazardous as acculturation, but the very rawness of nature and the expansive landscape were and remain part of the myth of Texas.

The symposium evaluation forms yield a conformation of future research possibilities. While the function of the symposium was primarily interpretative and exploratory rather than informative or instructive, participants willingly identified research topics needed but not found within the limits of a two-day conference. Beyond the call for more biographies, more regional, as well as urban-rural, concentration, including far west Texas and the Russian-Germans of Texas, and more family history-genealogy (from sixty-five to seventy participants [20 percent] attended the genealogy workshop held in conjunction with the symposium), the most fruitful area of further investigation would seem to be a continuing analysis and identification of the source of Texas-German ideals, opinions, and thought patterns. We continue to probe the manner of transfer of ideas from Germany to Texas, the shift of the Texas Germans from an initially agrarian economy to a broader range of subsistence, and the disruption of this process caused by the Civil War and two World Wars. So essential is this study to an understanding of the culture that we have felt the need to include two essays in this volume not originally given in the Southwest

Appraisal and Outlook

Symposium: "Goethe on the Guadalupe" and "The German Woman in Frontier Texas."

Additional social and demographic descriptions must provide a foundation for synchronic and diachronic investigations of the interaction of the German Texan with other ethnic groups, for example, with the Mexican Texans or the Czech Texans. Not to be excluded is the encounter of the German Texan with the native American, expanding and continuing a theme already touched by Biesele.[4] Included under this aegis might well be a causative study of the German Texans who went on to California, Mexico, or St. Louis, or who returned to Germany. The function of social organizations (*Schützenvereine, Kegelvereine, Gesangvereine,* etc.) as an assimilatory factor and as descriptors of a values system should progress beyond historical description. The need for a purely descriptive or cataloging treatment of certain artistic and folklore themes is urgent, but such treatment should then also attempt to explain and define the significance of, for example, music, painting, photography, architecture, folk medicine, the decorative and culinary arts, crafts, tools, practice of agriculture and conservation, journalism, literature, or technology or science for the time, the place, and the ethic considered. The same holds true for some needed historical investigations, namely the Texas-German part in the Mexican War of 1846, in Reconstruction Texas, or, for that matter, on the researchers of the Texas Germans (Biesele, Haas, Oheim, Ransleben, et al.).

Finally, the importance of the educational system cannot be overlooked. The schools of the Texas Germans were set apart by location, by textbooks, and sometimes by language, not to mention by curriculum and teachers. El-Beheri's[5] description of the German-English school of San Antonio is an example worthy of imitation, not simply because of its analytic approach, but also because of its blending of past and present educational values. Of course, it is necessary to provide a German-language foundation for any research on the German Texans; without question, German language study should be a part of every level of instruction from elementary through continuing education wherever it is desired; and surely, a German-Texan culture component can be added as a part of curriculum from preschool onward. One participant suggested the possibility of advanced students serving internships in German-Texan communities in order to experience the German-Texan manner of living and to conduct research.

In conclusion, we must ask to what degree the Texan response of an Ernst Kapp, Richard Petri, Ferdinand Lindheimer, or Ottilie Fuchs Goeth was typical of the German migrant. As Heinen pointed out, not all German migrants were highly educated, not all had the same motives for immigration or reacted to Texas in the same way. Not all were kept from writing books because they were too busy making a living. However, Walker found a motive common to the Forty-Eighters and the "general crowd" alike in the urge to escape a crushing bureaucracy. Seeking home-peace-stability, the Biedermeier ideals, the migrant found them—or failed to find them—in a Texas version defined by his own determination, organic environment, and the course of Texas history. Succeeding generations adapted that version to their own needs or perceptions of needs. Perhaps the Texas-born generations of the German immigrants better define German-Texan culture, for they preserve the traditions described by G. Jordan, Abernethy, and Ragsdale, in large measure without contact with or immediate knowledge of Germany. For them, Texas is the reality; Germany is, at most, the memory shared.

Notes and References

Chapter One

1. Friedrich Schlegel, *Dialogue on Poetry and Literary Aphorisms*, trans. and ed. Ernst Behler and Roman Struc (University Park: Pennsylvania State Univ. Press, 1968), pp. 43, 143.

2. Sigrid Bauschinger, Horst Denkler, and Wilfried Malsch, eds., *Amerika in der deutschen Literatur: Neue Welt-Nordamerika-USA* (Stuttgart: Reclam, 1975), pp. 63–74.

3. Karl Arndt, "The Harmony Society and Wilhelm Meisters Wanderjahre," *Comparative Literature*, 10 (1958), 196.

4. Thomas Carlyle, *Wilhelm Meister's Apprenticeship and Travels: Translated from the German of Goethe*, Vol. 25 in *The Works of Thomas Carlyle in Thirty Volumes*, Centenary Edition (New York: AMS Press, 1969), p. 11.

5. Arnold Bergstraesser, *Goethe's Image of Man and Society* (Chicago: Regnery, 1949), pp. 314–15.

6. Arndt, pp. 195–96, makes a rather cumbersome distinction when he discusses *Wilhelm Meister* not as a whole (as English readers have it in Carlyle's translation) but in terms of its three separate stages: *Wilhelm Meisters Theatralische Sendung* (1777), *Wilhelm Meisters Lehrjahre* (1821), and *Wilhelm Meisters Wanderjahre* (1826). The final interpretation of "America" as allegory is the same, but Arndt is able to identify a progression—and I feel a valid one—which Lange and other critics frequently pass over. Arndt writes,"*Wilhelm Meister* reflects the changing spirit of an age, and a study of its genesis from the *Theatralische Sendung* to the revised *Wanderjahre* reveals Goethe's decreasing faith in the future of Europe and his growing faith in America. The *Sendung* does not even mention America, while the *Lehrjahre* pictures America as a land of temporary adventure from which Lothario returns with the conviction, 'Hier oder nirgends ist America.' It was between 1821 and 1829 that the 'Americanization' of *Wilhelm Meister* set in, and the *Wanderjahre* changed completely from a work concerned with 'Wandern' to one concerned with 'Auswandern'" (p. 195). This distinction is crucial to Arndt's thesis associating the

Auswanderungsstaat of the *Wanderjahre* with Rapp's Harmonists, since he demonstrates that the *Wanderjahre* was written subsequent to Goethe's likely association with George Rapp in Württemberg. The "thorn in the flesh," though, of literary source study is that even firm proof of association merely "suggests" influence. With a man of Goethe's manifold interests, the source critic constantly risks oversimplification.

7. Carlyle, Vol. 24, p. 370.

8. Harold von Hofe, "August Wilhelm Schlegel's American Emigration Plans: Biographical-Literary Notes," *Wert und Wort: Festschrift fur Else M. Fleissner*, eds. Marion Sonnefeld et al. (Aurora, New York: Wells College, 1965), p. 23.

9. J. G. Robertson, *A History of German Literature*, 6th ed. by Dorothy Reich (Edinburgh: Blackwood, 1970), p. 360.

10. Robertson, p. 331.

11. George Steiner, in *After Babel: Aspects of Language and Translation* (London: Oxford Univ. Press, 1975), p. 80, writes of Wilhelm von Humboldt that, "like Goethe, he held the individual fact to be, as it were, shone through by the constant energies of universal, organic unity," For both brothers, Steiner continues, "it is the great weave and pulse of life itself that gives to each isolated phenomenon (isolated only because we may not yet have perceived the surrounding field of force) its meaning.... Ethnographers, anthropologists, linguists, statesmen, educators, the two brothers were a nerve-centre for humanistic and scientific inquiry."

12. William H. Goetzmann, *Exploration and Empire: The Explorer and the Scientist in the Winning of the American West* (New York: Knopf, 1966), p. 214.

13. Hofe, p. 30.

14. Regarding this association of noblemen it is interesting to note a comment by Arthur E. Bestor in the work *Backwoods Utopias: The Sectarian and Owenite Phases of Communitarian Socialism in America, 1663–1829* (Philadelphia: Univ. of Pennsylvania Press, 1950): "Students of Germanic institutions, notably Otto von Gierke, have traced this feeling for the group far back into medieval political philosophy and jurisprudence. Whereas the Roman codes were generally suspicious of associations, and granted the privilege of incorporation grudgingly, Germanic law, Gierke points out, was remarkable for the encouragement it gave to the formation of an association or fellowship (*Genossenschaft*)" (p. 16).

15. Duden's *Bericht über eine Reise nach den westlichen Staaten Nordamerikas*, Vol. 43, is quoted in Rudolph L. Biesele, *The History*

Notes and References

of the German Settlements in Texas: 1831–1861 (Austin: Von Boeckmann, 1930), p. 3.

16. Charles Sealsfield (Karl Postl), *The Making of an American. An Adaptation of Memorable Tales by Charles Sealsfield*, trans. Ulrich S. Carrington (Dallas: Southern Methodist Univ. Press, 1974), p. 27. Further references are given parenthetically in the text. See also A. Leslie Willson, "Another Planet: Texas in German Literature," *Texas and Germany: Crosscurrents*, ed. Joseph Wilson, Rice University Studies, 63, No. 3 (1977), 101–109.

17. Kleberg wrote this account in 1876; see Caroline Ernst von Hinüber, "Life of German Pioneers in Early Texas," *Texas State Historical Association Quarterly*, 2 (1899), fn. p. 228.

18. Biesele, *History of the German Settlements in Texas*, p. 69.

19. Otto W. Tetzlaff, "A Guide for German Immigrants," *Texas and Germany: Crosscurrents*, ed. Joseph Wilson, Rice University Studies, 63, No. 3 (1977), 14.

20. Letter to the Mainzer Adelsverein, February 1845, is quoted in Irene Marschall King, *John O. Meusebach: German Colonizer in Texas* (Austin: Univ. of Texas Press, 1967), p. 59.

21. German emigrants to the new land contracted with the society for the following, upon payment of fees: 1) passage and transportation; 2) a log cabin, or building materials, or a Mexican-style house; 3) 320 acres of land for a family, or 160 acres for a single man; 4) fencing material and seeds; 5) specified livestock; 6) the services of a community (church, hospital, mills, gins); and 7) a plow and a wagon.

22. Ottilie Fuchs Goeth, *Memoirs of a Texas Pioneer Grandmother (Was Grossmutter Erzaehlt: 1805–1915)*, trans. Irma Goeth Guenther (Austin: n.p., 1969), pp. 15–16.

23. Based on Moritz Tiling; see estimates in Terry G. Jordan, *German Seed in Texas Soil: Immigrant Farmers in Nineteenth-Century Texas* (Austin: Univ. of Texas Press, 1966), p. 50.

24. Frank J. Coppa and Thomas Curran, "From the Rhine to the Mississippi: The German Emigration to the United States," in *The Immigrant Experience in America*, The Immigrant Heritage of America, ed. Cecyle S. Neidle (Boston: Twayne, 1976), p. 51.

25. According to Robert V. Hine in *California's Utopian Colonies* (New Haven: Yale Univ. Press, 1966), "A utopian colony consists of a group of people who are attempting to establish a new social pattern based upon a vision of the ideal society and who have withdrawn themselves from the community at large to embody that vision in experimental form" (p. 5).

26. Arthur Eugene Bestor, *Backwoods Utopias: The Secretarian and Owenite Phases of Communitarian Socialism in America, 1663–1829* (Philadelphia: Univ. of Pennsylvania Press, 1950), p. 1.
27. Henry Nash Smith, *Virgin Land: The American West as Symbol and Myth* (Cambridge: Harvard Univ. Press, 1950), p. 170.
28. King, pp. 23–24.
29. King, p. 30.
30. Letter to Count Castell, Berlin, 24 October 1844, is quoted in King, p. 32.
31. King, pp. 145–48.
32. King, p. 173.
33. Georg Bunsen, Gustav Bunsen (who was killed in the Texas Revolution), and A. Berchtelmann, Lindheimer's colleagues from the Erziehungsantalt; Gustav Körner, later lieutenant-governor of Illinois and law associate of Abraham Lincoln; and Georg Engelmann and his brothers Theodor and Adolf—eminent botanists.
34. Victor Wolfgang von Hagen, *The Germanic People in America* (Norman: Univ. of Oklahoma Press, 1976), p. 280.
35. Samuel W. Geiser, *Naturalists of the Frontier* (Dallas: Southern Methodist Univ. Press, 1948), p. 136.
36. Geiser, *Naturalists of the Frontier*, pp. 137–39. For a picture of Lindheimer's contributions to Asa Gray's botanical research, see William H. Goetzmann, *Exploration and Empire*, pp. 321–23. See also A. Hunter Dupree, *Asa Gray* (Cambridge: Belknap Press, 1959), pp. 185–96, 211–12, 252–63.
37. Ferdinand von Roemer, *Texas: With Particular Reference to German Immigration and The Physical Appearance of the Country*, trans. Oswald Mueller (1935; rpt. Waco: Texian, 1967), p. 137.
38. Auguste Ervendberg Wiegreffe, "Pioneer Times in New Braunfels," *San Antonio Express*, 8 September 1935, interview by Sarah S. McKeller.
39. Geiser, *Naturalists of the Frontier*, p. 147. Letter from Gray Herbarium to the Institute of Texan Cultures, 5 July 1967.
40. Geiser, *Naturalists of the Frontier*, p. 150.
41. Between his graduation in 1842 and his death in 1891, Ferdinand von Roemer published over 350 items; for further information, see Frederic W. Simonds, "Dr. Ferdinand von Roemer, the Father of the Geology of Texas; His Life and Work," *American Geologist*, 29 (1902), 131–40. Although Roemer's name is omitted in Goetzmann's *Exploration and Empire*, his investigations in Texas of earth-shaping forces and geological history would almost serve

Notes and References

as a model of the subsequent geological reconnaissances undertaken throughout the West and Southwest.

42. Roemer, p. 137. Further references to this work are given parenthetically in the text.

43. Geiser, *Naturalists of the Frontier*, p. 171.

44. Louis Reinhardt, "The Communistic Colony of Bettina," *Texas State Historical Association Quarterly*, 3 (1899), 33–34.

45. Letter from Count Castell to Meusebach, Wiesbaden, 28 January 1847 (Solms-Braunfels Archiv, Sophienburg, New Braunfels).

46. Bestor, p. 14.

47. Reinhardt, p. 34. Bestor attempts to clarify a confusion of terms in recent scholarship: "The very year 1840 that saw the birth of the word *communism* saw also the creation of the terms *communitarian* and *communitarianism*.... These words derived immediately from *community*, and they soon came to signify a system of social reform based on small communities" (viii).

48. Reinhardt, p. 34.

49. Ibid., pp. 34–35. Apparently seven members dropped out before leaving Germany.

50. Bestor, p. 3.

51. Cited in Bestor, p. 13.

52. Wilhelm Hermes, "To the Emigration Company Land on the Llano, Experiences of a German Immigrant in Texas," November 1846, is quoted in Oscar Haas, *The History of New Braunfels and Comal County, 1844–1946* (Austin: Hart, 1968), pp. 42–43.

53. Reinhardt, p. 39.

54. Ibid.

55. Henry B. Dielmann, "Dr. Ferdinand Herff, Pioneer Physician and Surgeon," *Southwestern Historical Quarterly*, 57 (1954), 268–69.

56. Dielmann, p. 276.

57. For a lengthier treatment, see Arthur L. Finck's translation of Herff's work (Thesis, Univ. of Texas, 1949), pp. 24–29.

58. Carl J. Friedrich, in "The European Background," in *The Forty-Eighters: Political Refugees of the German Revolution of 1848*, ed. Adolf D. Zucker (New York: Columbia, 1950), p. 12, maintains, in an interesting comparison, that "the continuing influence of Goethe and the German idealistic philosophers, as represented by the Forty-Eighters, can be seen in the Middle West by the St. Louis Movement in Philosophy to which Goethe's *Faust* appealed particularly. The deep link between the final views of Faust and the outlook of the settlers in America was constantly stressed by Denton J. Snider, a prominent writer in the movement. Snider wrote:

Faust becomes the settler, the frontiersman on a vast ocean of savagery, he becomes the American, transforming a wild continent into the habitable abode of rational man. Often we have said, much oftener have we thought, that this Second Part of *Faust* in many portions seems an American Book, or rather the *Mythus* of America, in its settlement and conquest, as well as in its spiritual significance. That old Europe has not fully appreciated the book, cannot perhaps; but here we can see the mythical forms turning to living facts before our eyes.

59. Franz Kettner, "Letters of a German Pioneer in Texas," *Southwestern Historical Quarterly*, 69 (1965), 465–66, trans. Terry G. Jordan and Marlis Anderson Jordan.
60. Carl Wittke, *Refugees of Revolution: The German Forty-Eighters in America* (Westport, Conn.: Greenwood, 1952), p. 78.
61. Ibid., p. i.
62. Biesele, *History of the German Settlements in Texas*, p. 172.
63. Friedrich Kapp is quoted in Wittke, *Refugees of Revolution*, p. 119.
64. Theodore Huebener, *The Germans in America* (Philadelphia: Chilton, 1962), pp. 102–103.
65. Paul C. Ragsdale, "Ottomar von Behr," *The Handbook of Texas*, Vol. 3, Eldon Stephen Branda, ed. (Austin: Texas State Historical Association, 1976), p. 1070.
66. August Siemering, "Sisterdale," trans. from MS in Dresel file, San Antonio Public Library. (Further references to Siemering's account of Sisterdale come from this source.)
67. Adolf E. Zucker, "Biographical Dictionary of the Forty-Eighters," in *The Forty-Eighters: Political Refugees of the German Revolution of 1848* (New York: Columbia Univ. Press, 1950), p. 288.
68. Siemering, "Sisterdale."
69. Hans-Martin Sass, "Die philosophische Erdkunde des Hegelianers Ernst Kapp: Ein Beitrag zur Wissenschaftstheorie und Fortschrittsdiskussion in der Hegelschule," *Hegel-Studien*, ed. Friedhelm Nicolin and Otto Pöggeler (Bonn: Bouvier, 1973), pp. 163–81. For the impact of such works as Kapp's, see Herbert Marcuse, "Der Einfluss der deutschen Emigration auf das amerikanische Geistesleben: Philosophie und Soziologie," *Jahrbuch für Amerikastudien*, 10 (1965), 27–33.
70. Ernst Kapp, "Letter," 1849, trans. Oscar Haas, *New Braunfels Herald and Zeitung*, 20 July 1972.
71. Ida Kappell Kapp, "Letter," Comaltown, 13 January 1850, trans. Oscar Haas, *New Braunfels Herald and Zeitung*, 20 July 1972. Further references are given parenthetically in the text.

Notes and References

72. Georg Carl Willrich, Letter; Mt. Eliza, Fayette County, Texas, 1850; trans. Minnie Groos Wilkins (San Antonio: n.p., 1952).
73. Friedrich Kapp is quoted in Wittke, *Refugees of Revolution*, p. 115.
74. Friedrich Kapp is quoted in Hagen, p. 293.
75. Friedrich Kapp is quoted in Lawrence S. Thompson and Frank X. Braun, "The Forty-Eighters in Politics," in *The Forty-Eighters: Political Refugees of the German Revolution of 1848*, ed. Adolf E. Zucker (New York: Columbia Univ. Press, 1950), p. 121.
76. Friedrich Kapp is quoted in Hagen, p. 229.
77. Goeth, p. 23.
78. Friedrich Kapp is quoted in Wittke, *Refugees of Revolution*, p. 92.
79. August Siemering, "Texas, Her Past, Her Present, Her Future," trans. from *Texas Vorwärts*, 1894.
80. *History of the German Settlements in Texas*, p. 202.
81. Resignation as officer of the Provisional Army of the Confederate States, Rebel Archives, Record Division, War Dept.
82. John W. Sansom is quoted in Guido E. Ransleben, *A Hundred Years of Comfort in Texas: A Centennial History* (San Antonio: Naylor, 1954), p. 105. John L. Waller, *Colossal Hamilton of Texas: A Biography of Andrew Jackson Hamilton, Militant Unionist and Reconstruction Governor* (El Paso: Texas Western, 1968), p. 36.
83. Siemering, "Texas."
84. Goeth, p. 48.
85. Friedrich Kapp is quoted in Wittke, *Refugees of Revolution*, p. 92.
86. Flach, pp. 52, 8.

Chapter Three

1. Ernst Kapp, *Philosophische oder vergleichende allgemeine Erdkunde als wissenschaftliche Darstellung der Erdverhältnisse und des Menschenlebens nach ihrem inneren Zusammenhang*, Vol. I (Brunswick, 1845), p. 27.
2. Ibid., p. 37f.
3. See Hegel's concept of constructing a human environment through "taking-possession" and through "formation" of raw material in his *"Philosophy of Right"* Sect. 59ff and Sect. 56; as to Hegel's sketch of a Philosophy of Environment cf. H. M. Sass, "Hegel's Concept of Dialectics and the Meditations in the Field of Objective Spirit," in: *Proceedings of the Villanova Hegel Congress*, ed. D. P. Verene (New York: Humanities Press, 1978).

4. Not only the artificial production but also the universality of their availability belongs to the culture of space. "Oyster and turtle-soups can thus be enjoyed in every city of the continent. And the Scotchman eats his favorite dishes in East-India as freshly prepared as if they had just left his native kitchen" *Vergleichende* ..., Vol. II, p. 401f.

5. "Roads are a propaganda of mankind; therefore they transfigure the soil." The 600 miles of railroad, built in England from 1830–1845 are "now [1845!] no longer only single pieces of railroad, but whole nets of railroad; they are circulation-lines of national vital power"; and "charts and compass are a triumph of the mind over the bodies of water." Kapp, in 1845, also considered the problem of building air-ways for airplanes solvable in principle; cf. *Vergleichende*..., Vol. II, pp. 405–409, 424.

6. Kapp's concept of nature corresponds with that of John Passmore, *Man's Responsibility for Nature* (London, 1974), who stresses the fragility of nature—including man's nature—too.

7. "*Language* itself is the most transparent material in which the mind shows up," Vol. II, p. 431. "*Industry* in a higher sense is on the whole the establishment of the sovereignty of the mind over a material world through work." *Vergleichende*..., Vol. II, p. 435.

8. "The transfiguration of nature will be its perfection, effectuated by the work of the human being." *Vergleichende*..., Vol. II, p. 439f. The term "universal telegraphics" (*universelle Telegraphik*) originates with Carl Ritter.

9. *Vergleichende*..., Vol. II, p. 441. Compare his technological optimism and his anthropological approach to technology: "Machines may earn the money in the future, man will work in creative pleasure in order to find himself again as a rational being—not as machine—in work" (p. 443).

10. *Vergleichende*..., p. 441ff.

11. *Neu-Braunfelser Zeitung* (May 19, 1854), p. 2; *San Antonio Zeitung* (May 20, 1854), p. 2; a translation was printed in *Western Texas* (San Antonio, June 1, 1854), p. 1. This translation has been edited at nine spots for clarity by Glen E. Lich; most of these corrections involved prepositions or faulty grammatical constructions which impaired reading.

12. E. Kapp, *Grundlinien einer Philosophie der Technik. Zur Entstehungsgeschichte der Kultur aus neuen Gesichtspunkten* (Brunswick, 1877), p. v.

13. As a result of his pioneering experiences in Sisterdale, Texas, Kapp theorizes that the American form of the axe might be the

prototype for organ-projection of the human arm which intends to form the wilderness into the home of man; by their taming the wilderness with the axe and not with the gun, the American continent truly had become a home for the immigrants, he outlined; as to his "philosophy of the axe," cf. E. Kapp, *Philosophie der Technik*, p. 252f.

14. "The fact that man in an unconscious way transfers forms and functions and standards of the body into the tools, comes to his consciousness only at the end of this process," E. Kapp, *Philosophie der Technik*, p. vf; cf. also p. 16. The *Philosophie des Unbewussten* (1869) of Eduard von Hartmann had influenced Kapp; but already early in 1845 he had described how techniques had been developed *out of man*, the *Mikrokosmos*, in order to transfigure the *Makrokosmos* by culture and humanity.

15. Kapp demonstrates this point by giving a sectional drawing of an eye nerve along with a drawing of a submarine telegraph cable; cf. E. Kapp, *Philosophie der Technik*, pp. 139–54.

16. Marx published the first volume of his voluminous fragment *Das Kapital* in 1867.

17. Cf., for the roots of the Marxian concept of history as class-war history, H. M. Sass, "The Concept of Revolution in Marx's Dissertation," *Philosophical Forum*, 11 (1978).

18. Cf. Jacques Ellul, *La technique ou l'enjeu du siècle* (Paris, 1954). Kapp, on the other hand, develops strictly the counter-thesis to Ellul's proposition.

19. E. Kapp, *Philosophie der Technik*, p. 342; Kapp quotes F. Reuleaux, *Theoretische Kinematik. Grundzuege einer Theorie des Maschinenwesens* (Brunswick, 1875).

20. L. Mumford, *Technics and the Nature of Man, Philosophy and Technology*, ed. E. Mitcham and R. Mackay (New York, 1972), pp. 78–85; cf. also L. Mumford, *Technics and Civilization* (London, 1934).

21. E. Kapp, *Der konstituierte Despotismus und die konstitutionelle Freiheit* (Hamburg, 1849.), pp. 8, 82, 85.

22. E. Kapp, *Philosophie der Technik*, p. 344. Kapp names especially military formations and postal services as unavoidable sub-elements of the state; cf. also pp. 335–45. If the colleges and universities were closed for a short time, the state would not come into danger immediately, he points out; but if the army were liquidated within a relatively short time, the internal and the external enemies would destroy the state; E. Kapp, *Philosophie der Technik*, p. 337.

23. Trans. by Glen E. Lich.

Chapter Four

1. August Meitzen, *Das deutsche Haus* (Berlin: Dietrich Reimer, 1882), p. 3.
2. Previous works on German folk architecture in the Texas Hill Country include Terry G. Jordan, "German Houses in Texas," *Landscape* 14, No. 1 (1964), 24–26; Sylvia Lorraine Rusche Cook, "The Rock Houses of Fredericksburg, Texas, 1846–1910," (Thesis, University of New Mexico, 1975); Edith Margaret Hanna, "The Indigenous Architecture of Fredericksburg, Texas" (Thesis, North Texas State University, 1942); and Hubert G. H. Wilhelm, "German Settlement and Folk Building Practices in the Hill Country of Texas," *Pioneer America*, 3, No. 2 (1971), 15–24.
3. See, for example, Rudolph L. Biesele, *The History of the German Settlements in Texas 1831–1861* (Austin: Von Boeckmann-Jones, 1930) and Terry G. Jordan, *German Seed in Texas Soil* (Austin: Univ. of Texas Press, 1966).
4. Terry G. Jordan, "The Pattern of Origin of the Adelsverein German Colonists," *Texana*, 6 (1968), 245–57.
5. A good introduction to this diversity of architectural types is Wilhelm Müller-Wille, "Haus- und Gehöftformen in Mitteleuropa," *Geographische Zeitschrift*, 42 (1936), 121–38.
6. A concise treatment of eastern American folk architecture is Fred B. Kniffen, "Folk Housing: Key to Diffusion," *Annals, Association of American Geographers*, 55 (1965), 549–77. On Anglo floor plans, see also Terry G. Jordan, *Texas Log Buildings: A Folk Architecture* (Austin: Univ. of Texas Press, 1978), pp. 105–48.
7. Cook, "Rock Houses of Fredericksburg," p. 108.
8. O. Schwindrazheim, *Deutsche Bauernkunst* (Vienna and Leipzig: Deutscher Verlag für Jugend und Volk, 1931), p. 149.
9. Cook, "Rock Houses of Fredericksburg," p. 108.
10. Hubert G. H. Wilhelm, "Organized German Settlement and Its Effects on the Frontier of South-Central Texas" (Diss., Louisiana State University, 1968), pp. 69–70.
11. Jordan, *Texas Log Buildings*, p. 183.
12. Ibid., pp. 46–47.
13. Seth Eastman, *A Seth Eastman Sketchbook, 1848–1849* (Austin: Univ. of Texas Press, 1961), p. 53.
14. (Gillespie County Historical Society), *Pioneers in God's Hills* (Austin: Von Boeckmann-Jones, 1960), pp. 129, 237.
15. Cook, "Rock Houses of Fredericksburg," p. 130.
16. Wilhelm, "Organized German Settlement," p. 71.

Notes and References

17. *Seth Eastman Sketchbook*, pp. 53, 56, 57.
18. Cook, "Rock Houses of Fredericksburg," p. 108.
19. Henry J. Kauffman, "Architecture of the Dutch Country," paper read at the annual meeting of the Pioneer America Society, Lancaster, Pennsylvania, October 15, 1976.
20. Charles van Ravenswaay, *The Arts and Architecture of German Settlements in Missouri: A Survey of a Vanishing Culture* (Columbia: Univ. of Missouri Press, 1976), pp. 107–298.
21. Thomas Carter, "German-American Stone Houses in Franklin County, Indiana," paper read at the annual meeting of the Pioneer America Society, Lancaster, Pennsylvania, October 16, 1976; van Ravenswaay, *Arts and Architecture of German Settlements in Missouri*, pp. 179–219.

Chapter Six

1. Dr. and Mrs. Ernst Kapp, "*Briefe aus der Comalstadt 1850*," *Jahrbuch der Neu-Braunfelser Zeitung fuer 1936* (New Braunfels: Zeitung, 1936), p. 33.
2. Julius Dresel, File, Oscar Haas Archives, New Braunfels.
3. Rosa Kleberg, "Some of My Early Experiences in Texas," *Texas State Historical Association Quarterly*, 1 (April 1898), p. 289.
4. Louise Romberg Fuchs, *Reminiscences (Erinnerungen)*, Gertrude Franke, trans. (San Antonio, n.p., 1936), p. 9.
5. Willis W. Pratt, ed., *Galveston Island* (Austin: Univ. of Texas Press, 1967), p. 23.
6. Julius Schuetze, "Diary" (Ms.), Mrs. R. H. Bayer (Austin), pp. 7–15.
7. Adolph Douai, Papers, 1819–1908 (Austin: Barker Texas History Center, University of Texas at Austin).
8. Rosa Kleberg, "Experiences in Texas, II," *Texas State Historical Association Quarterly*, 2 (October 1898), p. 173.
9. Guido Ransleben, *A Hundred Years of Comfort in Texas* (San Antonio: Naylor, 1954), p. 137.
10. Melinda Koester, "Mt. Elisa, the George Carl Willrich home, Bluff, Fayette County, Texas, 1975," Measured drawings and photographs (Round Top, Texas: Winedale Museum, University of Texas at Austin, 1975).
11. Frederick Law Olmsted, *A Journey through Texas* (New York: Dix, Edwards & Co., 1857), p. 189.
12. Besides these, there are also a number of other portraits of the Texas-German woman. James Patrick McGuire, *Iwonski In*

Texas, Painter and Citizen (San Antonio: San Antonio Museum Association, 1976), pp. 38, 41, 49, 54, 81.

13. Pauline Pinckney, *Painting in Texas, The Nineteenth Century* (Austin: Univ. of Texas Press, 1967), pp. 84, 85.

14. McGuire, p. 64.

15. Ibid., p. 41.

16. Egon Tausch, "Reflections," KGNB Radio Station, New Braunfels, February 26, 1978.

17. "Disguises Unmasked," New Braunfels *Herald and Zeitung*, May 18, 1978, pp. 1B, 6B.

18. Interview with Mrs. Alfred Liebscher, New Braunfels, Texas, May 21, 1978.

19. For more details, see my book *The Golden Free Land* (Austin: Landmark Press, 1976). See also Olmsted, *Journey through Texas*, p. 193.

Chapter Seven

1. Max Amadeus Paulus Krueger, *Second Fatherland: The Life and Fortunes of a German Immigrant*, ed. Marilyn McAdams Sibley (College Station: Texas A&M Univ. Press, 1976), p. 112.

2. Lucy A. Erath, "Memoirs of Major George Bernard Erath," *Southwestern Historical Quarterly*, 26 (1923), 207–33, 255–80; 27 (1923) 27–51, 140–63.

3. *Texas Is the Place for Me*, trans. Ella Urbantke Fischer (Austin: Pemberton, 1970).

4. See, for example, *Gustav Dresel's Houston Journal. Adventures in North America and Texas. 1837–1841*, ed. and trans. Max Freund (Austin: Univ. of Texas Press, 1954), pp 74–75.

5. See Crystal Sasse Ragsdale, *The Golden Free Land. The Reminiscences and Letters of Women on an American Frontier* (Austin: Landmark, 1976), pp. 1–39. This annotated anthology has an extensive bibliography.

6. Benno von Roeder, "Life of Emilie von Roeder," Louis Lenz Collection, University of Texas; cited from Dorothy E. Justman, *German Colonists and their Descendants in Houston including Usener and Allied Families* (Quanah/Wichita Falls: Nortex, 1974), p. 36.

7. Rosa Kleberg, "Some of My Early Experiences in Texas," recorded and trans. Rudolph Kleberg, Jr., *Quarterly of the Texas State Historical Assciation*, 1 (1898), 302; also in Ragsdale, *Golden Free Land*, p. 28.

8. Ottilie Goeth, née Fuchs, *Memoirs of a Texas Pioneer Grand-*

mother (Was Grossmutter erzaehlt) 1805–1915, ed. and trans. Irma Goeth Guenther (Austin: self-published, 1969), p. 21

9. Ragsdale, *Golden Free Land*, p. 85, fn. 18.
10. Goeth, *Memoirs*, p. 118.
11. Ragsdale, *Golden Free Land*, pp. 53–54, 64–66, 83–86.
12. Ibid., pp. 69–70.
13. Goeth, *Memoirs*, p. 29.
14. Ragsdale, *Golden Free Land*, p. 79.
15. My translation; cf. Irene Marschall King, *John O. Meusebach* (Austin: Univ. of Texas Press, 1967), pp. 23–25, 88, and the plate opposite p. 66; Lucy Meusebach Marschall's sketch in *Pioneers in God's Hills*, I (Austin: Von Boeckmann-Jones, 1960), pp. 141–42.
16. Marschall, p. 142. Adolf Fuchs also admired these lines, and set them to music—see Goeth, *Memoirs*, pp. 116 and 140, fn. 18.
17. Ernst Kapp, "Letter," 1849, trans. Oscar Haas, *New Braunfels Herald and Zeitung*, 20 July 1972.
18. Waltraud Bartscht, "'Da waren Deutsche auch dabei!' The Story of a Texas-German Family," *Texas and Germany: Crosscurrents*, ed. Joseph Wilson, *Rice University Studies*, 63/3 (1977), 42–43.
19. Goeth, *Memoirs*, p. 11.
20. Ibid., p. 41.
21. Ibid., p. 45.
22. Cat Spring Agricultural Society, *The Cat Spring Story* (San Antonio: Lone Star, 1956), pp. 54–55.
23. Ibid., p. 54.
24. *Pioneers in God's Hills*, I, p. 183.
25. Ibid., p. 228.
26. See Vera Flach, *A Yankee in German-America. Texas Hill Country* (San Antonio: Naylor, 1973), p. 50; Glenn G. Gilbert, *Linguistic Atlas of Texas German* (Austin: Univ. of Texas Press, 1972), p. 15.
27. The example in Flach, *Yankee*, p. 104, is extreme—the books burned were in Latin and Greek.
28. The library contained books in French, Spanish, and English, as well as German. The latter included, besides technical and reference works, history and mathematics, selected and collected works by Franz Arago, Wilhelm Busch, Gustav Frenssen, Gustav Freytag, Emmanuel Geibel, J. W. Goethe, Paul Grabein, Heinrich Heine, Hans Hopfen, G. E. Lessing, C. F. Meyer, G. C. Pfeffel, Fritz Reuter, Friedrich Schiller, Karl v. Steinhausen, L. Uhland, C. Viebig, Ernst v. Wildenbruch, and Heinrich Zschokke. These probably represent only a portion of the Altgelt-Coreth holdings;

most were acquired after the families came to Texas the first time (there were several returns to Germany).
29. Ferdinand H. Lohmann, *Comfort* (Comfort: Fellbaum, 1904), p. 45.
30. Ibid., p. 46.
31. F. H. Lohmann, *Die deutsche Sprache* (Chicago: Koelling & Klappenbach, 1904), pp. 29–30.
32. Guido F. Ransleben, *A Hundred Years of Comfort in Texas. A Centennial History* (San Antonio: Naylor, 1954), p. 166.
33. Flach, *Yankee*, pp. 100–101.
34. Cf. Julius Schuetze, "Diary," listed in Ragsdale, *Golden Free Land*, p. 193.
35. *Pioneers in God's Hills*, II (Austin: Von Boeckmann-Jones, 1974), p. 160.
36. Gilbert J. Jordan and Terry G. Jordan, *Ernst and Lisette Jordan: German Pioneers in Texas* (Austin: Von Boeckmann-Jones, 1971), pp. 30–31.
37. Helen Jordan Zesch, "Peter Jordan," *Ernst and Lisette Jordan*, p. 72.
38. Frederick C. Chabot, *With the Makers of San Antonio* (San Antonio: Artes Graficas, 1937), pp. 375, 381, 298, 403, 401, 410, respectively.
39. Cf. *Pioneers in God's Hills*, I, pp. 226–27; Ferdinand H. Lohmann, *Texas-Blüten. Gedichte* (Utica, N.Y., and Leipzig: American Authors' Agency and H. G. Wallmann, n.d. [1906]) and *To My Darling and Other Poems* (New York: Broadway Publishing, 1910)—two-thirds of the latter poems are translations from German.
40. Lota M. Spell, *Music in Texas* (Austin: 1936; New York: AMS, 1973), pp. 92–100; and "The Early German Contribution to Music in Texas," *American-German Review*, 12/4 (April 1946), 8–10; Oscar Haas, *A Chronological History of the Singers of German Songs in Texas* (New Braunfels: self-published, 1948).
41. Hubert Heinen, "Autobiography. Comfort, Texas. 1872–1965" (n.p.: n.p., n.d.), p. 25 (a copy is deposited in the Learning Resources Center, Southwest Texas State University, San Marcos, Texas).
42. Ibid., p. 28.
43. Ransleben, *Comfort*, pp. 166, 193.
44. Gilbert, *Linguistic Atlas*, p. 15, XIX, 14; the notes do not usually give the names of the informants—references by name to persons interviewed are based on inference.
45. John R. Fuchs, *A Husband's Tribute to His Wife* (San Antonio: Naylor, 1938), p. 4.

Notes and References

46. Ibid., pp. 215–16.
47. *Cactus*, XV (Austin: Von Boeckmann-Jones, 1908), p. 177.
48. Gilbert, *Linguistic Atlas*, pp. 8–19.
49. Ibid., p. 9, IX, 15.
50. Personal communication with Glenn E. Gilbert, who has given me a copy of the taped interview, made in Comfort in 1962. During the interview, the question was put whether Goethe and Schiller were read in school, and the answer, though indirect, was apparently no.
51. Gilbert, *Linguistic Atlas*, p. 11, XIII, 13.
52. Ibid., p. 15, XIX, 15.
53. Ibid., p. 16, XXI, 6.
54. Ibid., p. 16, XX, 12.
55. Ibid., pp. 10, X, 7; 15, XIX, 16 and 17.
56. Ibid., p. 16, XX, 15.
57. See, for example, Hedwig Schroeter, *Else: ein Lebensbild aus Texas* (San Antonio: Texas Free Press, 1926).

Chapter Ten

1. Rudolph L. Biesele, *The History of German Settlements in Texas, 1831–1861* (Austin: n.p., 1930); Terry G. Jordan, "The German Settlement of Texas after 1865," *Southwestern Historical Quarterly*, 73 (1969–70), 193–212.
2. Biesele, pp. 1–22, and Robert W. Shook, "German Migration to Texas 1830–1850: Causes and Consequence," *Texana*, 10, No. 3 (1972), 226–43.
3. J. Frank Dobie, *The Mustangs* (New York: Bramhall, 1952), pp. 164–68.
4. Frederick Law Olmsted, *Journey through Texas* (Austin: Von Boeckmann-Jones, 1962), p. 95.
5. Caroline von Hinüber, "Life of German Pioneers in Early Texas," *Quarterly of the Texas State Historical Association*, 2, No. 3 (Jan. 1899), 232.
6. Irene Marschall King, *John O. Meusebach* (Austin: Univ. of Texas Press, 1967), pp. 92–94, 102–103.
7. Ibid., pp. 155–56, and Moritz Tiling, *History of the German Element in Texas and from 1820–1850* (Houston: n.p., 1913), p. 92.
8. King, *John O. Meusebach*, p. 67.
9. Good descriptions and discussions of the treaty can be found in the following: King, *John O. Meusebach*, pp. 111–23; Guido E. Ransleben, *A Hundred Years of Comfort in Texas* (San Antonio:

Naylor, 1954), pp. 9–14 (contains the proceedings of the treaty); Ferdinand Roemer, *Texas*, Oswald Mueller, trans. (San Antonio: Standard, 1935), pp. 220–73 (he was there.).

10. King, *John O. Meusebach*, pp. 118–19.

11. Olmsted, *Journey through Texas*, pp. 130–32.

12. Several accounts of the Nueces Massacre are presented in Ransleben, *A Hundred Years of Comfort in Texas*, Chapter 6, pp. 79–126.

13. Don H. Biggers, *German Pioneers in Texas* (Fredericksburg: Fredericksburg Publishing Co., 1925), p. 59.

14. Ibid.

15. Ibid., p. 71.

16. Carl von Solms-Braunfels, *Texas, 1844–1845*, trans. unnamed (Houston: Anson Jones, 1936), p. 100.

17. Gustav Dresel, *Houston Journal: Adventures in North America and Texas 1837–1841*, Max Freund, trans. (Austin: Univ. of Texas Press, 1954), pp. 90–92.

18. *Funk & Wagnalls Standard Dictionary of Folklore, Mythology, and Legend*, 2 Vols. (New York: Funk & Wagnalls, 1949), Vol. 1, pp. 229–30.

19. Roemer, *Texas*, pp. 48, 215.

20. Julia Estill, "Customs among the German Descendants of Gillespie County," *Coffee in the Gourd*, PTFS 2, 1923 (Dallas: SMU Press, Facsimile Reprint, 1969), pp. 70–73.

21. Terry Jordan, "The Old World Antecedent of the Fredericksburg Easter Fires," *Folklore of Texas Cultures*, PTFS 38 (Austin: Encino, 1974), pp. 151–54.

22. William A. Owens, *Texas Folk Songs*, PTFS 23 (Austin: The Texas Folklore Society, 1950), p. 157.

23. Ransleben, *A Hundred Years of Comfort in Texas*, p. 108; Roemer, *Texas*, p. 251; and Olmsted, *Journey through Texas*, p. 100.

24. Leon Hale, "A Lesson on Playing Mühle," *Some Still Do*, PTFS 39 (Austin: Encino, 1975), pp. 74–76.

25. Christine Boot, "Home and Farm Remedies and Charms in a German Manuscript from a Texas Ranch," *Paisanos*, Publications of the Texas Folklore Society 41 (Austin: Encino, 1978), 111–31.

26. George R. Nielson, "Folklore of the German-Wends in Texas," Publications of the Texas Folklore Society 30 (Dallas: SMU Press, 1961), pp. 248–52.

27. Carl von Solms-Braunfels, *Texas, 1844–1845*, p. 95.

28. Von Hinüber, "Life of German Pioneers in Early Texas," p. 229.

Notes and References

29. Roemer, *Texas*, p. 93.
30. Olmsted, *Journey through Texas*, p. 170.
31. Terry Jordan, "German Houses in Texas," *Landscape*, 14 (Autumn 1964), 24–26.
32. Olmsted, *Journey through Texas*, p. 67 fn.
33. Carl von Solms-Braunfels, *Texas, 1844–1845*, p. 137.

Chapter Eleven

1. Glenn G. Gilbert, *Linguistic Atlas of Texas German* (LATG) (Austin: Univ. of Texas Press, 1972).
2. As have all the immigrant languages in the United States. For a characterization of what an immigrant language is, see Heinz Kloss, *The American Bilingual Tradition* (Rowley, Mass.: Newbury, 1977); and Einer Haugen, *Bilingualism in the Americas*, Publication of the American Dialect Society, 26 (University, Alabama, 1956).
3. I owe the suggestion regarding Afrikaans to Joseph Wilson of Rice Univ.; see *Texas and Germany: Crosscurrents*, Rice Univ. Studies, 63, No. 3, (1977), v. See also the entries for Schuchardt in John E. Reinecke et al., *A Bibliography of Pidgin and Creole Languages* (Honolulu: Univ. Press of Hawaii, 1975). For Gastarbeiterdeutsch see Wolfgang Klein, *Sprache ausländischer Arbeiter* (Göttingen: Vandenhoeck & Ruprecht, 1975).

Chapter Twelve

1. *Dimension*, 1, 2 [1968], 306.
2. *Dimension*, 1, 2 [1968], 307. Trans. Christopher Middleton; all other translations in this essay are by A. Leslie Willson.
3. Günter Kunert, "Zabriskie Point—Das Gesicht einer Landschaft," *Film und Fernsehen*, 7 (1975).
4. Ibid.
5. Günter Kunert, *Der andere Planet* (Berlin: Aufbau Verlag, 1974), p. 28.
6. Horst Bienek, "Vögel gehen ins Dunkel sterben," *Süddeutsche Zeitung*, 2/3 February 1974, p. 108.
7. Christian Wallner, *Freund und Feind, Gedichte und Notate* (Salzburg: Winter, 1978), pp. 116–19.
8. Fred Viebahn, in *Jahrbuch 2* (Cologne: Braun, 1977), pp. 57–58.

Chapter Thirteen

1. Patricia Herminghouse, "German-American Studies in a New

Vein: Resources and Possibilities," *Die Unterrichtspraxis* 9, No. 2 (Fall 1976), 6.

2. George Wilkins Kendall, *Narrative of the Texan Santa Fé Expedition* (New York: Harper & Brothers, 1844), I, pp. 69–70.

3. Crystal Sasse Ragsdale, *The Golden Free Land* (Austin: Landmark Press, 1976), pp. 30–31.

4. Rudolph L. Biesele, "The German Settlers and the Indians in Texas, 1844–1860," *Southwestern Historical Quarterly* 31 (1927–28), 116–29.

5. Mary Mathis El-Beheri and Susan Clayton, "High School Students Research History of German-English School in San Antonio," *Die Unterrichtspraxis* 8, No. 2 (Fall 1975), 62–66; and 1978 Southwest Symposium papers. In this volume, we have attempted to provide models for interpretive treatments and to suggest avenues of approach; descriptive and instructive papers of the symposium are included in a second volume, *Retrospect and Retrieval: The German Element in Review. Essays on Cultural Preservation* (Ann Arbor: Univ. Microfilms Intl., 1978).

Selected Bibliography

DENNIS GIBBONS and GLEN E. LICH

This bibliography has been compiled for teachers and students of American studies, regional history, and ethnic or cross-cultural studies.

Certainly during recent years these interdisciplinary approaches have acquired a new vogue in this country. Some justification for this interest in cultural studies and preservation can be found in changing political perspectives, broader grassroots tolerance for heterogeneity, and growing interest in primitive antiques, folklore, and genealogy. A number of innovative curricular programs have ridden through on that wave of new interest.

Some productive pilot programs in Texas German studies were guided by a pioneer effort of the Southwest Educational Development Laboratory, *Germans in Texas*, Texas Heritage Unit, Ethnic Heritage Studies Program, with three volumes: a Teacher's Guide, a Student Text, and a Resource Guide (Austin, 1974–75). The results of a couple of years of experience are evident in a slightly later publication of the Texas Education Agency, Division of Curriculum Development, Foreign Language Section, *German: Guidelines for Levels I and II* (Austin, Sept. 1976). Its major value is its integrated approach to teaching cultural awareness. One of the first articles that applied these methods and areas (primarily local history and cultural appreciation) within the context of an ongoing language project was an informative report by Mary M. El-Beheri and Susan Clayton, "High School Students Research History of German-English School in San Antonio," *Die Unterrichtspraxis* 8 (1975), 62–66.

Within the larger context of German-American studies, probably the best article of recent years is one written by Patricia Herminghouse, "German-American Studies in a New Vein: Resources and Possibilities," *Die Unterrichtspraxis* 9 (1976), 3–14. A large part of that issue, incidentally, was devoted to teaching German-American studies; two other outstanding articles are William D. Keel and Barbara A. Bopp, "Some Suggestions for a Course on the German Heritage of America" (pp. 18–24); and LaVern J. Rippley, "The German-Americans: A Course Proposal" (pp. 24–30). A more specialized study, based on an upper-division crosscultural course at Southwest Texas State University, is Dona Reeves and Glen E. Lich, "Germans along the Guadalupe: An Approach to the Study of Cultural Diversity," *Die Unterrichtspraxis* 10 (1977), 33–39. The most recent additions to a growing list of curricular applications are found in Louis E. Brister, "Exploring German-American Culture in the Community," *Die Unterrichtspraxis*, 11 (1978), 48–52, and Alexander Waldenrath, "The Role of German-American Culture in Teaching German," *Schatzkammer*, 2 (1976), 26–32. A supplementary student reader is Karl Arndt, *Early German-American Narratives* (New York: American Book Co., 1941).

An attempt to bring together a number of resources and possibilities for regional history and ethnic or crosscultural studies is a recent publication edited by Dona B. Reeves and Glen E. Lich, *Retrospect and Retrieval: The German Element in Review. Essays on Cultural Preservation* (Ann Arbor: Univ. Microfilms Intl., 1978).

This bibliography contains slightly under 750 entries. *Section 1*: Selected Introductory Readings contains 96 selected items on German and American socioeconomic, political, cultural, and intellectual history, as well as general histories of Texas, the Southwest, and the West. *Section 2*: German Settlement of Texas (100 items) is restricted to analytical and descriptive histories applying to Texas-German migration in general and to overall patterns of settlement and dispersal. *Section 3*: Local Histories is a sampling of 88 items on specific colonies, communities, and countries, primarily in the two German belts of central and southwest Texas. *Section 4*: Language, Literature, and Press (97 items) includes a number of German-American works which afford an overview for Texas-German studies. *Section 5*: The Fine Arts, with only 27 items, covers one of the weaker aspects of Texas-German scholarship. Here especially is a great deal of untilled ground. The same holds true for *Section 6*: Religion, Folklore, and Folklife; although this grouping has the second-largest number of items (108) it covers an area almost as broad as ethnicity itself. The vast amount of Pennsylvania-Dutch scholarship, for example, affords a number of research models for a wide range of material and oral investigation. *Section 7*: Politics contains 32 items. *Section 8*: Commerce and Business lists

Selected Bibliography

only 11 items, but several of these, in particular the one by T. Jordan, *German Seed in Texas Soil*, are very comprehensive studies. An attempt was made in Section 9: Biographies, Genealogies, Letters, and Memoirs to list as much as possible (124 items) in the hope that preliminary investigation of these entries will uncover additional resources in this area. *Section 10*: Centers and Repositories lists 14 major locations. *Section 11*: Societies includes 11 organizations for cultural preservation among Texas Germans, Russian-Germans, and German Americans in general. The last category, *Section 12*: Bibliographies and Reference Works, lists 38 essential items.

Section 12 does not list bibliographies which have appeared in periodicals or checklists of theses and dissertations. The "Bibliography Americana Germanica" (formerly published in *German Quarterly* and now being revived in the *Journal of German-American Studies*), as well as the checklist of Texas theses and dissertations in the *Southwestern Historical Quarterly*, are starting places for the researcher, but there are many others as well. Likewise unlisted in this bibliography (because of length), but not to be overlooked as sources, are numerous professional journals, yearbooks, and almanacs, as well as German- and English-language newspapers of central and southwest Texas which publish or have published feature items on local history and biography. Many of the journals, yearbooks, and newspapers cited with specific articles elsewhere in this bibliography continue to publish similar material.

One of the great unworked areas of Texas-German research is newspapers. At least sixteen towns and cities (Austin, Bastrop, Bellville, Brenham, Comfort, Cuero, Dallas, Fredericksburg, Galveston, Giddings, LaGrange, New Braunfels, San Antonio, Seguin, Shiner, and Victoria) published one or more German newspapers, the last of which ceased publication in German in 1952. These need to be collected, examined, and indexed—possibly as the groundwork of a regional study like Carl Wittke, *The German Language Press in America*, cited in Section 4.

1. Selected Introductory Readings

ADAMS, EPHRAIM D., ed. *British Diplomatic Correspondence Concerning the Republic of Texas, 1838–1846*. Austin: Texas State Historical Assn., 1918.

ALMONTE, JUAN N. "Statistical Report on Texas." Ed. and trans. by C. E. Castañeda. *Southwestern Historical Quarterly*, 28 (1924–25), 177–222.

ANCHOR, ROBERT. *Germany Confronts Modernization: German Culture and Society*. Civilization and Society: Studies in Social, Economic, and Cultural History. Lexington, Massachusetts: D. C. Heath, 1972.

BARKER, EUGENE C. *Mexico and Texas. 1821–1835*. Dallas: P. L. Turner, 1928.

BENNET, MARION T. *American Immigration Policies: A History*. Washington: Public Affairs Press, 1964.

BILLIGMEIER, ROBERT HENRY. *Americans from Germany: A Study in Cultural Diversity*. Belmont, Calif.: Wadsworth, 1974.

BILLINGTON, RAY A. *America's Frontier Culture: Three Essays*. College Station: Texas A & M Univ. Press, 1977.

———. *The Far Western Frontier*. New York: Harper, 1956.

———. *Westward Expansion: A History of the American Frontier*. 3rd ed. New York: Macmillan, 1967.

BÖHMER, GÜNTER. *Die Welt des Biedermeier*. Munich: Kurt Desch, 1968.

BOERNER, PETER. "Amerikabilder der europäischen Literatur: Wünschprojektion und Kritik." *Amerikastudien*, 23 (1978), 40–50.

BRAUNS, ERNST L. *Amerika und die moderne Voelkerwanderung*. Potsdam: H. Vogler, 1833.

CANSTATT, OSCAR. *Die deutsche Auswanderung, Auswandererfuersorge und Auswandererziele*. Berlin-Schoeneberg: Ernst Hahn, 1904.

CHAMBERS, WILLIAM TROUT. *Texas—Its Land and People*. Austin: Steck, 1952.

COMMAGER, HENRY S. *Immigration and American History: Essays in Honor of Theodore C. Blegen*. Minneapolis: Univ. of Minnesota Press, 1961.

CONVERSE, C. L. *German Immigrant*. Boston: Humphries, 1953.

COPPA, FRANK J., and THOMAS CURRAN, eds. *The Immigrant Experience in America*. The Immigrant Heritage of America. Boston: Twayne, 1976.

DINNERSTEIN, LEONARD, and F. JAHER. *A History of Ethnic Minorities in America*. New York: Appleton-Century-Crofts, 1970.

DOERRIES, REINHARD R. "The Americanizing of the German Immigrant: A Chapter from U. S. Social History." *Amerikastudien*, 23 (1978), 51–59.

DRACHSLER, JULIUS. *Democracy and Assimilation: The Blending of Immigration Heritages in America*. Rpt. Westport, Conn.: Negro Univ. Press, 1972.

EBY, FREDERICK. *The Development of Education in Texas.* New York: Macmillan, 1925.

FAUST, ALBERT BERNHARDT. *Das Deutschthum in den Vereinigten Staaten in seiner geschichtlichen Entwickelung.* Leipzig: G. B. Teubner, 1912. A translation of Vol. 1 of the author's *The German Element in the United States.*

―――. *Das Deutschthum in den Vereinigten Staaten in seiner Bedeutung für die amerikanische Kultur.* Leipzig: G. B. Teubner, 1912. A translation of Vol. 2 of the author's *The German Element in the United States.*

―――. *The German Element in the United States with Special Reference to its Political, Moral, Social, and Educational Influence.* 2 vols. Boston: Houghton Mifflin, 1909.

FLEISCHMANN, CARL LUDWIG. *Plan für Deutsche Auswanderung und Ansiedlung (beziehungsweise einer Reihe von Ansiedlungen) in den Vereinigten Staaten von Nordamerika.* Stuttgart: F. Köhler, 1849.

FRIESEN, GERHARD K., and WALTER SCHATZBERG, eds. *The German Contribution to the Building of the Americas.* Studies in Honor of Karl J. R. Arndt. Hanover, New Hampshire: Clark Univ. Press, 1977.

GAGERN, HANS C. VON. *Ueber die Auswanderung der Deutschen.* Frankfurt am Main: Fr. Wilmans, 1817. A short, reflective pamphlet designed to call national attention to the emigration of 1816–17.

GLAZER, N. and D. MOYNIHAN. *Beyond the Melting Pot.* Boston: MIT Press, 1963.

GOETZMANN, WILLIAM. *The American Hegelians: An American Intellectual Episode in the History of Western America.* New York: Knopf, 1973.

GOETZMANN, WILLIAM H. *Exploration and Empire: The Explorer and the Scientist in the Winning of the American West.* New York: Knopf, 1966.

GREELEY, ANDREW M. *Ethnicity in the United States: A Preliminary Reconnaissance.* New York: Wiley, 1974.

GREENE, JOHN. "American Science Comes of Age: 1780–1820." *Journal of American History,* 55 (1968), 22–41.

HAGEDORN, HERMANN. *The Hyphenated Family: An American Saga.* New York: Macmillan, 1960.

HAGEN, VICTOR VON. *Der Ruf der Neuen Welt. Deutsche bauen Amerika.* Munich: Droemer, Knaur, 1970.

———. *The Germanic People in America.* Norman: Univ. of Oklahoma Press, 1976. Translation of the above.
HANDLIN, OSCAR. *Children of the Uprooted.* New York: Braziller, 1966.
———. *Immigration as a Factor in American History.* Englewood Cliffs, N.J.: Prentice-Hall, 1959.
———. *Race and Nationality in American Life.* New York: Little, 1957.
———. *The Uprooted: The Epic Story of the Great Migrations that Made the American People.* Boston: Little, Brown, 1951.
HANSEN, MARCUS L. *Atlantic Migration. 1607–1860.* Rpt. Gloucester, Mass.: Peter Smith, 1972.
HATCHER, MATTIE AUSTIN. *The Opening of Texas to Foreign Settlement. 1801–1820.* Univ. of Texas Bulletin No. 2714. Austin: Univ. of Texas, 1927.
HAWGOOD, JOHN A. *The Tragedy of German-America.* New York: Putnam, 1940.
HENDERSON, MARY V. "Minor Empresario Contracts for the Colonization of Texas." *Southwestern Historical Quarterly*, 32 (1928), 1–28.
HOGAN, WILLIAM RANSOM. *The Texas Republic: A Social and Economic History.* Norman: Univ. of Oklahoma Press, 1946.
HUEBENER, THEODORE. *The Germans in America.* Philadelphia: Chilton, 1962. An abbreviated overview.
JESSEN, HANS, ed. *Die deutsche Revolution 1848–49 in Augenzeugenberichten.* Munich: DTV, 1973.
JONES, HOWARD MUMFORD. *O Strange New World: American Culture—The Formative Years.* New York: Viking, 1964.
JORDAN, TERRY G. "Population Origins in Texas, 1850." *Geographical Review*, 59 (1969), 83–102.
KAPP, ERNST. *Grundlinien einer Philosophie der Technik.* Brunswick: G. Westermann, 1877. Rpt., Düsseldorf: Stern-Verlag, 1978.
———. *Vergleichende Allgemeine Erdkunde....* 2 vols. Brunswick: n.p., 1868. Rpt., Düsseldorf: Stern-Verlag (in preparation).
KAPP, FRIEDRICH. *Aus und ueber Amerika. Thatsachen und Erlebnisse.* Berlin: J. Springer, 1876.
———. *Geschichte der deutschen Einwanderung in Amerika.* New York: Steiger, 1867.
KENT, DONALD. *The Refugee Intellectual.* New York: Columbia Univ. Press, 1953.
KLETT, ADA. "Belleville Germans Look at America." *Journal of the Illinois Historical Society*, 40 (1947), 23–37.

Selected Bibliography

KLOSS, HEINZ. *Atlas of the 19th and 20th Century German-American Settlements.* Marburg: Elwert, 1974.

KOERNER, GUSTAV. *Das deutsche Element in den Vereinigten Staaten von Nordamerika. 1818–1848.* Cincinnati: A. E. Wilde, 1880.

KRUMPELMANN, JOHN T. "Duke Bernhard of Saxe-Weimar: An Emissary of Goethe to the American South." *South Central Bulletin*, 30 (1970), 201–203.

KUNZ, VIRGINIA BRAINERD. *The Germans in America.* In America Series. Minneapolis: Lerner, 1966. Illustrated, good for highschool or elementary libraries.

MARCUSE, HERBERT. "Der Einfluss der deutschen Emigration auf das amerikanische Geistesleben: Philosophie und Soziologie." *Jahrbuch fuer Amerikastudien*, 10 (1965), 27–33.

MARSCHALK, PETER. *Deutsche Überseewanderung im 19. Jahrhundert. Ein Beitrag zur soziologischen Theorie der Bevölkerung.* Stuttgart: E. Klett, 1973.

NAU, JOHN F. *The German People of New Orleans.* Leiden, Netherlands: Brill, 1958.

NORDHOFF, CHARLES. *The Communistic Societies of the United States: From Personal Visit and Observation....* 1875; rpt. New York: Schocken, 1965.

OCHS, DEBBIE. "Germans in Illinois: Belleville Was First." *Illinois History*, 23 (1970), 127.

O'CONNOR, RICHARD. *The German-Americans, An Informal History.* Boston: Little, Brown, 1968.

OLMSTED, FREDERICK LAW. *The Cotton Kingdom.* 2 vols. Ed. Arthur M. Schlesinger. New York: Knopf, 1953.

―――. *A Journey through Texas: or, A Saddle-Trip on the Southwestern Frontier.* New York: Dix, Edwards, & Co., 1857. Rpt., Austin: Univ. of Texas Press, 1978.

PAUL WILHELM, DUKE OF WÜRTTEMBERG. *Travels in North America. 1822–1824.* Trans. E. Robert Nitske. Ed. Savoie Lottinville. The American Exploration and Travel Series, 63. Norman: Univ. of Oklahoma Press, 1973.

PILTZ, THOMAS, ed. *Die Deutschen und die Amerikaner. The Americans and the Germans.* München: Heinz Moos, 1977.

POCHMANN, HENRY A. *German Culture in America: Philosophical and Literary Influences. 1600–1900.* Madison: Univ. of Wisconsin Press, 1957.

―――. *New England Transcendentalism and St. Louis Hegelianism.* Philadelphia: Carl Schurz Memorial Foundation, 1948.

RICHARDSON, RUPERT N. *Texas: The Lone Star State.* New York: Prentice-Hall, 1943.

RIPPLEY, LAVERN J. *The German-Americans.* The Immigrant Heritage of America. Boston: Twayne, 1976.

———. "A Look at Americans of German Descent." *The Cultural Revolution in Foreign Language Teaching: A Guide for Building the Modern Curriculum.* Ed. Robert C. Lafayette. Skokie, Illinois: National Textbook, 1975. 72–90.

ROEMER, FERDINAND. *Die Kreidebildungen von Texas und ihre organischen Einschluesse.* Bonn: A. Marcus, 1852.

ROPER, LAURA. "Frederick Law Olmsted and the Western Texas Free Soil Movement." *American Historical Review,* 56 (1950), 58–64.

SASS, HANS-MARTIN. "Die Philosophische Erdkunde des Hegelianers Ernst Kapp: Ein Beitrag zur Wissenschaftstheorie und Fortschrittsdiskussion in der Hegelschule." *Hegel-Studien.* Ed. Friedhelm Nicolin and Otto Pöggeler. Bonn: Bouvier, 1973. 163–81.

———. *Ludwig Feuerbach in Selbstzeugnissen und Bilddokumenten.* Rowohlts Monographien. Reinbeck bei Hamburg: Rowohlt, 1978.

SCHLAUCH, WOLFGANG and BARBARA. *The United States and the Federal Republic of Germany. Contacts and Relations in Historical and Cultural Perspective.* Philadelphia: AATG, 1977.

SCHULZ-BEHREND, GEORGE. "Communia, Iowa, a Nineteenth-Century German-American Utopia." *Iowa Journal,* 48 (1950), 27–54.

SCHWELIEN, JOACHIM H. *Encounter and Encouragement. A Bicentennial Review of German-American Relations.* Bonn: Universitäts-Buchdruckerei, 1976.

SEWARD, RUDY RAY. "Ethnic Families during the Nineteenth Century: Afro-Americans, Germans, and Mexicans in Texas." Thesis, North Texas State Univ., 1977.

SMITH, HENRY NASH. *Virgin Land: The American West as Symbol and Myth.* Cambridge: Harvard Univ. Press, 1950.

STOETZNER, FRIDEL. *The Transplanted.* New York: McGraw-Hill, 1966.

STRUCK, WOLF-HEINO. *Die Auswanderung aus dem Herzogtum Nassau 1806–66: Ein Kapitel der modernen politischen und sozialen Entwicklung.* (Geschichtliche Landeskunde, 4.) Wiesbaden: F. Steiner, 1966.

STUMPP, KARL. *The German Russians.* New York: Atlantic Forum, 1967.

TURNER, FREDERICK JACKSON. *The Frontier in American History.* New York: Holt, 1958.

Selected Bibliography

VAGTS, ALFRED. *Deutsch-Amerikanische Rueckwanderung.* Heidelberg: C. Winter, 1962.

WALKER, MACK. *Germany and the Emigration. 1816–1885.* Cambridge: Harvard Univ. Press, 1964.

WEBB, WALTER PRESCOTT. *The Great Frontier.* Intro. by Arnold J. Toynbee. Austin: Univ. of Texas Press, 1964.

———. *The Great Plains.* Boston: Ginn, 1931.

———, and H. BAILEY CARROLL, eds. *The Handbook of Texas.* 3 vols. Austin: Texas State Historical Assn., 1952, 1976.

WELLEK, ALBERT. "Der Einfluss der deutschen Emigration auf die Entwicklung der nordamerikanischen Psychologie." *Journal of the History of Behavioral Sciences,* 4 (1968), 207–29.

WHEELER, KENNETH W. *To Wear a City's Crown: The Beginning of Urban Growth in Texas. 1836–1865.* Cambridge: Harvard Univ. Press, 1968.

WILK, GERARD. *Americans from Germany.* New York: German Information Center, 1976. Also available in German translation as *Deutsch-Amerikanische Biographien.* New York: German Information Center, 1976.

WITTKE, CARL. "Fissures in the Melting Pot." *The Immigration of Ideas: Studies in the North Atlantic Community.* Rock Island: Augustana Historical Society, 1968.

WOLFE, JONATHAN JAMES. "Background of German Immigration." *Arkansas Historical Quarterly,* 25 (1966), 354–85.

2. German Settlement of Texas

ANDREWS, RENA MAZYCK. "German Pioneers in Texas: Civil War Period." Thesis, Univ. of Chicago, 1929.

Auswanderung nach Hoch Texas. Zürich: Orell, Füssli, 1855.

BEHR, OTTOMAR VON. *Guter Rath für Auswanderer nach den Vereinigten Staaten von Nord America mit besonderer Berücksichtigung von Texas... nach eigner Erfahrung geschrieben.* Leipzig: Robert Friese, 1847.

BENJAMIN, GILBERT GIDDINGS. *The Germans in Texas: A Study in Immigration.* Americana Germanica, 11. Philadelphia: Univ. of Pennsylvania; New York: D. Appleton, 1909. Rpt., Austin: Jenkins, 1974.

BERGHAUS, HEINRICH. "Der Freistaat Texas." *Allgemeine Länder- und Völkerkunde.* Stuttgart: Hoffmann, 1844. VI, 358–94.

BEYER, MORITZ. *Das Auswanderungsbuch oder Führer und Rathgeber* bei der Auswanderung nach Nordamerika und Texas. Leipzig: Baumgartner, 1846.

BIESELE, RUDOLPH L. "The German Settlers and the Indians in Texas, 1844–1860." *Southwestern Historical Quarterly*, 31 (1927), 116–29.

———. *The History of the German Settlements in Texas, 1831–1861*. Austin: Von Boeckmann-Jones, 1930.

———. "The San Saba Colonization Company." *Southwestern Historical Quarterly*, 33 (1930), 169–83.

BLASIG, ANNE. *The Wends of Texas*. San Antonio: Naylor, 1954.

BLUMBERG, CARL. "The True Effectiveness of the Mainz Society for Emigration to Texas as Described in a Letter of November 3, 1846." *Texana*, 7 (1969), 295–312.

———. *Die wahre Wirksamkeit des Mainzer Vereins für die Auswanderung nach Texas geschildert in einem Briefe vom 3. November 1846*. . . . n.p.: n.p., 1847.

BOPP, MARIE-JOSEPH. "Die elsaessische Auswanderung nach Texas." *Der Elsass Kalender*, 7 (1959), 147–53.

BROMME, TRAUGOTT. "Der Freistaat Texas." *Rathgeber für Auswanderungslustige. Wie und wohin sollen wir auswandern; nach den Vereinigten Staaten . . . oder dem Freistaat Texas*. . . . Stuttgart: Hoffmann, 1846.

———. "Der Staat Texas." *Hand- und Reisebuch für Auswanderer nach den Vereinigten Staaten von Nord-Amerika, Texas*. . . . 5th ed. Bayreuth: Buchner, 1848.

CALDWELL, LILLIAN MOERBE. *Texas Wends, Their First Half Century*. Salado, Texas: Anson Jones, 1961.

CARL, PRINZ ZU SOLMS-BRAUNFELS. "Berichte des Prinzen Karl zu Solms-Braunfels an den Mainzer Adelsverein." *Kalender der Neu-Braunfelser Zeitung fuer 1916*. New Braunfels, Texas: Zeitung, 1916. 15–64.

———. *Texas, Geschildert auf seine geographischen, socialen, und uebrigen Verhaeltnisse*. Frankfurt am Main: Sauerländer, 1846.

———. *Texas. 1844–1845*. Houston: n.p., 1936. This is a translation of the above work.

CASTRO, HENRI. *Colonisation au Texas (Amerique du Nord): Castroville (25 Miles Ouest de San Antonio de Bexar), Fondee le 3 Septembre 1844. Colonisation in Texas (Nord Amerika). Castroville (25 Meilen Westlich von San Antonio de Bexar), Gerguendet den 3. September 1844*. Antwerp: J.-E. Buschmann, 1845.

———. *Le Texas*. Antwerp: J.-E. Buschmann, 1845.

———. *Texas im Jahre 1845: Castrostadt, eine franzoesische Colonie,*

Selected Bibliography

welche . . . am Flusse Medina . . . durch Heinrich Castro begründet worden ist. . . . n.p.: n.p., 1845.

CASTRO, LORENZO. *Immigration from Alsace and Lorraine: A Brief Sketch of the History of Castro's Colony.* San Antonio: Herald Office, 1871.

CLAREN, OSCAR VON. "Ein Brief aus dem soeben gegruendeten Neu-Braunfels." *Kalender der Neu-Braunfelser Zeitung fuer 1920.* New Braunfels, Texas: Zeitung, 1920. 46–52.

CONSTANT, L. *Texas: Das Verderben deutscher Auswanderer in Texas unter dem Schutze des Mainzer Vereins.* Berlin: Reimer, 1847.

DECORDOVA, J. *The Texas Immigrant and Traveller's Guide Book.* Austin: DeCordova and Frazier, 1856.

Der Auswanderer nach Texas. Ein Handbuch und Rathgeber für die, welche sich in Texas ansiedeln wollen, unter besonderer Berücksichtigung derer, welche sich dem Mainzer oder Antwerpener Verein anvertrauen. . . . Bremen: C. Schunemann, 1846.

DEUTSCH-TEXANISCHE EINWANDERUNGS-GESELLSCHAFT. *Texas voran! Handbuch von Texas.* Houston: The Gesellschaft, 1907.

DUNT, DETLEF. *Reise nach Texas, nebst Nachrichten von diesem Lande; fuer Deutsche, welche nach Amerika zu gehen beabsichtigen.* Bremen: Carl W. Wiehe, 1834.

DUVERNOY, GUSTAV. *Freude nach Leid; oder, Die Ansiedler in Texas.* Regensburg: F. Pustet, 1868.

ENGERRAND, GEORGE C. *The So-Called Wends of Germany and Their Colonies in Texas and in Australia.* Univ. of Texas Bulletin No. 3417, Bureau of Research in the Social Sciences, Study No. 7. Austin: Univ. of Texas, 1934.

ETZLER, HERBERT. "Zur deutschen Einwanderung in Texas." *Zeitschrift fuer Kulturaustausch,* 19 (1969), 20–24.

FOLLENIUS, PAUL, and FRIEDERICH MUENCH. *Aufforderung an Teutsche Auswanderer zu einer groesseren und gemeinschaftlichen Ansiedlung in den Freistaaten von Nordamerika.* Giessen: Ricker, 1833.

FRANZ, GEORG. *Die Auswanderung der Deutschen nach Texas, Nordamerika und Ungarn. Eine Mahnung an die Nation.* Muenchen: G. Franz, 1844.

GERHARD, H. *Kolonie "Deutschburg." Deutsche Kolonie an der Matagorda Bay, Texas.* Lincoln, Nebraska: n.p., 1911.

GERMAN EMIGRATION CO. *Memorial of the Creditors of the German Emigration Company to the Legislature of the State of Texas.* Houston: Telegraph Office, 1855.

"German Texans." *Texan Observer,* 13 December 1974, pp. 1–4.

"Germans in Texas." *New York Daily Tribune*, 4 January 1856, p. 3.

Gesellschaft zur Ansiedelung Deutscher in Texas. *Plan zur Uebersiedelung Deutscher in Texas.* Biebrich am Rhein: n.p., 1849.

GEUE, CHESTER WILLIAM, and ETHEL HANDER. *A New Land Beckoned: German Immigration to Texas, 1844–1847.* New and enl. ed. Waco, Texas: Texian, 1972.

GEUE, ETHEL HANDER. *New Homes in a New Land: German Immigration to Texas: 1847–1861.* Waco: Texian, 1970.

GRUND, FRANCIS JOSEPH. *Handbuch und Wegweiser fuer Auswanderer nach den Vereinigten Staaten von Nordamerika und Texas.* 2nd ed. Stuttgart and Tuebingen: J. G. Cotta, 1846.

HERFF, FERDINAND VON. *Die geregelte Auswanderung des deutschen Proletariats mit besonderer Beziehung auf Texas.* Frankfurt am Main: Varrentrapp, 1850.

HERFF, FERDINAND CHARLES VON. *The Regulated Emigration of the German Proletariat with Special Reference to Texas.* Trans. Arthur L. Finck. San Antonio: Trinity Univ., 1978.

HERRMANN, MARIA. "The Restoration of Historical Fredericksburg." *Texas and Germany: Crosscurrents.* Ed. Joseph Wilson. *Rice Univ. Studies*, 63, No. 3 (1977), 119–39.

HOUSTON AND TEXAS CENTRAL RAILWAY COMPANY. *Texas the Best Land for the Emigrant.* . . . n.p.: n.p., 1885

JORDAN, TERRY G. "The German Element in Texas: an Overview." *Texas and Germany: Crosscurrents.* Ed Joseph Wilson. *Rice Univ. Studies*, 63, No. 3 (1977), 1–11. This is the definitive article-length treatment of German movement to and in Texas, along with discussions of cluster migration, dominant personalities, and immigrant letters.

———. "The German Settlement of Texas after 1865." *Southwestern Historical Quarterly*, 73 (1969), 193–212.

———. "The Pattern of Origins of the Adelsverein German Colonists." *Texana*, 6 (1968), 245–57.

KAPP, FRIEDRICH. "Die Geschichte der deutschen Ansiedelungen des westlichen Texas und dessen Bedeutung fuer die Vereinigten Staaten." *Atlantische Studien von Deutschen in Amerika*, 1 (1853), 173 ff.

———. "The History of Texas, Early German Colonization, Princes and Nobles in America. The Future of the State, a Lecture by Frederick Kapp." *New York Daily Tribune*, 20 January 1855, p. 6.

KEETH, KENT. "Sankt Antonius: Germans in the Alamo City in the 1850's." *Southwestern Historical Quarterly*, 76 (1972), 183–202.

KINGSBURY, W. G. *Beschreibung von Sued-, West- und Mittel- Texas.*

Selected Bibliography

. . . Trans. Albert Burckhardt. n.p.: Galveston, Harrisburg u. San Antonio Eisenbahn, 1878.

KLEBERG, RUDOLPH. *Beschreibung des Counties DeWitt und seinen Hülfsquellen. Ein Handbuch für Einwanderer.* Cuero, Texas: Cuero Star Office, 1887?

―――. *Description of the Resources of DeWitt County, Texas. The Immigrant's Handbook. New Homes for the Industrious Farmers and Stockraisers.* Cuero, Texas: Cuero Star Office, 1887? Translation of above.

KLOTZBACH, KURT. *Wagenspur nach Westen: Deutsche Pioniere in Texas.* Göttingen: Fischer, 1974.

KORDUEL, A. *Der sichere Fuehrer nach und in Texas.* . . . Rottweil am Neckar: J. P. Setzer, 1846.

KUBY, ERICH. "Die Deutschen in Amerika." *Stern*, series beginning 5 February 1976.

LAFRENTZ, L. F. "Deutsche Ansiedlungen in Comal County nach der Gruendung von New-Braunfels." *Jahrbuch der Neu-Braunfelser Zeitung fuer 1929.* New Braunfels, Texas: Zeitung, 1929. 15–30.

―――. "Die Deutschen in Texas vor der Massen-Einwanderung im Jahre 1844." *Deutsch-Texanische Monats-Hefte.* A series of articles in Vol. 11 (1906) through Vol. 12 (1908).

LICH, GLEN. *The German Texans.* San Antonio: The Univ. of Texas Institute of Texan Cultures, 1980.

LOVING, SOLON OLLIE. "A History of the Fisher-Miller Land Grant from 1842–1860." Thesis, Univ. of Texas at Austin, 1934.

MEUSEBACH, JOHN O. *Answer to Interrogatories in Case No. 396, . . . Mary C. Paschal et al., vs. Theodore Evans, District Court of McCulloch County, Texas November term, 1893.* Austin: E. Von Boeckmann, 1894 and Austin: Pemberton, 1964.

PREUSCHEN, DR. *Ueber die Colonisation von Texas.* Frankfurt: Heller und Rohm, 1846.

RATHER, ETHEL Z. "DeWitt's Colony." *Texas State Historical Association Quarterly*, 8 (1904), 95–192.

REGENBRECHT, ADALBERT. "The German Settlers of Millheim (Texas) before the Civil War." *Southwestern Historical Quarterly*, 20 (1916), 28–34.

REINHARDT, LOUIS. "The Communistic Colony of Bettina." *Texas State Historical Association Quarterly*, 3 (1899), 33–40.

ROEMER, FERDINAND. "Ein Ausflug von Neu-Braunfels nach San Antonio in Jahre 1846." *Neu-Braunfelser Zeitung Kalender*, 1911, pp. 17–32.

———. "Eine Reise von Houston nach Neu-Braunfels vor 63 Jahren." *Neu-Braunfelser Zeitung Kalender*, 1909, pp. 17–37.
———. *Texas mit besonderer Rücksicht auf deutsche Auswanderung.* Bonn: A. Marcus, 1849. An eyewitness account of the Adelsverein settlements.
———. *Texas, with Particular Reference to German Immigration and the Physical Appearance of the Country.* Trans. Oswald Mueller. San Antonio: Standard, 1935. Rpt., Waco, Texas: Texian, 1967.
ROSENBERG, WILLIAM VON. *Kritik der Geschichte des Vereins zum Schutze der Deutschen Auswanderer nach Texas.* Austin: n.p., 1894.
ROSS, GEORG M. VON. *Der Nordamerikanische Freistaat Texas, nach eigener Anschauung und nach den neuesten und besten Quellen fuer deutsche Auswanderer.* Rudolstadt: G. Froebel, 1851.
SCHERPF, G. A. *Entstehungsgeschichte und gegenwaertiger Zustand des neuen, unabhaengigen, amerikanischen Staates Texas.* . . . Augsburg: Matth. Rieger, 1841.
SCHUETZ, KUNO DAMIAN VON. *Texas: Rathgeber fuer Auswanderer nach diesem Lande.* . . . Wiesbaden: Chr. W. Kreidel, 1847.
SCHUFFLER, R. HENDERSON. "Germans Who Went West." *American-German Review*, 33 (1967), 10–13.
SCHULTZ, JOH. HEINR. SIEGFRIED. *Die deutsche Ansiedelung in Texas.* . . . Bonn: Friedrich Encke, 1845.
SHOOK, ROBERT W. "German Migration to Texas 1830–1850: Causes and Consequences." *Texana*, 10 (1972), 226–43.
SIBLEY, MARILYN MCADAMS. *Travelers in Texas. 1761–1860.* Austin: Univ. of Texas Press, 1967.
SIEMERING, A. *Texas als Ziel deutscher Auswanderung.* . . . Hamburg: J. F. Richter, 1882.
———. "Texas, Her Past, Her Present, Her Future." Trans. from *Texas Vörwarts*, 10 August–12 October 1894. Dresel File in San Antonio Public Library and photocopy at the Institute of Texan Cultures.
SOERGEL, ALWIN H. *Neueste Nachrichten aus Texas: Zugleich ein Huelferuf an den Mainzer Verein zum Schutze deutscher Einwanderer in Texas.* Eisleben: Georg Riechardt, 1847.
"Spiegel-Report über die Deutschen in Nordamerika." *Spiegel,* 27 October 1975, pp. 162–74.
STAEHLEN, C. *Neueste Nachrichten, Erklaerungen u. Briefe der Auswanderer von Texas.* Heilbronn: n.p., 1846.

STEINERT, W. *Nordamerika vorzueglich Texas im Jahre 1849.* Berlin: K. W. Krueger, 1850.

STRUBBERG, FRIEDRICH ARMAND. *Friedrichsburg, die Colonie des deutschen Fuersten-Vereins in Texas.* 2 vols. Leipzig: Friedrich Fleischer, 1867. A fanciful account.

TETZLAFF, OTTO W. "A Guide for German Immigrants." *Texas and Germany: Crosscurrents.* Ed. Joseph Wilson. *Rice Univ. Studies,* 63, No. 3 (1977), 13–19.

TILING, MORITZ. *History of the German Element in Texas from 1820–1850, and Historical Sketches of the German Singer's League and the Houston Turnverein from 1853–1913.* Houston: M. Tiling, 1913.

TREU, GEORG. *Das Buch der Auswanderung, enthaltend . . . der Bekanntmachungen . . . des Texas-Vereins. . . .* Bamberg: Fraenkischer Merkur, 1848.

VEREIN ZUM SCHUTZE DEUTSCHER EINWANDERER IN TEXAS. *Comite-Bericht des Vereines zum Schutze deutscher Einwanderer in Texas.* Wiesbaden: J. A. Stein, 1850.

———. *Ein Handbuch fuer deutsche Auswanderer. Mit besonderer Ruecksicht auf diejenigen, welche ihre Ueberfahrt und Ansiedlung durch Hilfe des Vereins . . . bewirken wollen.* Bremen: A. D. Geisler, 1846.

———. *Instruction fuer deutsche Auswanderer nach Texas, nebst der neuesten Karte dieses Staates. . . .* Berlin: D. Reimer, 1851.

———. *Gesammelte Aktenstuecke des Vereins zum Schutze deutscher Einwanderer in Texas.* Mainz: Victor von Zabern, 1845.

WALTHER, F. E. *Texas in sein wahres Licht gestellt, als geeignetster Colonisationsplatz fuer deutsche Auswanderer. . . .* Dresden and Leipzig: Arnold, 1848.

WAUGH, JULIA NOTT. *Castro-ville and Henry Castro, Empresario.* San Antonio: Standard Print, 1934.

WIEGREFFE, AUGUSTE ERVENDBERG. "Pioneer Times in New Braunfels." *San Antonio Express,* 8 September 1835. Interviewed by Sarah S. McKeller.

WILBANKS, ELSIE MONTGOMERY, and AUSTIN H. MONTGOMERY, JR. "The Other Germans." *Texana,* 9 (1971), 230–48.

WILHELM, HUBERT. "Organized German Settlement and its Effects on the Frontier of South Central Texas." Diss., Louisiana State Agricultural and Mechanical College, 1968.

WOOSTER, RALPH A. "Foreigners in the Principal Towns of Ante-Bellum Texas." *Southwestern Historical Quarterly,* 66 (1962), 208–20.

WREDE, FRIEDRICH W. VON. *Sketches of Life in the United States of North America and Texas.* Comp. Emil Drescher. Trans. Chester W. Geue. Waco, Texas: Texian, 1970.

3. Local Histories

ALEXANDER, FRANCES. *Orphans on the Guadalupe.* Quanah-Wichita Falls, Texas: Nortex, 1971.
"Austin County." *Schuetze's Jahrbuch fuer Texas . . . fuer 1883.* Austin: A. Schuetze, 1882.
BARKLEY, MARY STARR. *A History of Central Texas.* Austin: n.p., 1970.
———. *History of Travis County and Austin. 1839–1899.* 2nd ed. Austin: Steck, 1967.
BATTE, LELIA M. *History of Milam County, Texas.* San Antonio: Naylor, 1956.
BELLEVILLE WOCHENBLATT. *Austin County. Beilage zum Bellville Wochenblatt, den alten Texanern gewidmet und den jungen Texanern zu Nutz und Frommen.* Bellville, Texas: Wochenblatt, 1899?
BENNETT, BOB. *Kerr County, Texas. 1856–1956.* San Antonio: Naylor, 1956.
BIERSCHWALE, MARGARET. "Mason County, Texas. 1845–1860." *Southwestern Historical Quarterly,* 52 (1940), 379–97.
BIESELE, RUDOLPH L. "Early Times in New Braunfels and Comal County." *Southwestern Historical Quarterly,* 50 (1946), 75–92.
———. "The First German Settlement in Texas." *Southwestern Historical Quarterly,* 34 (1931), 334–39.
———. "Industry: The First German Settlement in Texas." *Deutsch-Amerikanische Geschichtsblätter,* 32 (1932), 523–28.
BILLINGSLY, W. C. "Llano County." *The Texas Almanac for 1867. . . .* Galveston: Richardson, 1866. 132.
BOETHEL, PAUL C. *History of Lavaca County.* San Antonio: Naylor, 1936. Rev. ed., Austin: Von Boeckmann-Jones, 1959.
BRIGHT, MARGARET DOROTHEA. "The Social Development of Houston, Texas. 1836–1860." Thesis, Univ. of Texas at Austin, 1940.
CAT SPRING AGRICULTURAL SOCIETY. *The Cat Spring Story.* San Antonio: Lone Star, 1956.
CHABOT, FREDERICK C. *With the Makers of San Antonio: genealogies of the early Latin, Anglo-American, and German families with occasional biographies, each group being prefaced with a brief historical sketch and illustrations.* Yanaguana Society publication 4. San Antonio: Artes Graficas, 1937.

Selected Bibliography

CLAUSS, C. HUGO. "Boerne und das Cibolo-Thal in Kendall County." *Schuetze's Jahrbuch fuer Texas . . . Fuer 1882*. Austin: A. Schuetze, 1881. 29–31.

COMFORT MIDDLE SCHOOL. *Those Comforting Hills*. 2 vols. Comfort, Texas: Comfort News, 1975, 1976.

COOLEY, A. O. "Gillespie County." *Texas Almanac for 1867. . . .* Galveston: Richardson, 1866. 109–10.

CURTIS, SARA KAY. "A History of Gillespie County, Texas. 1846–1900." Thesis, Univ. of Texas at Austin, 1943.

DABNEY, EDGAR ROBERT. "The Settlement of New Braunfels and the History of Its Earlier Schools." Thesis, Univ. of Texas at Austin, 1927.

DAVIS, T. H. "Llano County." *The Texas Almanac for 1861. . . .* Galveston: Richardson, 1860. 172–73.

Diamond Jubilee Souvenir Book of Comfort, Texas, Commemorating 75th Anniversary, August 18, 1929. . . . n.p.: n.p., 1929.

DIETRICH, WILFRED O. *The Blazing Story of Washington County*. Brenham, Texas: Banner-Press, 1950. Rev. ed., Wichita Falls, Texas: Nortex, 1973.

DOBIE, DUDLEY R. "A History of Hays County, Texas." Thesis, Univ. of Texas at Austin, 1932.

DUNLEVY, A. "Colorado County." *Texas Almanac for 1859. . . .* Galveston: Richardson, 1858. 170–71.

EDWARDS, WALTER F. *The Story of Fredericksburg: Its Past, Present, Points of Interest and Annual Events*. Fredericksburg: Texas: Fredericksburg Chamber of Commerce, 1969.

EICHHOLZ, W. T. "Die deutschen Ansiedlungen am Colletto." *Schuetze's Jahrbuch fuer Texas . . . fuer 1884*. Austin: A. Schuetze, 1883. 83–86.

ERLENMEYER, A. and P. M. MÜLLER. "Gillespie." *Texas Almanac for 1858. . . .* Galveston: Richardson, 1857. 65–66.

ESTILL, JULIA. *Fredericksburg, in the Texas Hill Country*. Comp. and issued by Fredericksburg Chamber of Commerce. Fredericksburg, Texas: Fredericksburg Publishing Co., 1946.

FELKER, REX A. *Haskell: Haskell County and Its Pioneers*. Quanah, Texas: Nortex, 1975.

FORNELL, EARL. "The German Pioneers of Galveston Island." *American German Review*, 22 (1956), 15–17.

FORNELL, EARL WESLEY. *The Galveston Era: The Texas Crescent on the Eve of Secession*. Austin: Univ. of Texas Press, 1961.

FRANK, SAMUEL H. "Comal." *Texas Almanac for 1859. . . .* Galveston: Richardson, 1858. 169–70.

"The Germans in Texas. The Germans in Fredericksburg, their First Settlement and Present Prosperous Condition." *Texas Almanac for 1872.* Galveston: Richardson, 1871. 76–77.

GILLESPIE COUNTY HISTORICAL SOCIETY. *Pioneers in God's Hills: A History of Fredericksburg and Gillespie County. People and Events.* 2 vols. Austin: Von Boeckmann-Jones, 1960, 1974.

GOLD, ELLA AMANDA. "The History of Education in Gillespie County." Thesis, Univ. of Texas at Austin, 1945.

GRAY, SARAH SAM. "The German-American Community of Fredericksburg, Texas and Its Assimilation." Thesis, Univ. of Texas at Austin, 1929.

HAAS, OSCAR. *The History of New Braunfels and Comal County, 1844–1946.* Austin: Steck, 1968.

HASSKARL, ROBERT A. *Brenham, Texas, 1844–1958.* Brenham, Texas: Banner-Press, 1958.

HUNTER, J. MARVIN. *100 Years in Bandera. 1853–1953.* Bandera, Texas: Frontier Times, 1936.

HUSON, HOBART. *Refugio: A Comprehensive History of Refugio County from Aboriginal Times to 1953.* 2 vols. Woodsboro, Texas: Rooke Foundation, 1953.

JOHNSON, JEWEL R. *A City on a Hill: A Story of a Community, a Church, a People. . . .* n.p.: n.p., 1974? Germans in Coupland, Texas.

JORDAN, TERRY G. "The German Element of Gillespie County, Texas." Thesis, Univ. of Texas at Austin, 1961.

KENNEY, MARTIN M. *An Historical and Descriptive Sketch of Austin County, Texas . . . forming the Centennial Address, Delivered at the Celebration near Bellville, July 4th, 1877* [sic]. Brenham, Texas: Banner, 1876.

KNAPIK, JANE. *Schulenburg: 100 Years on the Road. 1873–1973. With Brief Histories of Old Lyons and High Hill.* Quanah, Texas: Nortex, 1973.

Kurze Beschreibung des 75. Jubilaeums und Geschichte der Llano-Gemeinde. Fredericksburg, Texas: Fredericksburg Publishing Co., 1931.

LAWLER, RUTH C. *The Story of Castroville. . . .* n.p.: n.p., 1957.

LEE COUNTY HISTORICAL SURVEY COMMITTEE. *History of Lee County, Texas.* Quanah, Texas: Nortex, 1974.

LESLIE, THEODORE H. "The History of Lavaca County Schools." Thesis, Univ. of Texas at Austin, 1935.

LOHMANN, FERDINAND H. *Comfort: ein Kurzer Überblick über das Leben und Treiben der Bewohner von der Gründungszeit bis*

Selected Bibliography

zur Gegenwart. Festschrift zur fünfzigjährigen Jubelfeier der Ansiedelung. Comfort, Texas: W. Fellbaum, 1904.

LOTTO, FRANK. Fayette County: Her History and Her People. Schulenburg, Texas: The Author, 1902.

MALSCH, BROWNSON. Indianola: The Mother of Western Texas. Austin: Shoal Creek, 1977.

MASON COUNTY HISTORICAL COMMISSION. Mason County Historical Book. . . . n.p.: n.p., 1976.

MEYER, J. G. "Die Colonie Neu Baden in Robertson County." Schuetze's Jahrbuch fuer Texas . . . fuer 1883. Austin: A. Schuetze, 1882. 146–60.

MOELLERING, ARWERD MAX. "A History of Guadalupe County, Texas." Thesis, Univ. of Texas at Austin, 1938.

MURPHREE, NELL. A History of DeWitt County. Ed. Robert W. Shook. Victoria, Texas: n.p., 1962.

O'KEEFE, RUTH JONES. Archer County Pioneers: A History of Archer County, Texas. Hereford, Texas: Pioneer, 1969.

PENNIGER, ROBERT. Fredericksburg, Texas . . . The First Fifty Years. Trans. Charles L. Wisseman. Fredericksburg, Texas: Fredericksburg Publishing Co., 1971. Translation of Fest-Ausgabe zum 50-jährigen Jubiläum der Gründung der Stadt Friederichsburg. Fredericksburg: A. Hillmann, 1896.

PENNINGTON, MAY AMANDA. The History of Brenham and Washington County. Houston: Standard, 1915.

POLK, STELLA GIPSON. Mason and Mason County: A History. Austin: Pemberton, 1966.

RAMSDELL, CHARLES. San Antonio: A Historical and Pictoral Guide. Austin: Univ. of Texas Press, 1959.

RANCK, JAMES E. "Mason County." Texas Almanac for 1867. . . . Galveston: Richardson, 1866. 135–36.

RANSLEBEN, GUIDO E. A Hundred Years of Comfort in Texas: A Centennial History. San Antonio: Naylor, 1954. Rev. and enl. ed., San Antonio: Naylor, 1974.

RAY, WORTH S. Austin Colony Pioneers, Including History of Bastrop, Fayette, Grimes, Montgomery, and Washington Counties, Texas. Austin: Pemberton, 1970.

ROEMER, FERDINAND. "Neu-Braunfels im Jahre 1846, nach eigener Beobachtung geschildert." Neu-Braunfelser Zeitung Kalendar, 1910, pp. 17–40.

ROSE, VICTOR M. Some Historical Facts in Regard to the Settlement of Victoria, Texas, Its Progress and Present Status. Laredo, Texas: Daily Times Print, 1883. Rpt., San Antonio: n.p., 1961.

ROSENTHAL, A. J. "Fayette County." *Schuetze's Jahrbuch fuer Texas . . . fuer 1883*. Austin: A. Schuetze, 1882.

ST. ROMAIN, LILLIAN SCHILLER. *Western Falls County, Texas*. Austin: Texas State Historical Assn., 1951.

SCHMIDT, CHARLES F. *History of Washington County*. San Antonio: Naylor, 1949.

SCHNELLE, ANNIE KELLERSBERGER. *Yesterdays*. Ed. Irma Goeth Guenther. Marble Falls: Highlander Press, 1974. A short history of the Cypress Mill Area.

SCHUCHARD, ERNST. *100th Anniversary Pioneer Flour Mills, 1851–1951: A Scrapbook of Pictures and Events in San Antonio during the Last 100 Years*. San Antonio: n.p., 1951.

SCOTT, ZELMA. *A History of Coryell County, Texas*. Austin: Texas State Historical Assn., 1965.

SEELE, HERMANN. "Die deutsche Colonie New Braunfels im Mai 1845." *Schuetze's Jahrbuch fuer Texas . . . fuer 1884*. Austin: A. Schuetze, 1883. 93–104.

———. "Ein Beitrag zur Geschichte von Neu Braunfels." *Schuetze's Jahrbuch fuer Texas . . . fuer 1882*. Austin: A. Schuetze, 1881. 31–65.

———. *A Short Sketch of Comal County, Texas*. New Braunfels, Texas: Zeitung, 1885.

SIEMERING, A. "Die lateinische Ansiedlung in Texas: The Latin Settlement in Texas." Trans. C. W. Geue. *Texana*, 5 (1967), 126–31.

SMITH, ALEX. *The First 100 Years in Cooke County*. San Antonio: Naylor, 1955.

STEINFELD, CECILIA. *San Antonio Was: Seen through a Magic Lantern. Views from the Slide Collection of Albert Steves, Sr*. San Antonio: San Antonio Museum Assn., 1978.

TAYLOR, IRA T. *The Cavalcade of Jackson County*. San Antonio: Naylor, 1938.

TAYLOR, WILLIAM CHARLES. *A History of Clay County*. Austin: Jenkins, 1972.

THURMOND, A. S. "Goliad County." *The Texas Almanac for 1867*. Galveston: Richardson, 1866. 110–11.

TRENCKMANN, W. A. *Austin County: . . .* Bellville, Texas: Wochenblatt, 1899.

TYLER, GEORGE W. *The History of Bell County*. San Antonio: Naylor, 1936.

WEINERT, WILLIE MAE. *An Authentic History of Guadalupe County*. Seguin, Texas: Enterprise, 1951.

WEYAND, LEONIE RUMMEL, and HOUSTON WADE. *An Early History of Fayette County.* LaGrange, Texas: Journal, 1936.
WHARTON, CLARENCE R. *History of Fort Bend County.* San Antonio: Naylor, 1939.
WILLIAMS, MARJORIE L., ed. *Fayette County: Past and Present.* By the students of LaGrange High School. Austin, 1976.

4. Language, Literature, and Press

ALBRECHT, ERICH. "Nordamerika." *Grundriss zur Geschichte der deutschen Dichtung aus den Quellen.* By Karl Goedeke. Rev. ed. Berlin: Akademie-Verlag, 1966. 15, 516–661.
ARNDT, KARL. "The Harmony Society and Wilhelm Meisters Wanderjahre." *Comparative Literature,* 10 (1958), 193–202.
AUFDERHEIDE, ELFRIEDE. "Das Amerikaerlebnis in den Romanen von Charles Sealsfield." Diss., Univ. of Goettingen, 1945.
BAUSCHINGER, SIGRID, HORST DENKLER, and WILFRIED MALSCH, eds. *Amerika in der deutschen Literatur: Neue Welt—Nordamerika—USA.* Stuttgart: Reclam, 1975.
BERGSTRAESSER, ARNOLD. *Goethe's Image of Man and Society.* Chicago: Regnery, 1949.
BIENEK, HORST. "Vögel gehen ins Dunkel sterben." *Süddeutsche Zeitung,* 2/3 February 1974, p. 108.
BORNEMANN, FELIX. *Sealsfield-Bibliographie. 1945–1965.* Stuttgart: Verlag der Charles Sealsfield-Gesellschaft, 1966.
BURZLE, J. A. "Balduin Möllhausen: A Forgotten German Romantic of the American West." Paper read at a German-Americana meeting, SCMLA, Hot Springs, 1977.
CAZDEN, ROBERT E. *German Exile Literature in America. 1933–1950. A History of the Free German Press and Book Trade.* Chicago: ALA, 1970.
CLARDY, CATHERINE JANE (JONES). "A Description and Analysis of the German Language Spoken in New Braunfels, Texas." Thesis, Univ. of Texas at Austin, 1954.
DESCZYK, GERHARD. *Amerika in der Phantasie deutscher Dichter.* Chicago: n.p., 1935.
DICKSON, PAUL. "Das Amerikabild in der deutschen Emigrantenliteratur seit 1933." Diss., Univ. of Munich, 1956.
DIETEL, GUENTHER. "Studien zur Aufnahme der deutschen Literatur in Amerika. 1919–1939." Diss., Univ. of Jena, 1952.
DOUAI, ADOLF. *Fata Morgana.* St. Louis, 1858.
———. *Land und Leute in der Union.* Berlin: O. Janke, 1864.

EIKEL, FRED. "New Braunfels German: Parts I and II." *American Speech*, 41 (1966), 5–16, 254–60.

———. "The New Braunfels German Dialect." Thesis, Johns Hopkins Univ., 1954.

———. "The Use of Cases in New Braunfels German." *American Speech*, 24 (1949), 278–81.

ENGELHARDT, SUSAN GAY MALLOY. "English Loans in the German of Die Neu-Braunfelser Zeitung. 1853–1935." Thesis, Univ. of Texas at Austin, 1969.

ETZLER, T. HERBERT. "German-American Newspapers in Texas with Special Reference to the Texas Volksblatt. 1877–1879." *Southwestern Historical Quarterly*, 57 (1954), 423–31.

———. "Texas Volksblatt. 1877–1889." *American-German Review*, 19 (1953), 16–17.

FAUST, ALBERT BERNHARDT. *Charles Sealsfield (Carl Postl), Der Dichter beider Hemisphären: Sein Leben und seine Werke.* Weimar: E. Felber, 1897.

FRIESEN, GERHARD. "Adolph Douai's Literary Activities." *Journal of German-American Studies*, 13 (1978), 25–38.

GILBERT, GLENN. "Dative vs. Accusative in the German Dialects of Central Texas." *Zeitschrift für Mundartforschung*, 32 (1965), 288–96.

———. "English Loanwords in the German of Fredericksburg, Texas." *American Speech*, 40 (1965), 102–12.

———. "The German Dialect in Kendall and Gillespie Counties, Texas." Thesis, Harvard Univ., 1963.

———, ed. *The German Language in America: A Symposium.* Austin: Univ. of Texas Press, 1971.

———. *Linguistic Atlas of Texas.* Austin: Univ. of Texas Press, 1972. (Deutscher Sprachatlas: Regionale Sprachatlanten, Nr. 5.)

———. "Origin and Present-Day Location of German Speakers in Texas." *Problems in Applied Educational Sociolinguistics: Readings on Language and Culture Problems of U.S. Ethnic Groups.* Ed. Glenn G. Gilbert and Jacob Ornstein. The Hague: Mouton, 1978. 119–29.

———. "Origin and Present-Day Location of German Speakers in Texas: A Statistical Interpretation." *Texas and Germany: Crosscurrents.* Ed. Joseph Wilson. *Rice Univ. Studies*, 63, No. 3 (1977), 21–34.

———. *Texas Studies in Bilingualism: Spanish, French, German, Czech, Polish, Serbian and Norwegian in the Southwest.* (Studia

Linguistica Germanica, 3). Berlin: De Gruyter, 1970. Contains three articles on the Texas-German dialect.

GOVIER, ROBERT ALLEN. "German Poetry in New Braunfels, Texas." Thesis, Univ. of Texas at Austin, 1962.

HATFIELD, HENRY, and J. MERRICK. "Studies of German Literature in the United States. 1939–1946." *Modern Language Review*, 43 (1948), 353–92.

HENRY, MARGUERITE KELLER. "Friedrich Gerstaecker, Itchy Feet." Paper read at a German-Americana meeting, SCMLA, Hot Springs, 1977.

JORDAN, E. L. *America, Glorious and Chaotic Land: Charles Sealsfield Discovers the Young United States*. Englewood Cliffs, N.J.: Prentice-Hall, 1969.

JORDAN, GILBERT J. "The Texas German Language of the Western Hill Country." *Texas and Germany: Crosscurrents*. Ed. Joseph Wilson. *Rice Univ. Studies*, 63, No. 3 (1977), 59–71.

KAISER, LEO. "German Verse in Missouri Churchyards." *Zeitschrift fuer Kulturaustausch*, 12 (1962), 319–22.

KLOSS, HEINZ. *The American Bilingual Tradition*. Rowley, Massachusetts: Newbury, 1977.

KOPP, W. L. *German Literature in the United States. 1945–1960*. Chapel Hill, N.C.: Univ. of North Carolina Press, 1967.

KORNBLUTH, MARTIN. "The Reception of Wilhelm Meister in America." *Symposium*, 13 (1959), 128–34.

KOSCH, WILHELM. *Deutsches Literatur-Lexikon: Biographisches und bibliographisches Handbuch*. 2 Aufl. 4 vols. Bern: Francke, 1947–58.

KUNERT, GÜNTER. *Der andere Planet. Ansichten von Amerika*. Berlin: Aufbau Verlag, 1974.

———. "Zabriskie Point—Das Gesicht einer Landschaft." *Film und Fernsehen*, 7 (1975).

LANDA, B. "The American Scene in Friedrich Gerstaecker's Works of Fiction." Diss., Univ. of Minnesota, 1953.

LAWRENCE, ELWOOD. "The Immigrant in American Fiction." Diss., Western Reserve Univ., 1944.

LEHMANN, WINFRED. "Lone Star German." *Texas and Germany: Crosscurrents*. Ed. Joseph Wilson. *Rice Univ. Studies*, 63, No. 3 (1977), 73–81.

LOHMANN, FERDINAND H. *Die deutsche Sprache: Was koennen wir beitragen zu ihrer Erhaltung in diesem Lande*. Chicago: Koelling & Klappenbach, 1904.

———. *Texas-Bluethen*. Utica, N.Y.: American Author's Agency, 1912.
MIYOSHI, MASAO. *The Divided Self: A Perspective on the Literature of the Victorians*. New York: New York Univ. Press, 1969.
PASCAL, ROY. *The German Novel*. Toronto: Univ. of Toronto Press, 1956.
PASCHAL, R. L. "Shall German Be Taught in Our Schools?" *Texas Outlook* (1930).
POCHMANN, HENRY. "Early German-American Journalistic Exchanges." *Huntington Library Quarterly*, 11 (1948), 161–79.
PRAHL, AUGUSTUS. "Friedrich Gerstaecker: The Frontier Novelist." *Arkansas Historical Quarterly*, 14 (1955), 43–50.
RAUNICK, SELMA METZENTHIN. *Deutsche Schriften in Texas*. 2 vols. San Antonio: Freie Presse für Texas, 1935–36.
———. "German Verse in Texas." *Southwest Review*, 18 (1932), 38–49.
———. "Johannes Christlieb Nathanael Romberg, German Poet of Texas." *American German Review*, 12 (1946), 32–35.
———. "One Hundred Years Neu-Braunfelser Zeitung." *American German Review*, 19 (1953), 15–16.
———. "A Survey of German Literature in Texas." *Southwestern Historical Quarterly*, 33 (1929), 134–59.
———. "Was Haben die deutschen Einwanderer und deren Nachkommen in Texas auf dem Gebiet der Dichtkunst geleistet?" Thesis, Univ. of Texas at Austin, 1922.
REED, CARROL. "Gender of English Loanwords in Pa. German." *American Speech* (1942).
REISS, HANS. *Goethe's Novels*. Coral Gables, Florida: Univ. of Miami Press, 1969.
ROBERTSON, J. G. *A History of German Literature*. 6th ed. by Dorothy Reich. Edinburgh: Blackwood, 1970.
ROMBERG, ANNIE. "A Texas Literary Society of Pioneer Days." *Southwestern Historical Quarterly*, 52 (1948), 60–65.
ROMBERG, JOHANNES. *Gedichte*. Ed. Alfred Wagner. Dresden: Pierson, 1900.
ROUCEK, JOSEPH. *The Immigrant in Fiction and Biography*. New York: Bureau for Intercultural Education, 1945.
SCHAUMANN, HERMANN. "Grundzuege deutscher Lyrik in Amerika." Diss., Cornell Univ., 1934.
SCHLEGEL, FRIEDRICH. *Dialogue on Poetry and Literary Aphorisms*. Trans. and ed. Ernst Behler and Roman Struc. University Park: Pennsylvania State Univ. Press, 1968.

SEALSFIELD, CHARLES. *The Cabin Book: or National Characteristics.* New York: St. John & Coffin, 1871.
———. *Life in Texas.* Philadelphia: Colon and Adriance, 1845.
———. *Life in the New World: or Sketches of American Society.* New York: J. Winchester, 1842.
———. *The Making of an American. An Adaptation of Memorable Tales by Charles Sealsfield.* Trans. Ulrich S. Carrington. Dallas: Southern Methodist Univ. Press, 1974.
———. *Nathan, der Squatter-Regulator, oder Der Erste Amerikaner in Texas.* Zurich: Friedrich Shulthess, 1837.
SEELE, HERMANN. *Die Cypresse und Gesammelte Schriften.* New Braunfels, Texas: Zeitung, 1936.
SHEEHAN, AGATHA, SISTER. "A Study of the First Four Novels of Texas." Thesis, Catholic Univ. of America, 1939.
SPILLER, ROBERT E., ed. *Literary History of the U.S.* New York: Macmillan, 1948.
STERNFELD, WILHELM, and EVA TEIDEMANN. *Deutsche Exil-Literatur. 1933–45: Eine Bio-bibliographie.* Heidleberg: Lambert Schneider, 1962.
TOEPPERWEIN, HERMAN. *Rebel in Blue: A Novel of the Southwest Frontier. 1861–1864.* New York: Morrow, 1963.
TOLZMANN, DON HEINRICH. "Deutschamerikanische Dichtung. 1675–1973." *Der Milwaukee Herold*, 2 August 1973.
TRAVIS, D. C. "Texas Symposium: The German Language in America." *Die Unterrichtspraxis*, 2 (1969), 104–12.
VINES, MARY JO. "A Pioneer Poet of Texas." *American-German Review*, 14 (1948), 28–30. About Marie Weisselberg (1835–1911).
VOGEL, STANLEY MORTON. *German Literary Influences on the American Transcendentalists.* Yale Studies in English, V. 127. New Haven: Yale Univ. Press, 1955.
WARD, ROBERT ELMER. "The Case for German-American Literature." *The German Contribution to the Building of the Americas: Studies in Honor of Karl J. R. Arndt.* Eds. Gerhard K. Friesen and Walter Schatzberg. Worcester, Massachusetts: Clark Univ. Press, 1977. 373–89.
———. *Deutsche Lyrik aus Amerika.* New York: Literary Society Foundation, Inc., 1969.
———. "Deutsches Buehnenwesen in Amerika." *German-American Studies*, 5 (1972), 53–54.
———. *Dictionary of German-American Creative Writers from the*

17th Century to the Present. Vol. I: Bibliographical Handbook. Cleveland, Ohio: German-American Publishing Co., 1978.

———. "Symposium ueber deutsche Kultur in den Vereinigten Staaten." *Der Deutsch-Amerikaner* (December 1973).

WARNER, CHARLES DUDLEY, ed. "Elisabeth Brentano (Bettina v. Arnim), 1785–1859." *Library of the World's Best Literature*, 6 (1902), 2348–49.

WEBER, PAUL C. *America in Imaginative German Literature in the First Half of the Nineteenth Century.* New York: Columbia Univ. Press, 1926.

WELLEK, RENÉ. *Confrontations: Studies in the Intellectual and Literary Relations Between Germany, England, and the United States during the Nineteenth Century.* Princeton: Princeton Univ. Press, 1965.

WILLSON, A. LESLIE. "Another Planet: Texas in German Literature." *Texas and Germany: Crosscurrents.* Ed. Joseph Wilson. *Rice Univ. Studies*, 63, No. 3 (1977), 101–109.

WILSON, JOE. "The German Language in Texas." *Schatzkammer der deutschen Sprachlehre, Dichtung und Geschichte*, 2 (1976), 43–49.

———. "The German Language in Central Texas Today." *Texas and Germany: Crosscurrents.* Ed. Joseph Wilson. *Rice Univ. Studies*, 63, No. 3 (1977), 47–58.

———. "The Texas German of Lee and Fayette Counties." *Rice Institute Pamphlet*, 47 (1960), 83–98.

WITTKE, CARL. *The German Language Press in America.* Lexington: Univ. of Kentucky, 1957.

———. "The Immigrant Theme on the American Stage." *Mississippi Valley Historical Review*, 39 (1952), 211–32.

———. "Melting-Pot Literature." *English Journal*, 7 (1946), 189–97.

WOOD, RALPH. "German-American Poetry." *American-German Review*, 23 (1957), 3.

5. The Fine Arts

AMON CARTER MUSEUM OF WESTERN ART, FORT WORTH, TEXAS. *Catalogue of the Collection, 1972.* Fort Worth: The Museum, 1973.

ASHFORD, GERALD. "Paintings of Old San Antonio." *San Antonio Express Magazine*, 5 August 1951.

BÖRSCH-SUPAN, HELMUT. *Caspar David Friedrich.* Trans. Sarah Twohig. New York: Braziller, 1974.

———. *Deutsche Romantiker. Deutsche Maler zwischen 1800 und 1850.* Munich: C. Bertelsmann, 1972.
BRION, MARCEL. *German Painting.* Trans. W. J. Strachan. New York: Universe Books, 1959.
BRYSON, A. "German Theatre Methods and Theory in Texas." *American-German Review,* 28 (1962), 25–29.
BUNEMANN, HERMANN. *Von Runge bis Spitzweg. Deutsche und Österreichische Malerei in der ersten Hälfte des 19. Jahrhunderts.* Königstein: Langewiesche, 1971.
CARVAJAL, CHRISTA LUISE. "German Theaters in Central Texas. 1850–1915." Diss., Univ. of Texas at Austin, 1977.
DAVIS, RONALD. "A History of Resident Opera in the American West." Diss., Univ. of Texas at Austin, 1962.
FINKE, ULRICH. *German Painting from Romanticism to Expressionism.* Boulder, Colorado: Westview, 1975.
FISK, FRANCES BATTAILE. *A History of Texas Artists and Sculptors.* Abilene, Texas, 1928.
GALLEGLY, JOSEPH S. "The Renaissance of the Galveston Theatre: Henry Greenwall's First Season. 1867–1868." *Southwestern Historical Quarterly,* 62 (1958), 442–56.
HARTMANN, HORST. *George Catlin und Balduin Moelhausen: Zwei Interpreten der Indianer und des alten Westens.* Berlin: Reimer, 1963.
HENDRICKS, GORDON. *Albert Bierstadt, Painter of the American West.* New York: Harry N. Abrams and Amon Carter Museum of Western Art, [1974].
HUTSON, ALICE. *From Chalk to Bronze: A Biography of Waldine Tauch.* Austin: Shoal Creek, 1978.
McDERMOTT, JOHN FRANCIS. *Seth Eastman, Pictorial Historian of the Indian.* Norman: Univ. of Oklahoma Press, 1961.
McGUIRE, JAMES PATRICK. *Iwonski in Texas: Painter and Citizen.* San Antonio: San Antonio Museum Assoc., 1976.
MEYERS, ESTELLE. "The Lives and Works of Hermann Lungkwitz and Richard Petri." Thesis, Univ. of Texas at Austin, 1933.
NEW YORK HISTORICAL SOCIETY. *Dictionary of Artists in America. 1564–1860.* New Haven: Yale Univ. Press, 1957.
NEWCOMB, W. W. *German Artist on the Texas Frontier: Friedrich Richard Petri.* Austin: Univ. of Texas Press, 1978.
NOVAK, BARBARA. *American Painting of the Nineteenth Century.* New York: Praeger, 1969.
PINCKNEY, PAULINE A. *Painting in Texas: The Nineteenth Century.* Austin: Univ. of Texas Press, 1967.

ROESSLER, HERMANN. "An American German Primitive Painter." *American-German Review*, 26 (1960), 29.

ROSENBLUM, ROBERT. *Modern Painting and the Northern Romantic Tradition: Friedrich to Rothko.* New York: Harper & Row, 1975.

SPELL, LOTA. "The Early German Contributions to Music in Texas." *American-German Review*, 12 (1946), 8–10.

SPELL, LOTA M. *Music in Texas.* Austin: n.p., 1936. Rpt., New York: AMS, 1973.

ZIEGLSCHMID, A. J. F. "Petri and Lungkwitz: Pioneer Artists in Texas." *American-German Review* (1942), 4–6.

6. Religion, Folklore, and Folklife

ABERNETHY, FRANCIS EDWARD. "Texas Folklore and German Culture." *Texas and Germany: Crosscurrents.* Ed. Joseph Wilson. *Rice Univ. Studies*, 63, No. 3 (1977), 83–99.

ALEXANDER, DRURY BLAKE. *Texas Homes of the Nineteenth Century.* Austin: Univ. of Texas Press, 1966.

BARRY, COLMAN. *The Catholic Church and German Americans.* Milwaukee: Bruce, 1953.

BEACH, WALTER, trans. and comp. *Souvenir of Golden Jubilee, Church of the Visitation, Westphalia, Texas, July 4 and 5, 1933.* From a German Diary by Martin Roessler. Austin: Capital, 1933.

BEWIE, WILLIAM HENRY. *Missouri in Texas: A History of the Lutheran Church—Missouri Synod in Texas. 1855–1941.* Austin: n.p., 1952.

BINDING, GÜNTHER, UDO MAINZER, and ANITA WIEDENAU. *Kleine Kunstgeschichte des deutschen Fachwerkbaus.* Darmstadt: Wissenschaftliche Buchgesellschaft, 1975.

BOATRIGHT, MODY C., et al. *The Family Saga and Other Phases of American Folklore.* Urbana: Univ. of Illinois Press, 1958.

BOGUSCH, E. R. "Superstitions of Bexar County." *Publications of the Texas Folklore Society*, 5 (1926), 112–25. Gathered among the German farmers of Bexar County.

BONEKAMP, W. *Schematismus der deutschen und der deutschsprechenden Priester sowie der deutschen Katholiken-Gemeinde in den Vereinigten Staaten.* . . . St. Louis: B. Herder, 1882.

BOOT, CHRISTINE. "Home and Farm Remedies and Charms in a German Manuscript from a Texas Ranch." *Paisanos.* Publications of the Texas Folklore Society, 41. Austin: Encino, 1978. 111–31.

BRACHER, FREDERICK A. *Ein Rueckblick in die Vergangenheit: ein*

Einblick in die gegenwaertige Gestalt: ein Ausblick in die Zukunft der Evangelisch-lutherischen Zions Gemeinde zur Fredericksburg, Texas. Fredericksburg, Texas: Fredericksburg Publishing Co., 1927.

BRIDENBAUGH, CARL. *The Colonial Craftsman.* New York: New York Univ. Press, 1950.

BUTLER, E. M. *The Saint-Simonian Religion in Germany.* London: Cambridge Univ. Press, 1926.

CARROLL, H. "A Texas Volksfest." *Southwestern Historical Quarterly,* 60 (1957), 412.

CLARK, SARA. "The Decoration of Graves in Central Texas with Seashells." *Diamond Bessie and The Shepherds.* Ed. Wilson M. Hudson. Texas Folklore Society Publications, 36 (1972), 33–43.

CONNOR, SEYMOUR V. "Log Cabins in Texas." *Southwestern Historical Quarterly,* 53 (1949–50), 105–16.

DEUTSCH RÖMISCH-KATHOLISCH CENTRAL-VEREIN. *Souvenir-Programm zur Andenken an die 64. General-Versammlung des Deutschen Römisch-Katholischen Central-Vereins Abgehalten zu San Antonio, Texas, am 12., 13., and 14. Sept. 1920.* San Antonio: Standard, 1920.

DEUTSCH-TEXANISCHER SÄNGERBUND. *Fest Lieder für das 36te Staats Sängerfest, Dallas, October, 1936....* n.p.: n.p., 1936?

―――. *Silver-jubilee 25th State Saengerfest of the German-Texan Singers' League Held at Dallas, Texas, April 25., 26., and 27., 1904.* Dallas: Sandell, 1904.

DOBIE, J. FRANK. *The Mustangs.* New York: Bramhall, 1952.

DOUGLASS, PAUL F. *The Story of German Methodism: Biography of an Immigrant Soul.* New York: The Methodist book concern, 1939.

ESTILL, JULIA. "Children's Games." *The Sky Is My Tipi.* Ed. Mody C. Boatright. Publications of the Texas Folklore Society, 22. Austin: Texas Folklore Society, 1949. 231–36. Games of children in Fredericksburg.

―――. "Customs among the German Descendants of Gillespie County (in 1923)." *The Folklore of Texan Cultures.* Ed. Francis E. Abernethy. Publications of the Texas Folklore Society, 38. Austin: Encino, 1974. The same essay appears in *Coffee in the Gourd.* Publications of the Texas Folklore Society, 2 (1923). Dallas: Southern Methodist Univ. Press (Facsimile Reprint), 1969.

―――. "The Enchanted Rock in Llano County." *Legends of Texas.*

Ed. J. Frank Dobie. *Publications of the Texas Folklore Society*, 3. Austin: Texas Folklore Society, 1924. 153–56.

———. "The Hermit of the Palo Alto." *American-German Review*, 13 (1946), 29–31.

———. "Indian Pictographs near Lange's Mill, Gillespie County, Texas." *Publications of the Texas Folklore Society*, 4. Austin: Texas Folklore Society, 1925. 103–14. About Indian encounters with German settlers.

FOIK, PAUL JOSEPH. *Early Plans for the German Catholic Colonization of Texas.* Austin: Texas Catholic Historical Society, 1934.

FREDERICKSBURG, TEX., ZION LUTHERAN CHURCH. *Commemorating the Centennial Anniversary of Zion Lutheran Church: Gus W. Sager, pastor, Fredericksburg, Texas. 1852–1952.* Fredericksburg, Texas: Fredericksburg Publishing Co., 1952.

FUHRMANN, JOSEPH P. *A Golden Jubilee History of the Sacred Heart Parish. 1889–1939, Muenster, Texas.* San Antonio: Standard, 1939.

GERLACH, H. *Festschrift zum 75-jaehrigen Jubilaeum der St. Marien-Gemeinde zu Friedrichsburg, Texas.* Fredericksburg, Texas: n.p., 1921.

"German Texans Perpetuate Heritage, Add to Mainstream." *People.* Institute of Texan Cultures at San Antonio, 1, No. 3 (1971).

GIDEON, SAMUEL E. "Sunday Houses in Texas." *Pencil Points* (April 1931), 276–81.

GLAZER, NATHAN. *American Judaism: A Historical Survey of the Jewish Religion in America.* Chicago: Univ. of Chicago Press, 1957.

GROTE, CHARLES H. *The History of the German Methodist Episcopal Church, South, Organized by Rev. Chas. A. Grote at Castell, Llano County, Texas, March 8, 1856.* Castell, Texas, 1931.

HAAS, OSCAR. *A Chronological History of the Singers of German Songs in Texas.* New Braunfels, Texas: New Braunfels Zeitung, 1948.

———. *The First Protestant Church: its History and its People. 1845–1955.* New Braunfels, Texas: Zeitung, 1955. Supplement. 1955–1965. New Braunfels, Texas: n.p., 1965.

HALE, LEON. "A Lesson on Playing Mühle." *Some Still Do.* Publications of the Texas Folklore Society, 39. Austin: Encino, 1975. 74–76.

HEIMSATH, CLOVIS. *Pioneer Texas Buildings: A Geometry Lesson.* Austin: Univ. of Texas Press, 1968.

HELT, RICHARD C. " 'Country-Musik?'—Some Notes on the Popular Music of Texas and the Gulf Coast in West Germany." *Texas*

and Germany: Crosscurrents. Ed. Joseph Wilson. Rice Univ. Studies, 63, No. 3 (1977), 111–18.
HEWES, LESLIE. "Cultural Fault Line in the Cherokee Country." Economic Geography, 19 (1943), 136–42.
HILDA, TEX., METHODIST CHURCH. History of the Hilda (Bethel) Methodist Church: Centennial. 1862–1962. San Marcos, Texas: Record, 1962.
HIRSCHLER, ERIC. Jews from Germany in the United States. New York: Farrar, Straus and Cudahy, 1956.
JEANE, DONALD G. "The Traditional Upland South Cemetery." Landscape, 18 (1969), 39–41.
JOHNSON, DOUGLAS W., PAUL R. PICARD, and BERNARD QUINN. Churches and Church Membership in the United States. Washington, D.C.: Glenmary Research Center, 1971.
JORDAN, ERVIN M. "The Work of the Methodist Episcopal Church, South, among the Germans in Texas." Thesis, Southern Methodist Univ., 1935.
JORDAN, GILBERT J. "Texas German Methodism in a Rural Setting." Perkins Journal, 31, No. 3 (1978), 1–21.
———. Yesterday in the Texas Hill Country. College Station: Texas A&M Univ. Press, 1979.
JORDAN, TERRY G. "Forest Folk, Prairie Folk: Rural Religious Cultures in North Texas." Southwestern Historical Quarterly, 53 (1976), 135–62.
———. "German Houses in Texas. . . ." Landscape, 14 (1964), 24–26.
———. "The Old World Antecedent of the Fredericksburg Easter Fires." The Folklore of Texan Cultures. Ed. Francis E. Abernethy. Publications of the Texas Folklore Society, 38. Austin: Encino, 1974, 151–54.
———. "Perceptual Regions in Texas." The Geographical Review, 68 (1978), 293–307.
———. Texas Log Buildings: A Folk Architecture. Austin: Univ. of Texas Press, 1978.
———. "The Traditional Southern Rural Chapel in Texas." Ecumene, 8 (1976), 6–17.
KING, C. RICHARD. Ghost Towns of Texas. San Antonio: Naylor, 1953.
KING, IRENE MARSCHALL. Comanches on the Peace-Path. Waco, Texas: Texian, 1970. This work is interesting because it shows a curiously ambivalent German attitude toward relations with

the Indians which surfaces again and again in Texas-German lore.

KLEIN, VICTOR. "Wedding Customs of the Germans in the Soviet Union." Trans. Dona B. Reeves. *American Historical Society of Germans from Russia Work Sheet*, 23 (1977), 43–47.

KNISPEL, MINNIE. *Establishment and Development of the Kyle German Baptist Community*. . . . n.p.: n.p., n.d.

KOWERT, ELISE. *Old Homes and Buildings of Fredericksburg*. Fredericksburg, Texas: Fredericksburg Publishing Co., 1977.

KROHN, KAARLE. *Folklore*. Trans. Roger L. Welsch. Austin: Univ. of Texas Press, 1971.

LANCASTER, CLAY. "Some Octagonal Forms in Southern Architecture." *Art Bulletin*, 27 (1946), 103–11.

LICH, GLEN E. "Animal Metaphors and Verbal Abuse: A Study of Social Relations and Values among German-Speaking Farmers on Cypress Creek, Kerr County, Texas." 1978. Copy in Learning Resources Center, Southwest Texas State University, San Marcos, Texas.

———. "Germans in the Hill Country: A Pictorial Essay on Immigration to Texas in the Nineteenth Century." *Journal of German-American Studies*, 11 (1976), 49–70.

———, and LERA TYLER. "When the Creeks Run Dry: Water Milling in the German Hill Country." *Built in Texas*. Ed. Francis E. Abernethy. Publications of the Texas Folklore Society, 42. Waco: E-Heart, 1979. 236–45.

LOVE, K. "German Winter Festivals in Fredericksburg, Texas." *American-German Review*, 16 (1949), 17–20.

MANKIN, CAROLYN. "Tales the German Texans Tell." *Singers and Storytellers*. Ed. Mody Boatright. Publications of the Texas Folklore Society, 30. Dallas: Southern Methodist Univ. Press, 1961. 260–65.

METHODIST EPISCOPAL CHURCH. *Deutsches Gesang- und Melodienbuch der Bischöflichen Methodisten-Kirche*. Cincinnati: n.p., 1888.

———. Conferences. Southern German. *Kurze Geschichte der Suedlich-deutschen Konferenz zum 50-Jaehrigen Jubilaeum. 1872–1922*. Seguin, Texas: n.p., [1922?].

MGEBROFF, JOHANNES. *Geschichte der Ersten Deutschen Evangelisch-Lutherischen Synode in Texas*. Chicago: Wartburg, 1902.

MOELLING, PETER AUGUST. *Reise-Skizzen in Poesie und Prosa, Gesammelt auf einer siebenmonatlichen Tour durch die Vereinigten*

Staaten von Nord-Amerika. Galveston: Office des "Apologeten," 1858.

MORSCH, PETER. *History of the First Fifty Years of Holy Family Church, Nazareth, Texas. 1902–1952. Golden Jubilee Celebration, August 21, 1952.* Nazareth, Texas: n.p., 1952.

MOSTER, THOMAS R. *A Diamond Jubilee History of the Sacred Heart Parish. 1889–1964.* Muenster, Texas. n.p.: n.p., 1964?

MUELLER, ESTHER L. "Log Cabins to Sunday Houses." *Diamond Bessie and the Shepherds.* Ed. Wilson M. Hudson. Publications of the Texas Folklore Society, 36. Austin: Encino, 1972. 51–60.

MURRAY, MYRTLE. "Home Life on Early Ranches of Southwest Texas." *Cattleman.* A series of articles, beginning in Vol. 24, No. 8, Jan. 1938, and ending in Vol. 27, No. 7, Dec. 1940.

MURTAGH, WILLIAM. "Half-Timbering in American Architecture." *Pennsylvania Folk Lore,* 9 (1958), 2–11.

NAIL, OLIN W., ed. *Texas Methodist Centennial Yearbook. 1834-1934.* Elgin, Tex.: n.p., 1934.

NEU BRAUNFELSER GEGENSEITIGER UNTERSTUETZUNGS-VEREIN. *Übersichtliche Darstellung über die Gründung, Entwicklung und das Wirken des Neu Braunfelser Gegenseitigen Unterstützungsverein: zur Feier des 25-Jährigen Bestehens Desselben. 1876–1901.* New Braunfels, Tex.: The Verein, 1901?

NEUMANN, ROY. *A Centennial History of St. Joseph's Church and Parish. 1868–1968.* San Antonio: n.p., 1968.

NEW BRAUNFELS, TEX., DEUTSCH-PROTESTANTISCHE KIRCHE. *Die Deutsch-Protestantische Kirche in Texas. Herausgegeben zum Besten des Waisen-Hauses in West-Texas zu Neu-wied. Neu-Braunfels, Texas.* Galveston: C. H. Büchner, 1850.

NEW BRAUNFELS, TEX., GYMNASTIC ASSOCIATION. *Statuten des Turn-Vereins von Neu-Braunfels. Rules, Regulations and By-laws of the Gymnastic Association of New Braunfels.* San Antonio: A. Siemering, 1874.

NEW BRAUNFELS, TEX., MÄNNECHOR. *Deutsches Volksliederbüchlein des New Braunfels Männerchors.* New Braunfels, Tex.: n.p,. 1935.

NIELSON, GEORGE. "Folklore of the German-Wends in Texas." *Singers and Storytellers.* Ed. Mody Boatright. Publications of the Texas Folklore Society, 30. Dallas: Southern Methodist Univ. Press, 1961. 248–59.

OWENS, WILLIAM A. *Texas Folk Songs.* Publications of the Texas Folklore Society, 23. Austin: Texas Folklore Society, 1950.

PARISOT, P. F., and C. J. SMITH. *History of the Catholic Church in*

the *Diocese of San Antonio, Texas*. San Antonio: Carrico & Bowen, 1897.
PARISOT, PIERRE FOURIER. *The Reminiscences of a Texas Missionary*. San Antonio: Johnson, 1899.
REINERT, AL. "Closing Down LaGrange." *Texas Monthly*, 1, No. 9 (1973), 46–53.
REFF, ARTHUR. "Beginnings of Lutheranism in Houston, Texas." *Concordia Historical Institute Quarterly*, 26 (1953), 49–77.
———. "The Lutheran Church in America a Century Ago." *Concordia Historical Institute Quarterly*, 20 (1947), 63–79.
RIPPLEY, LAVERN. *Of German Ways*. Minneapolis: Dillon, 1970.
ROUND TOP, TEX., BETHLEHEM LUTHERAN CHURCH. *A Centennial History of Bethlehem Lutheran Church, Round Top, Texas*. Comp. Martin H. Obst, John C. Banik, and others. Ed. Sue Watkins Grasty. Austin: Von Boeckmann-Jones, 1966.
SCHMIDT, BRUNO C. "A History of the Southern German Conference." Thesis, Southern Methodist Univ., 1935.
SCHMIDT, CURT E. *Oma & Opa: German-Texas Pioneers*. New Braunfels, Tex.: Folkways, 1975.
SCHREIBER, ALBERT M. *Mesquite Does Bloom: An Historical Account of the First Fifty Years of St. Mary's Parish and Community, Windthorst, Texas. 1892–1942*. San Antonio: Standard, 1942.
SMITHSONIAN INSTITUTION. Folklife Program, Office of American and Folklife Studies. *Family Folklore: Interviewing Guide and Questionnaire*. Comp. Holly Cutting-Baker, Amy Kotkin, and Margaret Yocum. Unfortunately this guide is only seven pages long; otherwise superb.
STEINFELDT, CECILIA, and DONALD LEWIS STOVER. *Early Texas Furniture and Decorative Arts*. San Antonio: Trinity Univ. Press, 1973.
STEINMETZ, ROLLIN, and C. RICE. *Vanishing Crafts and Their Craftsmen*. New Brunswick: Rutgers Univ. Press, 1959.
STOVER, DONALD L. *Tischlermeister John*. San Antonio: San Antonio Museum Assoc., 1978.
SWEET, WILLIAM. *Religion on the American Frontier: A Collection of Source Material*. Chicago: Univ. of Chicago Press, 1931–46.
TAYLOR, LONN, and DAVID B. WARREN. *Texas Furniture: The Cabinetmakers and Their Work. 1840–1880*. Austin: Univ. of Texas Press, 1975.
TRENCKMANN, WILLIAM. *Christmas in Troubled Times*. Trans. Anders Saustrup. Round Top, Tex.: The Friends of Winedale, 1976.
VIEBAHN, FRED. *Jahrbuch 2*. Cologne: Braun, 1977. 57–58.

VOGT, EVON, and HYMAN RAY. *Water Witching U.S.A.* Chicago: Univ. of Chicago Press, 1959.

WALBE, JOHN. *A Diamond Jubilee History of Saint Peter's Parish. 1892–1967, Lindsay Texas.* Dallas: n.p., 1967.

WALLNER, CHRISTIAN. *Freund und Feind. Gedichte und Notate.* Salzburg: Winter, 1978. 116–19.

WEBB, WALTER PRESCOTT. "Christmas and New Year in Texas." *Southwestern Historical Quarterly,* 44 (1940–41), 357–79.

WHITE, J. ROY. *Limestone and Log: A Hill Country Sketchbook.* Austin: Encino, 1968.

WIEDERAENDERS, ROBERT, and WALTER TILLMANNS. *The Synods of American Lutheranism.* St. Louis: Lutheran Historical Conference, 1968.

WOLF, F. X. *Centennial of St. Mary's Parish, Fredericksburg, Texas. 1846–1946. A Concise History of St. Mary's Parish.* Fredericksburg, Tex.: Fredericksburg Publishing Co., 1946.

ZIEHE, HEINZ C. *A Centennial Story of the Lutheran Church in Texas.* 2 vols. Seguin, Texas: South Texas Print., 1951–54.

7. Politics

BAKER, T. S. "America as the Political Utopia of Young Germany." *Americana Germanica,* 1, No. 2 (1897), 62–102.

BARKER, EUGENE C. "The Influence of Slavery in the Colonization of Texas." *Southwestern Historical Quarterly,* 28 (1924–25), 1–33.

BEALS, CARLETON. *Brass-Knuckle Crusade: The Great Know-Nothing Conspiracy. 1820–1860.* New York: Hastings, 1960.

BESTOR, ARTHUR. *Backwoods Utopias: The Sectarian and Owenite Phases of Communitarian Socialism in America. 1663–1829.* Philadelphia: Univ. of Pennsylvania Press, 1950.

BIESELE, RUDOLPH L. "The Texas State Convention of Germans in 1854." *Southwestern Historical Quarterly,* 33 (1930), 247–61.

BINKLEY, WILLIAM CAMPBELL. *The Expansionist Movement in Texas. 1836–1850.* Berkeley: Univ. of California Press, 1925.

BRUNCKEN, ERNEST. *German Political Refugees in the United States during the Period from 1815–1860.* Chicago: n.p., 1904. Rpt., San Francisco: R. and E. Research Assoc., 1970.

CASSDORPH, PAUL. *History of the Republican Party in Texas. 1865–1965.* Austin: Pemberton, 1965.

CROSS, JASPER. "The Forty-Eighters and the Election of 1860." *History Bulletin,* 27 (1951), 79–80, 87–89.

ELLIOTT, CLAUDE. "Union Sentiment in Texas. 1861–1865." *Southwestern Historical Quarterly*, 50 (1946–47), 449–77.

EWING, FLOYD F. "Origins of Unionist Sentiment on the West Texas Frontier." *West Texas Historical Association Year Book*, 32 (1956), 21–29.

FRIEDEL, FRANK. "A German-American Observer at the Frankfurt Parliament of 1848." *American-German Review*, 15 (1949), 7–9.

FROEBEL, JULIUS. *Amerika, Europa und die politische Gesichtspunkte der Gegenwart*. Berlin: Springer, 1859.

———. *System der socialen Politik*. 2 vol. Mannheim: Grohe, 1847. Rpt., Aalen: Scientia, 1975.

———. *Theorie der Politik, als Ergebnis einer erneuerten Prüfung demokratischer Lehrmeinungen*. 2 vol. Wien: C. Gerald, 1861–64. Rpt., Aalen: Scientia, 1975.

———. *Die Wirtschaft des Menschengeschlechts auf dem Standpunkte der Einheit idealer und realer Interessen*. Leipzig: Wigand, 1870.

"German Unionists in Texas." *Harper's Weekly*, 20 January 1866.

GILLAN, DENNIS. "Some American Uses of Froebel." Diss., Rutgers State Univ., 1969.

HALL, ADA MARIE. "The Texas Germans in State and National Politics. 1850–1865." Thesis, Univ. of Texas, 1938.

HINE, ROBERT V. *California's Utopian Colonies*. New Haven: Yale Univ. Press, 1966.

KAPP, ERNST. *Der konstituirte Despotismus und die konstitutionelle Freiheit*. Hamburg: n.p., 1849.

KLOSS, HEINZ. "Volksgruppen- und Deutschtumforschung in den Vereinigten Staaten. 1939–1941. Versuche der Carl-Schurz-Gedaechtnisstiftung zur zentralen Zusammenfassung der deutsch-amerikanischen Forschung." *Volksforschung*, 5 (1942), 2–3, 193–97.

KOSSOK, MANFRED. "Prussia, Bremen and the Texas Question 1835 to 1845." *Texana*, 3 (1965), 227–69.

MCGRATH, PAUL, SISTER. *Political Nativism in Texas 1825–1860*. Washington, D. C.: Catholic Univ. of America, 1930.

MCKAY, SETH SHEPARD. *Texas Politics. 1906–1944: With Special Reference to German Counties*. Lubbock: Texas Tech Press, 1952.

SMRYL, FRANK H. "Unionism in Texas. 1856–1861." *Southwestern Historical Quarterly*, 68 (1964), 172–195.

WALLER, JOHN L. *Colossal Hamilton of Texas: A Biography of*

Selected Bibliography

Andrew Jackson Hamilton, Militant Unionist and Reconstruction Governor. El Paso: Texas Western Press, 1968.

WEBBER, EVERETT. *Escape to Utopia: The Communal Movement in America.* New York: Hastings, 1959.

WITTKE, CARL. "American Germans in Two World Wars." *Wisconsin Magazine of History,* 27 (1943), 6–16.

———. *German-Americans in the World War.* Columbus: Ohio State Archaeological and Historical Society, 1936.

———. *Refugees of Revolution: The German Forty-Eighters in America.* Philadelphia: Univ. of Pennsylvania Press, 1952.

ZUCKER, ADOLF E. *The Forty-Eighters: Political Refugees of the German Revolution of 1848.* New York: Columbia Univ. Press, 1950.

8. Commerce and Agriculture

BARON, STANLEY. *Brewed in America: A History of Beer and Ale in the U.S.* Boston: Little, Brown, 1962.

BLACK, WILLIAM L. *A New Industry: or Raising the Angora Goat, and Mohair, for Profit.* Fort Worth: Keystone, 1900.

BOGUE, ALLAN G. *From Prairie to Corn Belt.* Chicago: Univ. of Chicago Press, 1963.

CAT SPRING AGRICULTURAL SOCIETY. *Century of Agricultural Progress. 1856–1957.* Trans. A. L. Schuette, E. P. Krueger, and E. A. Miller. San Antonio: Lone Star, 1956.

ERICKSON, CHARLOTTE. *American Industry and the European Immigrant. 1860–1885.* Cambridge: Harvard Univ. Press, 1957.

GOODWYN, FRANK. *Life on the King Ranch.* New York: Crowell, 1951.

JORDAN, TERRY. "A Geographical Appraisal of the Significance of German Settlement in Nineteenth Century Texas Agriculture." Diss., Univ. of Wisconsin, 1965.

———. *German Seed in Texas Soil: Immigrant Farmers in Nineteenth-Century Texas.* Austin: Univ. of Texas Press, 1966.

NIEDERAUER, C. "Weinbau." *Schuetze's Jahrbuch fuer Texas... fuer 1884.* Austin: A. Schuetze, 1883. 71–72.

ROSENBLUM, GERALD. *Immigrant Workers: The Impact on American Labor Radicalism.* New York: Basic Books, 1973.

SCHUETTE, ARTHUR LUEDECKE. "The German Settlers of Cat Spring and Their Scientific Study of Agriculture." Thesis, Southwest Texas State Teachers College, 1945.

9. Biographies, Genealogies, Letters, and Memoirs

ACHENBACH, HERMANN. *Tagebuch meiner Reise nach der Nordamerikanischen Freistaaten oder: Das neue Kanaan.* Düsseldorf: G. H. Beyer and J. Wolf, 1835.

ALTGELT, EMMA MURCK. *Beobachtungen und Erinnerungen.* New Braunfels, Tex.: Neu Braunfelser Zeitung, 1930.

———. "Life Story." Guido Ernst Ransleben manuscript, Comfort, Tex. Trans. of the above memoir.

———. "Sketches of Life in Texas." Trans. and ed. H. Dielmann. *American-German Review*, 26 (1960), 40.

American Genealogical-Biographical Index to American Genealogical, Biographical and Local History Materials. Middletown, Conn.: Published under the auspices of an Advisory Committee representing the cooperating subscribing libraries by Godfrey Memorial Library, 1952–64.

BANTA, WILLIAM, and J. W. CALDWELL, JR. *Twenty-Seven Years on the Texas Frontier.* Rev. ed., 1893, rpt., Council Hill, Okla.: n.p., 1933.

BARBA, PRESTON ALBERT. *Balduin Moellhausen: The German Cooper.* Americana Germanica, 17. Philadelphia: Univ. of Pennsylvania; New York: D. Appleton, 1914.

———. *The Life and Works of Friedrich Armand Strubberg.* Americana Germanica, 16. Philadelphia: Univ. of Pennsylvania; New York: D. Appleton, 1913.

BARTLETT, JOHN RUSSELL. *Personal Narrative of Explorations and Incidents in Texas, New Mexico, California, Sonora, and Chihuahua.* 2 vols. New York: D. Appleton, 1854.

BARTSCHT, WALTRAUD. " 'Da Waren Deutsche Auch Dabei!' The Story of a Texas-German Family." *Texas and Germany: Crosscurrents.* Ed. Joseph Wilson. *Rice Univ. Studies*, 63, No. 3 (1977), 35–46.

BIESELE, RUDOLPH. "Dr. Ferdinand Roemer's Account of the Llano-San Saba Country." *Southwestern Historical Quarterly*, 62 (1958), 71–74.

———. "Prince Solms' Trip to Texas. 1844–1845." *Southwestern Historical Quarterly*, 40 (1936), 1–25.

BIGGERS, DON H. *German Pioneers in Texas.* Fredericksburg, Tex.: Fredericksburg Publishing Co., 1925.

BLUME, IRWIN H. *The First Hundred Years of the "Schuhmann" Family of Fayette, County, Texas.* Bellaire, Tex.: Blume, 1973.

BOHMFALK, JOHN HENRY. *The History of the Friede Bohmfalk*

Family, Nov. 7, 1848 to Aug. 21, 1966. San Antonio: n.p., 1966.
BOLLAERT, WILLIAM. *William Bollaert's Texas*. Ed. W. Eugene Hollon and Ruth Lapham Butler. The American Exploration and Travel Series, 21. Norman: Univ. of Oklahoma Press, 1956.
BRACHT, VIKTOR. *Texas in 1848*. Trans. and ed. Charles Frank Schmidt. San Antonio: Naylor, 1931. *Texas im Jahre 1848*. Elberfeld u. Iserlohn: J. Bädeker, 1849.
BRAMAN, D. E. E. *Braman's Information about Texas*. Philadelphia: J. B. Lippincott, 1858.
BROWN, JOHN HENRY. *Indian Wars and Pioneers of Texas*. Austin: L. E. Daniell, 1890?
BUETTNER, JOHANN G. *Briefe aus und ueber Nordamerika*... Vol. 1 Dresden and Leipzig: Arnold, 1847.
BUTSCHER, LOUIS C. "A Brief Biography of Prince Paul Wilhelm of Württemberg (1797–1860)." *New Mexico Historical Review*, 17 (1942), 181–225, 295–344.
DARST, MAURY. "Six Weeks to Texas." *Texana*, 6 (1968), 140–52.
DIELMANN, HENRY B. "Dr. Ferdinand Herff, Pioneer Physician and Surgeon." *Southwestern Historical Quarterly*, 57 (1954), 265–84.
———. "Elisabeth Ney, Sculptor." *Southwestern Historical Quarterly*, 45 (1961), 157–83.
———. "Emma Altgelt's Sketches of Life in Texas." *Southwestern Historical Quarterly*, 63 (1959–60), 363–84.
DOUAI, ADOLF. Papers, 1819–1908. Eugene C. Barker Texas History Center, Univ. of Texas at Austin.
DRESEL, GUSTAV. *Gustav Dresel's Houston Journal: Adventures in North America and Texas. 1837–1841*. Ed. and trans. Max Freund. Austin: Univ. of Texas Press, 1954.
DUDEN, GOTTFRIED. *Bericht ueber eine Reise nach den westlichen Staaten Nordamerika's... in Bezug auf Auswanderung und Uebervoelkerung....* 2nd ed. Bonn: E. Weber, 1834.
EHRENBERG, HERMANN. *Fahrten und Schicksale eines Deutschen in Texas*. Leipzig: O. Wigand, 1845. Originally published as *Texas und seine Revolution....* Leipzig, 1843, and published in 1844 as *Der Freiheitskampf in Texas im Jahre 1836*.
———. *With Milam and Fannin: Adventures of a German Boy in Texas' Revolution*. Trans. Charlotte Churchill. Ed. Henry Smith. Austin: Pemberton, 1968. Abridged translation of above.
ERATH, GEORGE BERNARD. *Memoirs of Major George Bernard Erath*. Dictated to and arranged by Lucy A. Erath. Austin: Texas State Historical Association, 1923.
ERHARD, CAYTON. "Cayton Erhard's Reminiscences of the Texan

Santa Fe Expedition, 1841." *Southwestern Historical Quarterly*, 66 (1963), 424–79.

FIERMAN, FLOYD. "Samuel J. Freudenthal, El Paso Merchant and Civic Leader: From the 1880s through the Mexican Revolution." *Southwestern Studies*, 3 (1965), 44.

FLACH, VERA. *A Yankee in German America: Texas Hill Country*. San Antonio: Naylor, 1973.

FRANKE, GERTRUDE. *A Goodly Heritage: The Story of Carl Siegesmund Bauer and His Descendants (1792–1975)*. San Antonio: Alamo Printing, 1975.

FROEBEL, JULIUS. *Aus Amerika: Erfahrungen, Reisen und Studien*. Leipzig: Weber, 1857–58.

———. *Die deutsche Auswanderung und ihre culturhistorische Bedeutung: Fuenfzehn Briefe an den Herausgeber der Allgemeinen Auswanderer-Zeitung*. Leipzig: Wagner, 1858.

FUCHS, JOHN R. *A Husband's Tribute to His Wife*. San Antonio: Naylor, 1938.

FUCHS, LOUISE ROMBERG. *Reminiscences (Erinnerungen)*. Trans. Gertrude Franke. San Antonio, 1936.

GEISER, SAMUEL WOOD. "A Chronology of Dr. Ernst Kapp." *Southwestern Historical Quarterly*, 50 (1946), 297–300.

———. "Dr. Ernst Kapp, Early Geographer in Texas." *Field and Laboratory*, 14, No. 1 (1946), 16–31.

———. *Naturalists of the Frontier*. 2nd ed. Rev. and enl., Dallas: Southern Methodist Univ. Press, 1948.

———. "William H. von Streeruwitz (1833–1916)." *Field and Laboratory*, 25 (Jan. 1957).

GIESECKE, WALTER. *Reminiscences and Adventures of Walter Giesecke*. Ed. Irma Goeth Guenther. Privately published in 1961. Copies in Texas State Archives and in Barker Texas History Library at the University of Texas.

GOETH, OTTILIE FUCHS. *Memoirs of a Texas Pioneer Grandmother (Was Grossmutter Erzaehlt): 1805–1915*. Trans. Irma Goeth Guenther. Austin: n.p., 1969.

———. *Was Grossmutter Erzaehlt*. San Antonio: The Passing Show Printing Co., 1915.

GOLDBECK, FRITZ. *Seit Fünfzig Jahren*. 2 vols. San Antonio: n.p., 1895–96.

GREENE, A. C. *The Last Captive: The Lives of Herman Lehmann*. Austin: Encino, 1972.

GREER, GEORGEANNA H., and HARDING BLACK. *The Meyer Family: Master Potters of Texas*. San Antonio: Trinity Univ. Press, 1971.

Selected Bibliography

GROOS, ANNA WILLRICH. *Recollections.* Trans. Minnie Groos Wilkins. San Antonio: n.p., 1953.

GUENTHER, CARL HILMAR. *Diary and Letters.* Trans. Regina Beckmann Hurst. San Antonio: Clegg, 1952.

HALL, HORACE M. "Horace M. Hall's Letters from Gillespie County, Texas. 1871–1873." Ed. Joseph S. Hall. *Southwestern Historical Quarterly*, 62 (1958–59), 336–55.

HECKE, J. VALENTIN. *Reise Durch die Vereinigten Staaten von Nordamerika in den Jahren 1818 und 1819.* 2 vols. Berlin: H. P. Petri, 1820–21.

HEINEN, HUBERT. "Autobiography. Comfort, Texas. 1872–1965." n.p.: n.p., n.d. Copy in the Learning Resources Center, Southwest Texas State University, San Marcos, Texas.

HERBST, CARL. "Seine Reden und Schriften." Comfort, Texas. This is an unpublished compilation of Herbst's speeches and writings. Date unknown.

HERFF, FERDINAND PETER. *The Doctors Herff: A Three-Generation Memoir.* 2 vols. San Antonio: Trinity Univ. Press, 1973.

HERMES, WILHELM. "Erlebnisse eines deutschen Einwanderers in Texas." *Kalender der Neu-Braunfelser Zeitung fuer 1922.* New Braunfels, Texas: Zeitung, 1922. 18–30.

HINUEBER, CAROLINE VON. "Life of German Pioneers in Texas." *Quarterly of the Texas State Historical Association*, 2 (1899), 227–32.

History of the Pfluger Family. 1803–1978. Pflugerville: n.p., 1978.

HOEHNE, FRIEDRICH. *Wahn und Ueberzeugung. Reise des Kupferschmiede-Meisters Friedrich Hoehne in Weimar ueber Bremen nach Nordamerika und Texas in den Jahren 1839, 1840 und 1841.* Weimar: Wilhelm Hoffman, 1844.

HOFE, HAROLD VON. "August Wilhelm Schlegel's American Emigration Plans: Biographical-Literary Notes." *Wert und Wort: Festschrift für Else M. Fleissner.* Eds. Marion Sonnenfeld et al. Aurora, N.Y.: Wells College, 1965.

HUBER, ALVIN O. "Frederick Armand Strubberg, Alias Dr. Shubbert: Townbuilder, Physician, and Adventurer. 1806–1866." *West Texas Historical Association Yearbook*, 38 (1962), 37–41.

INSTITUTE OF TEXAN CULTURES. "The German Texans." The Texians and the Texans. San Antonio, 1970.

JORDAN, GILBERT J., and TERRY G. JORDAN. *Ernst and Lisette Jordan: German Pioneers in Texas.* Austin: Von Boeckmann-Jones, 1971.

JUSTMAN, DOROTHY E. *German Colonists and their Descendants in*

Houston, Including Usener and Allied Families. Quanah, Texas: Nortex, 1974.

KAPP, DR. and MRS. ERNST. "Briefe aus der Comalstadt 1859." *Jahrbuch der Neu-Braunfelser Zeitung fuer 1936.* New Braunfels, Texas: Zeitung, 1936. 15–38.

KAPP, IDA KAPPELL and ERNST. "Letters." *New Braunfels Herald,* 20 July–19 October 1972. Trans. Oscar Haas.

KETTNER, FRANZ. "Letters of a German Pioneer in Texas." Ed. and trans. Terry G. Jordan and Marlis Anderson Jordan. *Southwestern Historical Quarterly,* 69 (1965–66), 463–72.

KING, IRENE MARSCHALL. *John O. Meusebach: German Colonizer in Texas.* Austin: Univ. of Texas Press, 1967.

KLEBERG, ROSA VON ROEDER. "Some of My Early Experiences in Texas." *Quarterly of the Texas State Historical Association,* 1 (1898), 297–302; 2 (1898), 170–73.

KNESCHKE, ERNEST HEINRICH. "Freiherren Meusebach." Library of Congress, Washington, D.C.

KOELTZOW, OTTO. "From the Brazos to the North Fork: The Autobiography of Otto Koeltzow." *Chronicles of Oklahoma,* 40 (1962), 100–149.

KOERNER, GUSTAV. *Memoirs of Gustav Koerner, 1809–1896.* 2 vols. Cedar Rapids, Iowa: Torch, 1909. Although Koerner was not a Texan, he was associated with Lindheimer and other Texan Dreissiger.

KOWERT, ART. "LBJ's Boyhood: Among the German-Americans in Texas." *American-German Review,* 34 (1968), 2–6.

KRUEGER, MAX AMADEUS PAULUS. *Second Fatherland: The Life and Fortunes of a German Immigrant.* Ed. Marilyn McAdams Sibley. College Station, Texas: Texas A&M Univ. Press, 1976. Originally published as *Pioneer Life in Texas: An Autobiography.* San Antonio: Clegg, 1930?

LENEL, EDITH. *Friedrich Kapp, 1824–1844. Ein Lebensbild aus den Deutschen und den Nordamerikanischen Einheitskämpfen.* Leipzig: J. C. Hinrichs, 1935.

LICH, GLEN ERNST. "Balthasar Lich, German Rancher in the Texas Hills." *Texana,* 12 (1974), 101–23.

LINN, JOHN J. *Reminiscences of Fifty Years in Texas.* New York: D. & J. Sadlier, 1883. Rpt., Austin: Steck, 1935.

LUDECUS, EDUARD. *Reise durch die mexikanischen Provinzen Tumalipas, Cohahuila und Texas im Jahre 1834.* Leipzig: J. F. Hartknoch, 1847.

LUHN, F. W. "Bericht des Farmers F. W. Luhn aus Holstein ueber

Selected Bibliography

seine Erfahrungen in Texas. . . ." *Jahrbuch der Neu-Braunfelser Zeitung fuer 1925.* New Braunfels, Texas: Zeitung, 1925. 27–42.

MOORE, A. W. "A Reconnaissance in Texas in 1846." *Southwestern Historical Quarterly,* 30 (1926), 252–71.

MOURSUND, JOHN S. *Blanco County Families for One Hundred Years.* Austin: n.p., 1958.

NAGEL, CHARLES. *A Boy's Civil War Story.* St. Louis: Eden, 1934.

OSTERMAYER, HEINRICH. *Tagebuch einer Reise nach Texas im Jahr 1848–1849.* . . . Biberach: Im Verlage des Verfassers, 1850.

OTTMERS REUNION COMMITTEE, GOTTFRIED. *The History of the Gottfried Ottmers Family.* Fredericksburg, Texas: Fredericksburg Publishing Co., 1955.

QUENSELL, CARL WILHELM ADOLPH. *From Tyranny to Texas: A German Pioneer in Harris County.* San Antonio: Naylor, 1975.

RABE, JOH. E. *Eine Erholungsfahrt nach Texas und Mexico. Tagebuchblaetter von Joh. E. Rabe.* Hamburg and Leipzig: Leopold Voss, 1893.

RAGSDALE, CRYSTAL SASSE, ed. *The Golden Free Land: Reminiscences and Letters of Women on an American Frontier.* Austin: Landmark, 1976.

RAUNICK, SELMA METZENTHIN, and MARGARET SCHADE. *The Kothmanns of Texas. 1845–1931.* Austin: Von Boeckmann-Jones, 1931.

"Reflections." KGNB Radio Station, New Braunfels, Texas, 1977— Broadcast and tapes available from Sophienburg Museum in New Braunfels.

ROBINSON, ROBERT R., JR. (ROBINSON-ZWAHR, ROBERT). *Die Bremerverwandtschaft in Deutschland und in Texas (The Bremers and Their Kin in Germany and in Texas).* Vol. I. Wichita Falls, Texas: Nortex, 1977.

ROEDER, FLORA L. VON. *These are the Generations: A Biography of the von Roeder Family and its Role in Texas History.* Houston: Baylor College of Medicine, 1978.

ROMBERG, ANNIE. *History of the Romberg Family.* Belton, Texas: Peter Hansborough Bell, 1960?

ROSENBERG, AMANDA FALLIER VON. *Letters. 1849–1850.* Trans. Walter Wupperman. Travis County Room, Austin Public Library, Austin.

ROSENBERG, WILHELM VON. *Letter. 1849.* Trans. Walter Wupperman. Travis County Room, Austin Public Library, Austin.

ROSENBERG-TOMLINSON, ALMA VON. *The Von Rosenberg Family of Texas.* Boerne, Texas: Toepperwein, 1949.

RUTLAND, WILLIE B., ed. *Sursum! Elisabet Ney in Texas.* Austin: 1977.
SANSOM, JOHN WILLIAM. *Battle of Nueces River in Kinney County, Texas, August 10th, 1862.* San Antonio: n.p., 1905?
SANTLEBEN, AUGUST. *A Texas Pioneer: Early Staging and Overland Freighting Days on the Frontiers of Texas and Mexico.* Ed. I. D. Affleck. New York: Neale, 1910. Rpt., Waco, Texas: W. M. Morrison, 1967.
SASS, HANS-MARTIN. "A Hegelian in Southwest Texas." *The Owl of Minerva*, 9, No. 2 (1977), 5–7.
SCHLECHT, FRIEDRICH. *Mein Ausflug nach Texas.* Bunzlau: Appun, 1851.
SCHROETER, HEDWIG. *Else: Ein Lebensbild aus Texas.* San Antonio: Texas Free Press, 1926.
SCHUETZE, JULIUS. "Diary, 1852–1864." Manuscript in possession of Mrs. R. H. Bayer, Austin, Texas.
―――. "Meine Erlebnisse in Texas." *Texas Vorwaerts*, 1 February 1884, 2.
SEELE, HERMANN. "Zwei Erinnerungsbilder aus der Zeit der deutschen Ansiedlung von West-Texas." *Schuetze's Jahrbuch fuer Texas . . . fuer 1883.* Austin: A. Schuetze, 1882. 44–61.
SHERIDAN, FRANCIS. *Galveston Island: The Journal of Francis Sheridan. 1839–1849.* Ed. Willis W. Pratt. Austin: Univ. of Texas Press, 1954.
SHOOK, ROBERT W. "The Battle of the Nueces, August 10, 1862." *Southwestern Historical Quarterly*, 66 (1962), 31–42.
SHUFORD, IRIS. *The Seven Timmermann Sisters: A Legend in Their Time.* Austin: Felix Shuford, 1976.
SIMONDS, FREDERIC W. "Dr. Ferdinand von Roemer, the Father of the Geology of Texas; His Life and Work." *The American Geologist*, 29 (1902), 131–40.
SMITH, OPHIA D. "A Trip to Texas in 1855." *Southwestern Historical Quarterly*, 59 (1955–56), 24–39.
SOERGEL, ALWIN H. *Fuer Auswanderungslustige! Briefe eines unter dem Schutze des Mainzer Vereins nach Texas Ausgewanderten.* Leipzig: Expedizion des Herold, 1847.
SOMMER, CARL VON. *Bericht ueber meine Reise nach Texas im Jahre 1846.* Bremen, Texas: Heyse, 1847.
STEPHENS, ROBERT W. *August Buchel: Texas Soldier of Fortune.* Dallas: n.p., 1970.
STOEHR, LOUISE ERNST. "Die erste deutsche Frau in Texas." *Der deutsche Pionier*, 16 (1884), 372–75.

STORK, ROSE MARIE and OLIVER. *Philip Peter Stork and His Descendants. 1798–1974.* Brenham, Texas: Hermann, n.d.

THRAN, JAKOB. *Meine Auswanderung nach Texas unter dem Schutze des Mainzer Vereins. Ein Warnungs-Beispiel fuer Auswanderungslustige.* Berlin: Eduard Krause, 1848.

URBANTKE, CARL. *Texas Is the Place for Me: The Autobiography of a German Immigrant Youth: Carl Urbantke, Founder of Blinn College.* Trans. Ella Urbantke Fischer. Austin: Pemberton, 1970.

VAN DER STUCKEN, FRANK. "Letters." Howard Moore, San Marcos, Texas.

VAN DER STUCKEN, SOPHIE SCHOENEWOLF. "Letters." Howard Moore, San Marcos, Texas.

WEBER, ADOLF PAUL. *Deutsche Pioniere. Zur Geschichte des Deutschthums in Texas.* San Antonio: Selbstverlag, 1894.

WIGGIN, EDITH E. *Anstandslehre fuer Schule und Haus.* Uebersetzt von Wilhelm Eilers. Nebst einem Anhang, enthaltend Geschichte und Biographien prominenter Deutsch-Texaner, gesammelt und bearbeitet durch W. Eilers. Austin: n.p., 1905.

WILLRICH, ELISE KUCKUCK, and GEORG CARL WILLRICH. *Letters. 1848–1850.* Ed. and trans. Minnie Groos Wilkins. San Antonio, 1952.

WISSEMAN, CHARLES L. *The Ludwig Ranzau Family.* Kerrville, Texas: n.p., 1972.

WURZBACH, EMIL FRIEDRICH. *Life and Memoirs of Emil Frederick Wurzbach to Which Is Appended Some Papers of John Meusebach.* Trans. Franz J. Dohmen. Yanaguana Society Publications, 3. San Antonio: Yanaguana Society, 1937.

10. Centers and Repositories

Comfort Museum. Comfort, Texas.
Daughters of the Republic of Texas Library at the Alamo, San Antonio, Texas.
Newberry Library. Chicago, Illinois.
 Rich source of German-American historical material.
Pioneer Memorial Museum. Fredericksburg, Texas.
The Rosenberg Library. Galveston, Texas.
San Antonio Public Library. Julius Dresel File. San Antonio, Texas.
Sophienburg Museum. New Braunfels, Texas. Archival repository of Solms-Braunfels Archives.
Southwest Texas State Univ. Brinkmann-Ransleben Collection. San Marcos, Texas.

Texas State Library and Archives. Lorenzo de Zavala Building. Austin, Texas.
Univ. of Kansas. Max Kade German-American Research and Document Center. Lawrence, Kansas. Midwestern German-Americana and German-American literature.
Univ. of Texas at Austin. Barker Texas History Center. Austin, Texas.
Univ. of Texas at Austin. Winedale Historical Center. Round Top, Texas.
Univ. of Texas Institute of Texan Cultures at San Antonio. San Antonio, Texas.
Witte Museum. San Antonio, Texas.

11. Societies

American Association of Teachers of German. Cherry Hill, New Jersey.
American Historical Society of Germans from Russia. Lincoln, Nebraska.
Deutsch Texanischer Saengerbund. San Antonio, Texas.
German-Texan Heritage Society. Southwest Texas State University. San Marcos, Texas.
Melus. The Society for the Study of the Multi-Ethnic Literature of the United States. East Texas State Univ., Commerce, Texas.
National Carl Schurz Association. Philadelphia, Pennsylvania.
Order of the Sons of Hermann in the State of Texas. San Antonio, Texas.
Society for German-American Studies. Cleveland, Ohio.
Texanischer Gebirgs-Saengerbund. San Antonio, Texas.
Verband deutschsprachiger Autoren in Amerika. Cincinnati, Ohio.
Volksfest Association of Texas. San Antonio, Texas.

12. Bibliographies and Reference Works

ARNDT, KARL JOHN RICHARD. *German-American Newspapers and Periodicals. 1732–1955: History and Bibliography.* 2nd ed. Rev., New York: Johnson Reprint, 1965.
BENNION, LOWELL. "German Migration and Colonization: Inventory and Prologue to Geographic Study." Diss., Syracuse Univ., 1963.
BERQUIST, JAMES M. *Germans in North America.* The Balch Institute Historical Reading-Lists, No. 18. Philadelphia: Balch Institute, 1975.
BRECHENMACHER, JOSEF KARLMANN. *Etymologisches Woerterbuch der deutschen Familiennamen.* Limburg an der Lahn: Starke, 1960–63.

CARROLL, H. BAILEY. *Texas County Histories: A Bibliography*. Austin: Texas State Historical Assoc., 1943.

———, and MILTON R. GUTSCH. *Texas History Theses*. Austin: Texas State Historical Assoc., 1955. Continued periodically as part of the *Southwestern Historical Quarterly*.

CLARK, THOMAS D. *Travels in the Old South*. 3 vols. Norman: Univ. of Oklahoma Press, 1959.

———. *Travels in the New South: A Bibliography*. 2 vols. Norman: Univ. of Oklahoma Press, 1962.

DAY, JAMES M. *The Map Collection of the Texas State Archives. Maps of Texas. 1827–1900*. Austin, 1964.

ELLIOTT, CLAUDE, ed. *Theses on Texas History*. Austin: Texas State Historical Assoc., 1955.

Familiengeschichtliche Bibliographie. Leipzig: Zentralstelle fuer Deutsche Personen und Familiengeschichte, 1928–62.

GLANZ, RUDOLPH. *The German Jew in America: An Annotated Bibliography Including Books, Pamphlets and Articles of Special Interest*. New York: Ktav, 1970.

GRIFFIN, A. P. C. *A List of Works Relating to the Germans in the United States*. Washington, D.C., 1904.

HUBACH, ROBERT. *Early Midwestern Travel Narratives: An annotated Bibliography. 1634–1850*. Detroit: Wayne State Univ. Press, 1961.

Immigrant Groups in the U.S. New York: Russel Sage Foundation, 1932.

Index to American Genealogies, and to Genealogical Materials Contained in all Works such as Town Histories, City Histories, Local Histories, Historical Society Publications, Biographies, Historical Periodicals, and Kindred Works, Alphabetically Arranged. Albany, N.Y.: Munsell, 1900. Contains 50,000 references.

JACKSON, W. H., and S. A. LONG. *The Texas Stock Directory or Book of Marks and Brands*. Vol. I. San Antonio: Herald, 1865.

JENKINS, JOHN H. *Cracker Barrel Chronicle: A Bibliography of Texas Town and County Histories*. Austin: Pemberton, 1965.

LOMAX, ALAN, and SIDNEY ROBERTSON. *American Folksong and Folklore: A Regional Bibliography*. New York: Progressive Ed. Assoc., 1942.

MÜLLER, FRIEDRICH. *Grosses deutsches Ortsbuch, vollständiges Gemeindelexikon. Enthält neben allen Städten und sonstigen Gemeinden die nicht selbstständigen Wohnplätze der Bundesrepublik und der DDR*. 12., vollständig überarb. und erweiterte

Aufl. Wuppertal-Barmen: 1958. Of value for genealogical research.

MULLINS, MARION. *The First Census of Texas, 1829–1836, to Which are Added Texas Citizenship Lists, 1821–1845, and Other Early Records of the Republic of Texas.* Washington, D.C.: [National Genealogical Society], 1959.

NEWBERRY LIBRARY. Edward E. Ayer Collection. *Catalog of the Edward E. Ayer Collection of Americana and American Indians.* Boston: Hall, 1961. Lists 90,000 items.

POCHMANN, HENRY A. *Bibliography of German Culture in America to 1940.* Ed. Arthur R. Schultz. Madison: Univ. of Wisconsin Press, 1953.

SCHULTZ, ARTHUR R. *Inventory of German-American Genealogies.* In press, 1978.

SMITH, CLIFFORD, and ANNA PISZCZAN-CZAJA SMITH. *Encyclopedia of German-American Genealogical Research.* New York: R. R. Bowker, 1976.

STERN, MALCOLM. *Americans of Jewish Descent.* Washington, D.C.: National Genealogical Society Quarterly, 1958.

———. *Americans of Jewish Descent: A Compendium of Genealogy.* Cincinnati: Hebrew Union College Press, 1960.

STREETER, THOMAS. *Bibliography of Texas. 1795–1845.* 5 vols. Cambridge: Harvard Univ. Press, 1955–60.

THOMPSON, LAWRENCE. "Travel Books on Texas Published in Foreign Countries. 1900–1950." *Southwestern Historical Quarterly,* 57 (1953), 202–21.

TOLZMANN, DON H. *German-Americana: A Bibliography.* Metuchen, N.J.: Scarecrow, 1975.

UNITED STATES CENSUS OFFICE. *Seventh Census, 1850. Eighth Census, 1860. Ninth Census, 1870. Tenth Census, 1880. Twelfth Census, 1900.* Washington, D.C.: U.S. Govt. Print. Office, 1850–1900.

UNITED STATES WORKS PROGRESS ADMINISTRATION. Division of Women's and Professional Projects. *Check List of Records Required or Permitted by Law in Texas.* San Antonio: The Historical Records Survey, 1937.

WARD, ROBERT ELMER. "Bibliographical Notes on German-American Culture." *Symposium on German Culture in America and Ohio.* Cleveland, 1973. 6–8.

———. *Dictionary of German-American Creative Writers: From the 17th Century to the Present.* Cleveland: German-American Publishing Co., 1978.

WIEDERAENDERS, ROBERT. "The Lutheran Church in North America: A Bibliography." *Lutheran Quarterly*, 10 (1959), 339–51.

WILLIAMS, ETHEL W. *Know Your Ancestors: A Guide to Genealogical Research.* Rutland, Vermont: C. E. Tuttle, 1961.

WINKLER, E. W. "The Vandale Collection of Texana." *Southwestern Historical Quarterly*, 54 (1950), 27–61.

WITTKE, CARL FREDERICK. *The Germans in America: A Student's Guide to Localized History.* New York: Teachers College Press, 1967.

About the Contributors

FRANCIS E. ABERNETHY is Professor of English at Stephen F. Austin State University. Previously he held positions at Lamar State College and LSU. A native of Oklahoma, he studied at the University of Neuchatel, Switzerland, and he earned the B.A. at Stephen F. Austin, and the M.A. and Ph.D. at Louisiana State University. Professor Abernethy has received numerous teaching awards and faculty grants and is a member of the Texas Institute of Letters. He has produced seven books, including *Tales from the Big Thicket, J. Frank Dobie, Observations and Reflections on Texas Folklore,* and *The Folklore of Texan Cultures.* He has published numerous scholarly articles for books and journals such as *Studies in English Renaissance Literature, Rice University Studies, Modern Drama, Tempo, Eleusis,* and *New Orleans Review.* Dr. Abernethy is Secretary-Editor of the Texas Folklore Society, Director of the Texas Folklife Festival, and a consultant to the Fort Worth Museum of Science and History. He is a member of the American Folklore Society, Texas Herpetological Society, South-Central Renaissance Society, South Central Modern Language Association, and East Texas Historical Association.

JOE B. FRANTZ is Walter Prescott Webb Professor of History and Ideas at the University of Texas. A native Texan, he holds the B.A., M.A., and Ph.D. from the University of Texas. He was a postdoctoral fellow in business history at Harvard, and has been visiting professor at the University of Chicago, Northwestern University, University of Colorado, University of Maine, Southern Methodist University, University of Chile, San Marcos University (Peru), Catholic University in Guayaquil, and Catholic University in Quito. He has served as Chairman of the Department of History at the University of Texas, Historical Adviser of the National Aeronautics and Space Administration, Vice-Chairman of the National Parks Advisory Board, presidential appointee of the National Historical Publications Commission, Director of the Texas State Historical Association for eleven years, Director of the Oral History Project at the University of Texas, and consultant in History to the White House.

About the Contributors

DENNIS GIBBONS is Collection Development Librarian at Stockton State College in Pomona, New Jersey. A native of Texas, Mr. Gibbons has studied at the University of Vienna and holds the B.A. from Rice University and the M.L.S. from the University of Texas.

GLENN G. GILBERT is Professor of Linguistics at Southern Illinois University. Previously he taught in the Department of Germanic Languages at the University of Texas. A native of Alabama, he earned the B.A. at the University of Chicago and the Ph.D. at Harvard University. He studied also at the University of Frankfurt and the University of Paris. He has been visiting professor at the University of Alberta, and Fulbright lecturer at Marburg and Mainz. The recipient of numerous teaching and research awards, Professor Gilbert is author of the *Linguistic Atlas of Texas German* and the editor of *Texas Studies in Bilingualism, The German Language in America*, and *Readings in Applied Educational Sociolinguistics*. He has written reviews and scholarly articles for journals such as *Zeitschrift für Mundartforschung, American Speech, Language, Lingua*, and *Zeitschrift für Dialektologie und Linguistik*. Professor Gilbert is a member of the American Dialect Society, Linguistic Society of America, and a Fellow of the American Anthropological Association.

HUBERT P. HEINEN is Associate Professor in the Department of Germanic Languages at the University of Texas. Previously he taught at the University of Pittsburgh. A native Texan, he earned the B.A. and Ph.D. from the University of Texas. Professor Heinen is a Fellow of the Southeastern Medieval Institute. He is author of *Die rhythmischmetrische Gestaltung des Knittelverses bei Hans Folz, Paths to German Poetry: An Introductory Anthology*, and *Basic Spoken German Grammar* (with Alan Pfeffer et al.). He has also written numerous encyclopedia entries for *Kindler Literatur Lexikon*, as well as articles, translations, and reviews in scholarly publications such as *Texas Studies in Literature and Language, Modern Austrian Literature, Amsterdamer Beiträge zur älteren Germanistik, Dimension, Modern Language Notes, Zeitschrift für Dialektologie und Linguistik, Speculum*, and *Germanistik*. Dr. Heinen has served as Secretary and Chairman of the German I Section of the South Central Modern Language Association, and he is a member of the Modern Language Association, American Association of Teachers of German, and Mediaeval Academy of America.

GILBERT J. JORDAN is a native of Mason County, Texas, where he spent his youth on a ranch in the German Hill Country and attended a bilingual elementary school. He holds the B.A. from Southwestern University, the M.A. from the University of Texas, and the Ph.D. from Ohio State University. After several years of teaching in the public schools of Texas, he became Professor of German at Southern Methodist University, where he taught until his retirement in 1968. Then he took a professorship at Sam Houston State University for an additional five years. He has published magazine articles and books in the field of German language and literature. After his second retirement he has been engaged in research and writing in the field of German Texana.

TERRY G. JORDAN, a sixth-generation Texan of German and southern Anglo-American descent, is a specialist in the folk-geography of his native state. His doctoral degree in cultural-historical geography was granted in 1965 by the University of Wisconsin at Madison, and since 1969 he has been Professor and Chairman of Geography at North Texas State University. He is author of *German Seed in Texas Soil*, a study of acculturation of German immigrant farmers in the nineteenth century, and he has published other books and numerous articles dealing with Texas ethnic and folk-geography. His latest book is *Texas Log Buildings: A Folk Architecture*. He belongs to Phi Beta Kappa and is a former Woodrow Wilson Fellow. In 1977 he was awarded the H. Bailey Carroll Award by the Texas State Historical Association.

GLEN E. LICH, formerly an Instructor in English at Southwest Texas State University, holds the B.A. from Southwestern University, the M.A. in German from the University of Texas, and the M.A. in English from Southwest Texas State University. He has also done undergraduate study at the University of Vienna, Austria. Mr. Lich is author of *The German Texans* (1980). He is a consultant for the University of Texas Institute of Texan Cultures at San Antonio and for the Gottfried Keller Center in Glattfelden, Switzerland, as well as associate editor of the *Journal of German-American Studies*. He is a member of the South Central Modern Language Association, Texas Folklore Society, American Studies Association, American Literary Translators Association, American Association of Teachers of German, and Texas State Historical Association. He is presently on the English faculty at the University of New Orleans.

JAMES PATRICK MCGUIRE is Director of Educational Services at the University of Texas Institute of Texan Cultures at San Antonio. A

About the Contributors

native Texan, he earned the B.A. at the University of Texas and the M.A. at St. Mary's University. Mr. McGuire is a research specialist on seven immigrant ethnic groups in Texas, including the Germans. He is author of *Iwonski in Texas: Painter and Citizen* and *Julius Stockfleth: Gulf Coast Marine and Landscape Painter*. Mr. McGuire is a member of the American Historical Association, Texas State Historical Association, Texas Folklore Society, American Association of Museums, San Antonio Conservation Society, and San Antonio Museum Association.

CRYSTAL SASSE RAGSDALE is a resident of Austin and New Braunfels, Texas. She was a research historian for the Institute of Texan Cultures and an editorial associate of *The Handbook of Texas* (Vol. III). Mrs. Ragsdale is author of *The Biegel Settlement, Fayette County, Texas, 1832–1880*, and editor of *The Golden Free Land: Reminiscences and Letters of Women on an American Frontier*.

DONA B. REEVES, Professor of German and past chairer of the Modern Languages Department at Southwest Texas State University, completed the M.A. and Ph.D. at the University of Texas at Austin. She has done postgraduate study at the University of California at Berkeley and at the Johannes Gutenberg Universität in Mainz, Germany. Professor Reeves has served as a consultant for the Texas Education Agency, the American Council on Teaching Foreign Languages, and the Institute of International Education. She is a member of the American Association of Teachers of German, Modern Language Association, South Central Modern Language Association, Texas Foreign Language Association, and American Council on the Teaching of Foreign Languages.

HANS-MARTIN SASS is Professor of Philosophy at Ruhr-Universität in Bochum and was recently visiting professor in the Department of Philosophy at Georgetown University. A native of Hagen, he holds the Ph.D. from the University of Muenster. Dr. Sass has served on the German UNESCO Commission in the section on Cultural Activities. He is Secretary General of the Allgemeine Gesellschaft für Philosophie in Deutschland and Vice-President of the Executive Committee of the Sixteenth World Congress of Philosophy. He has lectured in the United States and Germany on modern philosophy, religion, and existentialism, as well as on the writings of Spinoza, Hegel, and Marx. He has published numerous scholarly articles on Hegel, Feuerbach, and Heidegger, along with critical works on philosophy of religion, social philosophy, and philosophy of politics, environment, and technology. Presently, he is editing selected treatises for publication as an introduction to European philosophy of the nineteenth century.

LERA PATRICK TYLER holds the B.A. from Southwestern University in Georgetown, Texas. She is a graduate student in English at the University of New Orleans. She is a member of the Texas Folklore Society and the German-Texan Heritage Society.

MACK WALKER is Professor of History at The Johns Hopkins University. Previously he taught at Cornell and Harvard. A native of Massachusetts, he earned the A.B. at Bowdoin College and the Ph.D. at Harvard University. Professor Walker has published a number of bibliographies, book reviews, and scholarly papers in journals such as the *New England Quarterly, Political Science Quarterly, Central European History, Polish Review,* and *Journal of Modern History.* He is the author of *Germany and the Emigration; Metternich's Europe; Plombieres: Secret Diplomacy and the Rebirth of Italy;* and *German Home Towns: Community, Estate, and General Estate, 1648–1871.*

A. LESLIE WILLSON, educated in Texas and at Yale, is Professor of German and Chairman of the Department of Germanic Languages at the University of Texas. He has taught at Wesleyan (Connecticut), Northwestern, Duke, and Penn State, and has served on the faculty at Texas for seventeen years. His publications have been in the area of German Romanticism and contemporary German literature. Professor Willson is author of *A Mythical Image: The Ideal of India in German Romanticism* and editor of *A Schiller Symposium, Surveys and Soundings in European Literature* by Hermann J. Weigand, and *A Günther Grass Symposium.* He has translated widely since founding the bilingual literary magazine *Dimension* at Texas in 1968. He is a member of the Mainz Academy of the Sciences and Literature, and in the fall of 1976 he received the Officer's Cross of Merit, First Class, from the government of the Federal Republic of Germany.

Index

Abolitionist movement, 62, 66-67, 89-92, 191-96, 211-13
Adelsverein, 35-49, 58, 70, 122, 123, 161, 204, 208, 210, 258
Agassiz, Louis, 33
Agriculture, 60, 205, 261
Albert of Saxe-Coburg-Gotha, 54
Alsatians, 205
Altgelt, Agnes Coreth, 165
Altgelt, Emma Murck, 165
Altgelt Ernst, 165
Altgelt, Hermann, 165
Altgelt, Ottilie Coreth, 165
Amthor family, Hermann, 147
Anglo-American folk architecture, 110-12
Anglo-Americans, 221-24
Architecture, 103-20, 221-25, 259, 261
von Arnim, Bettina Brentano. See Brentano von Arnim, Bettina
Artists, 121-43, 262
Assimilation, 42, 49-50, 57, 65, 70, 77, 119-20, 168, 203-226, 222-26, 256-62

Bahr, C. O., 123
Bartlett, John Russell, 200
Battle of the Nueces, 69, 195, 211-12, 217
Bauch, Caroline, 147
Beckman, John, 123, 168
Behne, Augustus, 123
von Behr, Ottomar, 58-60, 66, 173, 200
Belleville, Illinois, 43-45
Bender, Hans, 254
Berchtelmann, A., 43
Bergman, Charles, 212

Berlin Academy of Sciences, 45
Berlin art academy, 122
Berlin circle, 33-34, 52
Berlin, University of, 32, 167
Bernhard of Weimar, 31
Bettina commune, 51-53, 56, 198, 200, 206
Biedermeier, 74-76, 79-81, 124, 129, 142-43, 262
Bienek, Horst, 245-46
Bierstadt, Albert, 121, 142
Biesele, Rudolph Leopold, 261
Biggers, D. H., 212
von Bismarck, Otto, 67, 199
von Blücher, Felix, 197
Bodmer, Carl, 33, 121, 142
Boerne, 53
Börne, Ludwig, 33, 53, 173
Boone, Rebecca, 144
Botanical investigation, 43-47, 197
Bowie, Jim, 209
Brenham, 155
Brentano, Clemens, 32
Brentano von Arnim, Bettina, 34, 41, 60, 200
Brinkmann, Rolf Dieter, 254
Brook Farm, 41, 200
Brossius, Hermann, 123
Büchner, Georg, 33
Bunson, Georg, 43
Bunson, Gustav, 43
Busch, Wilhelm, 174

Cabet, Etienne, 51, 56-57
Carl of Solms-Braunfels. See Solms-Braunfels, Carl of
Casino Club of San Antonio, 130, 152, 168
Cat Spring, 146-47, 204

Celebrations, 152-55
Civil War, 43, 54, 67-70, 122, 124, 129-30, 132, 142, 158, 163, 211-13, 222, 225, 258, 260
Classes. See Social classes
Clubs, social. See Social clubs
Comanche Treaty, 43, 50, 201, 208-209, 211, 216
Comfort, 68-69, 71, 112, 124, 129, 148, 165-66, 169-70, 212, 216-17
Comforter Leseverein, 165
Communism, 51-56, 191, 200, 206
Communitarian movement, 51-56, 200, 206
Congress of Vienna, 32
Cooper, James Fenimore, 33, 145
von Coreth family, 149, 165
Crèvecoeur, St. Jean de, 41
Cultural decline, 65-66, 70-71, 157-75, 203-26, 237-38, 256-62
Cultural preservation, 146-56, 157-75, 176-88, 203-26, 237, 256-62
Curley, James M., 196
Cypress Creek Damenleseverein, 166, 170
Czech Texans, 237, 261

Dances, 147-48, 215, 220
Darmstadt, 51, 53, 198
Darmstädter Farm commune, 53, 206
Degener, Edward, 62, 69
DeRyee, William, 129
Dies Buch gehört dem Konig (Bettina Brentano von Arnim), 34
Dispersal, 205
Dobie, J. Frank, 206-207
von Donop, Otto, 167
Douai, Adolf, 58, 62, 68-69, 147
Douai, Agnes von Beust, 147
Dreissiger, 43
Dresden art academy, 122, 135, 137-38, 149
Dresel, Gustav, 214
Dresel, Julius, 62, 69
Duden, Gottfried, 35

Düsseldorf art academy, 122, 131
Duff, James M., 212

East European immigrants, 77
Education, 43, 197-99, 237-40, 261-62
von Eichendorff, Joseph, 32
Engelmann, Adolf, 43
Engelmann, Georg, 43, 47
Engelmann, Theodor, 43
Engels, Friedrich, 56-57
Erath, George Bernard, 158
Ernst, Friedrich, 36-37, 204, 207, 210, 222
Ervendberg, Louis Cachand, 45, 48-49
Ethnic pluralism, 203-205, 237, 257-58

Fachwerk, 112
Families, 185
Faust (Goethe), 41, 63, 161-62
Feuerbach, Eleonore, 98
Feuerbach, Ludwig, 97-98
Fichte, Johann Gottlieb, 32
Fisher, Henry (Heinrich Fischer), 204
Fisher-Miller Grant, 204-205, 209, 216
Flach, Vera, 166
Floorplans, 106-11
Folk architecture, 103-20
Folk songs, 174, 176-77
Folklore and folklife, 176-88, 203-26, 259-61
Follenius, Paul, 29
Food, 156, 220
Fordtran, Charles, 222
Forty, The, 51-56, 197-98
Forty-Eighters, 53, 56-68, 138, 258, 262
Fourier, Charles, 51, 56-58
Franco-Prussian War, 70, 131
Frankfurter Putsch, 43, 194
Frederick, Prince of Prussia, 54
Frederick the Great, 30

Index

Fredericksburg, 112, 135, 137-41, 149, 158, 166, 205, 213, 215-16, 236
Freethinkers, 51, 58, 89-92, 159, 238
Freie Presse für Texas, 130, 169-70
Der Freie Verein, 58, 89-92
French Revolution, 30, 41
Friedrich, Caspar David, 135, 138
Friedrichsburger Wochenblatt, 173
Frisch, Max, 254
Froebel, Friedrich, 62
Froebel, Julius, 58, 62
Fuchs, Adolphus, 38, 160-61, 163, 170
Fuchs, John R., 170-71
Fuchs, Louise Romberg, 160-62
Fuchs, Patty Wenmohs, 170-71

Games, 180, 220
Garibaldi, Giuseppe, 58
Die Gartenlaube, 163, 165
Gentilz, Theodore, 143
Geological investigation, 45
Die geregelte Auswanderung des deutschen Proletariats (Herff), 56
German Catholics, 167
German English School (San Antonio), 132, 168
German Jews, 77
German Lutherans, 167
German Methodists, 159, 166-67
German nationalism, 41, 70-71
German unification, 70, 258
Germans in Mexico. *See* Mexico, Germans in
Germania Gesangverein, 124
Germania Society, 171
Giessen, University of, 51, 53-54, 198, 200
Giessener Gesellschaft, 29, 41, 258
Goeth, Carl, 174
Goeth, Ottilie Fuchs, 38, 70, 149, 160-63, 174, 262
Goeth, William, 161

von Goethe, Johann Wolfgang, 30-31, 34-35, 41, 63, 99, 159, 161-63, 173
Goyne, Minetta Altgelt, 165
Gray, Asa, 45, 47, 123
"Grays," 58
Greek Revolution, 58-59
"Greens," 58
Griesenbeck, Carl, 168
Grimm, Jakob and Wilhelm, 32, 41, 174
Groos, Friedrich, 168
Grundlinien einer Philosophie der Technik (E. Kapp), 92-93
Guenther, Carl Hilmar, 151
Guenther, Dorothea Wilhelmine Pape, 150-51
Guenther, Irma Goeth, 174-75
Guenther, John, 175
Guter Rath für Auswanderer (Behr), 60

Haas, Oscar, 261
Haas, William, 157-58
Habecker, Emil, 169
Hadra, Ida Weisselberg, 123
Half-timbering (Fachwerk), 112, 223, 259
Hamilton, Andrew Jackson, 69
Haseloff, Elise, 129
Die Hausfrau, 172-73
Healing, 186-87, 220-21, 261
Hegel, Georg Wilhelm Friedrich, 84, 92, 97
Heidelberg, University of, 51, 198, 200
Heine, Heinrich, 33, 173
Heinen, Hubert, 169
Herburger, Günter, 241, 254-55
von Herff, Ferdinand, 54-56, 133, 144-45, 197
Herff, Mathilde, 144-45
Hermann und Dorothea (Goethe), 161
von Hinueber, Caroline, 173, 222
Hitler, Adolf, 78

Hoffmann von Fallersleben, August, 41
Holekamp, Annie, 166
Holekamp, Fritz, 170
Holekamp, Ida, 170
Holidays, 152-55, 176-80, 214-16, 256-57
Holtz, Helmut, 123
Homes, 103-20, 221-25, 259
Hoppe, Adolf, 195
Hoppe, Louis, 124
Hübner, Julius, 135
von Humboldt, Alexander, 30, 32-33, 47, 60, 62, 130
von Humboldt, Wilhelm, 30, 32-33, 41, 67
Hunting, 207, 210
Hymns, 176-77

Indianola, 147, 205
Indians, 43, 50, 121-22, 142, 145, 158, 191, 201, 203-205, 208-11, 216
Industrial Revolution, 30, 74-76, 81, 206
Industry, 204, 222
"Inner Migration," 31-33, 74-76, 84-85
Irish-Catholics, 73
Ironclad Oath, 70
Italian-Americans, 77
von Iwonski, Carl G., 122-31, 142-43, 149-51

Jean Paul (Jean Paul Friedrich Richter), 163
Jefferson, Thomas, 31
Jews. *See* German Jews
Johnson, Uwe, 254
Joplin, Janis, 252
Jordan, Emma von Donop, 166-67
Jordan, Peter, 166

Kabale und Liebe (Schiller), 152
Kapp, Ernst, 56, 58, 62, 66, 69, 71, 82-99, 145, 162, 259, 262

Kapp, Friedrich, 58, 62, 65-67, 70-71, 97-98
Kapp, Ida, 64-65, 69, 88, 145
Kapp Putsch, 71
Kapp, Wolfgang, 71
Karl August of Weimar, 30
Kinkel, 58
Kleberg, Robert Justus, 36, 159, 204
Kleberg, Rosa von Roeder, 146, 148-49, 257-58
Kloss, Emil, 163
Kloss, Robert, 163
Koch, Augustus, 123
Koerner, Gustav, 43, 78
Der konstituirte Despotismus und die konstitutionelle Freiheit (E. Kapp), 62, 88
Kossuth, Lajos, 58
Krueger, Max, 157-58
Ku Klux Klan, 225
Kuechler, Jacob, 53
Kunert, Günter, 242-45

LaGrange, 148, 152
Lafayette, Marquis de, 31
Lamar, Mirabeau B., 257
Landscape, 36-37, 45-48, 51-52, 64, 121-22, 133-35, 141-42, 206, 223, 241-55, 260
Landscape painting, 124-43
Language, 52, 67-68, 145, 162, 167, 170-73, 225-26, 229-40, 260
Lanier, Sidney, 199-200
Latin Colonies, 51-53, 58-67, 82, 88-89, 140, 148-49, 165, 198, 200, 206
Latium, 206
Leatherstocking Tales (Cooper), 145
Legends, 206-13
Lehmann, Theodore, 124
Lenau, Nikolaus, 173
Lessing, Gotthold Ephraim, 163
Lessing, Karl Friedrich, 131
von Liebig, Justus, 33, 35

Index

Lindheimer, Ferdinand, 39, 43-47, 51-52, 67-68, 129, 156, 194, 197, 262
Linguistic Atlas (Gilbert), 172-74
Literary societies, 148, 220
Literature, 157-75, 241-55, 259, 261
Log building, 111-12
Lohmann Ferdinand H., 165-66
Longfellow, Henry Wadsworth, 145
Lungkwitz, Hermann, 123-24, 129, 137-43, 149, 151

McCarthy, Joe, 191
Maria Alexandra of Russia, 54
Marx, Karl, 56-58
Matthei, Arnold, 162
Maximilian von Wied-Neuwied. *See* Wied-Neuwied, Maximilian von
Mayröcker, Friederike, 254
Mazzini, Giuseppe, 58
Meckel, Christoph, 242, 245
Medicine, 89, 261
Menger, Rudolph, 168
Metternich, Prince, 38, 41
Meusebach family, 149
von Meusebach, Ottfried Hans (John O.), 39, 41-43, 47, 50, 67, 161, 197, 200-201, 208-11, 216, 217, 259
Mexican War, 43, 123, 158, 261
Mexicans, 191, 261
Mexico, Germans in, 69, 132, 195-96
Migration, 29-32, 35-39, 51-52, 56-58, 72-81, 83-84, 98-99, 105, 203-206, 258-59
Miller, Burchard (Mueller), 204-205
Möllhausen, Heinrich Baldwin, 33, 121, 142
Moelling, Peter A. 123
Moureau, Alwine vom Stein, 149
Moureau, Franz, 149
Moureau, Hulda, 149
Moureau, Thekla, 149

Münch, Friedrich, 29
Music, 216-17, 261
Nebel, Carl, 123
Neu-Braunfelser Zeitung (Lindheimer), 67-68, 129, 147, 152-58, 155, 170, 194
Neuser, William, 123
New Braunfels, 38, 54, 99, 112, 123-29, 140, 149, 158, 171, 200, 205, 217
New Harmony, 31
Nietzsche, Friedrich Wilhelm, 174
Nimitz Hotel, 213
Northern Romantic tradition, 122, 135, 138, 142-43
Nueces, Battle of. *See* Battle of the Nueces

Oheim, Frederic, 261
Olmsted, Frederick Law, 60, 149, 156, 200, 210, 217, 223-24
Oma and Opa (Schmidt), 181
Owen, Robert, 31, 52

Painting, 67-68, 147-48, 261
Palisado (picket) construction, 112
Paul of Württemberg, 33, 60, 63, 200
Pentenrieder, Erhard, 123
Petri, Elise, 139, 151
Petri, Marie, 151
Petri, Richard, 123-24, 134-37, 142-43, 151, 262
Petri, Teresa, 151
Philosophische oder vergleichende allgemeine Erdkunde (E. Kapp), 84
Photography, 129, 140, 149, 261
Political reform, 88-90, 191-202
Politics, 191-202
Polish Texans, 237
Pollhart, Frantz, 146
Portraiture, 129-37, 149-51
Postl, Karl. *See* Sealsfield, Charles
Prairie-Blume Society, 148
Prayers, 178-79, 183-84

Prohibition, 197
Proverbs, 181-82

Racism, 192-93
Ransleben, Guido Ernst, 261
Real family, 170
Reconstruction, 69-70, 123, 130, 213, 225, 261
Reform. *See* Political reform, Religious reform, Social reform
Religion, 45-49, 78-79, 92, 135, 159, 167, 176-80
Religious reform, 92
Republican Party politics, 130
Reuter, Fritz, 162, 165
Revolution, French. *See* French Revolution
Revolution, Greek. *See* Greek Revolution
Revolution, Industrial. *See* Industrial Revolution
Revolution of 1830, 29, 73
Revolution of 1848, 29, 38, 56-58, 73, 138
Revolution, Texas. *See* Texas Revolution
Richter, Adrian Ludwig, 135, 137-38
Rindisbacher Peter, 121
Ritter, Carl, 97
von Roeder, Joachim, 146
von Roeder, Louise Sacks, 159
von Roeder, Valeska, 146
von Roemer, Ferdinand, 39, 45-50, 209, 214-15, 217, 223
Rohrdorf, Carl, 123
Romberg, Johannes, 160
Rühmkorf, Peter, 254
Russian Germans, 260

San Antonio, 66, 89, 123-34, 138-41, 143, 149, 157, 168, 191, 196, 199-200, 205
San Antonio Zeitung (Douai), 62, 68
Santa Anna, 45, 159

Schenck sisters, 150
Schiller, Friedrich, 32, 157, 163, 170, 173
Schimmelphfennig, Hermann, 148
Schlecht, Clara, 162
Schlegel, Friedrich, 30
Schlegel, Wilhelm, 32
Schleicher, Gustav, 53-54, 152
Schmidt, Curt, 181
Schnerr, Frederick William, 163, 165
Schreiner, Emil, 211
Schroedter, Adolph, 131
Schroeter, Hedwig Klappenbach, 174
Schuchard, Carl, 123
Schuetze, Adolf, 147
Schuetze, Emilie, 147
Schuetze, Julius, 147
Schuetze, Louis, 147
Schurz, Carl, 78
Science. *See* Botanical investigation, Geological investigation, Medicine, Zoological investigation
Sealsfield, Charles (Karl Postl), 36
Shakespeare, William, 159, 163
Sheridan, Francis, 147
Shooting clubs, 208
Siemering, August, 58, 62-63, 66-69
Singing societies, 152, 168, 191, 199, 216-17
Sisterdale, 53, 58-67, 82, 88-89, 97-99, 140, 149, 165, 200, 206
Social classes, 49-50, 63, 73-81
Social clubs, 148, 199, 217, 259, 261
Social reform, 90-92, 198-200
Social uprooting, 29-32, 38, 41, 51
Sohn, August Wilhelm, 131
Solms-Braunfels, Carl of, 37-39, 45, 51, 197-98, 205, 207, 213, 226, 257
The Song of Hiawatha (Longfellow), 145
Spanish-American migrants, 77, 204

Index

Spiess, Hermann, 197
Staël, Madame de, 32
Steves, Albert, 168
Stone masonry, 114-15
Superstitions, 186-88, 220-21
Swiss Germans, 33, 121, 123

Technology and environment, 82-99, 259, 261
Tegener, Fritz, 211
Texas Museum, Scientific and Literary Association, 168
Texas Revolution, 45, 147, 158
Texas (Roemer), 47
Texas Vorwärts, 173
The Forty. *See* Forty, The
Theatre, 129, 152-55
Theissen, Gustav, 53, 58, 69
Thielepape, William C.A., 123, 130
Tusculum commune, 53, 206

"Union Loyal League," 69
Unionism, 67-69, 92, 191-96, 211-13, 217, 225
Urbantke, Carl, 159
Utopianism, 29-31, 39-41

Varnhagen von Ense, K. A., 41
Victorian architecture, 118
Viebahn, Fred, 252-54
Vienna, Congress of. *See* Congress of Vienna
Voting patterns, 196-202

Waelder, Frederick Jacob, 168
Wallace, Henry, 194
Wallner, Christian, 246-52
Walser, Martin, 254
Walter, Hulda, 168
Weddings, 180-81
Wehmeyer, Conrad, 165
Weimar, Bernhard of. *See* Bernhard of Weimar
Weimar government, 71
Weimar, Karl August of. *See* Karl August of Weimar
Wendel, John Oswald, 166
Wends, 205, 237
von Werner, Anton, 131
Westphal, Baron von, 58
von Wied-Neuwied, Maximilian, 33
Wilhelm II, 78
Wilhelm, Georg, 97
Wilhelm Meister (Goethe), 30, 41
Willrich family, George, 148
Women, 144-56, 259
World War I, 70, 78, 226, 260
World War II, 70, 78, 81, 172, 225, 260
Wueste, Louise, 123-34, 142-43
Württemberg, Paul of. *See* Paul of Württemberg
Wurzbach, Harry M., 196

Young Germany, 33, 38

Zink, Nicolas, 58
Zoological investigation, 43